THE NUREMBERG TRIALS

To

Last Tragedy of the Holocaust

Professor Pam MERTENS,

It is a pleasure having you as a colleague here at SSU. Thank you for your support and for you interest in my ideas.

Ellis Washington

Peace,

Ellis Washington

15 Oct. 2008

University Press of America,® Inc.

Lanham · Boulder · New York · Toronto · Plymouth, UK

4501 Forbes Boulevard
Suite 200
Lanham, Maryland 20706
UPA Acquisitions Department (301) 459-3366

Estover Road
Plymouth PL6 7PY
United Kingdom

Printed in the United States of America
British Library Cataloging in Publication Information Available

Library of Congress Control Number: 2008926470
ISBN-13: 978-0-7618-4108-1 (paperback : alk. paper)
ISBN-10: 0-7618-4108-3 (paperback : alk. paper)

™ The paper used in this publication meets the minimum requirements of American National Standard for Information Sciences—Permanence of Paper for Printed Library Materials, ANSI Z39.48—1984

DEDICATION

In memory of a great man . . .

That Titan of classical music—composer, Ludwig van Beethoven (1770-1827), following the *Zeitgeist* of the Age of Enlightenment in 1803 dedicated his monumental Symphony No. 3 in E flat major to the great revolutionary, Napoleon Bonaparte (1769-1821). However, when he heard that Napoleon had decreed himself Emperor of France in 1804, Beethoven, in his customary fit of rage, so violently scratched out the dedication to Napoleon that one can still see where he actually tore a hole in the original manuscript. Beethoven later rededicated his third symphony, *Eroica* (Heroic) . . .

In memory of a great man . . .

EPIGRAPH

To remain silent and indifferent is the greatest sin of all.

~ Elie Wiesel, Holocaust survivor

The central idea of Machiavelli is that the state power is not bound by the moral law. The law is not above the state, but below it.

~ Lord Acton

CONTENTS

ACKNOWLEGMENTS

Exceeding gratitude to a great, but unheralded intellectual, Attorney Che Ali Karega (1950 -) (a.k.a. Machiavelli), who during the preparation of an earlier draft of this manuscript as law review article, provided me with a peaceful, inviting environment in his home in Southfield, Michigan, where the only rule in his house is that any *true* intellectual pursuit is welcomed. I also thank Che for providing me a venue where I could be myself, where I could be like Plato's 'Philosopher-King,' where I could be a man of gravitas. . . where I could be a Black scholar without fear of envy or reprisals. Finally, thanks to Che for being my prime antagonist on innumerable occasions, and for his invaluable editorial advice on points of history, grammar, tone, and syntax. Regrettably, Machiavelli and I have parted again; (no doubt the fallout of opposing personality forces I deduce), but I *must* acknowledge his substantive contributions to this work nonetheless for without his keen intellect, iconoclastic disposition, and prescient ideas, this opus would have been exceedingly more deficient than in its present state.

The subtitle of this book came to me during a lunch discussion Machiavelli and I had at our favorite café (The Coffee Beanery in Southfield, MI) one beautiful morning on March 19, 2004. The conversation meandered around a number of diverse topics but finally settled on the subject of young Adolf Hitler; the aspiring artist studying in Vienna in the 1920s. I commented to Machiavelli that it was well documented that young Adolf the artist never painted people in his landscapes and drawings. On this part Machiavelli immediately remarked in his own inimitable style—

> The war [World War II] was kind of a metaphor of Hitler's geopolitical painting of Europe. Hitler viewed himself as the grand artist and when the painting was finished, there would be no [inferior] people left, but only Aryans to view his masterpiece.[1]

Next the conversation shifted to the proposed structure and scope of what I envisioned this book to be. I also grappled with what type of writing style I would utilize. On the latter point I found a kindred spirit with USC law professor and liberal pundit, Susan Estrich, who commented in a piece titled, *Writing Proverb* that she "was lucky enough to work for a brilliant man who taught me an enormous amount about law, writing, reasoning, argument, legal expression, getting to the point, keeping it simple, and the usefulness of short sentences." These are all good lessons to emulate in developing one's writing style. Long ago, perhaps due to my initial formal training in classical music (french horn), music theory, and musicology (history), I had patterned my writing approach not so much on the technique of other writers (of whom there are many I admire), but trying to put word against word in a similar manner as the great masters of classical music had done in times past with notes; geniuses like—Palestrina, Monteverdi, Verdi, Bach, Mozart, Beethoven, Brahms, Wagner, Strauss, Mahler, and others put note against note (like the intricately cut limestone blocks in a grand Gothic cathedral) to form counterpoint. This unorthodox approach to writing by inspiration of the classical masters of the arts is not without precedent. One of my favorite historians, that great British writer, Paul Johnson, had the following observations regarding inspiration of his own writing style—

> My grandfather used to say, "Learn to like art, music and literature deeply and passionately. They will be your friends when things are bad." It is true: at this time of year, when days are short and dark, and one hardly dares to open the newspapers, I turn, not vainly either, to the great creators of the past for distraction, solace and help.[2]

Likewise did I follow Johnson's admonitions and sought my Muse from the classical masters of the past, particularly in art music. In musical terms, I wanted my writing to sing; to have creativity, lyricism, harmony, interest, and depth. I wanted this opus to have the contrapuntal rigor of Johann Sebastian Bach's *Goldberg Variations* or *The Well-Tempered Clavier*, the grandeur and majesty of Richard Wagner's *Tristan und Isolde, Parsifal* or *Götterdammerüng*, but the succinctness and complexity of Anton Webern's minimalist and dense works like—*String Trio* (Opus 20), *Symphony* (Opus 21) or Alban Berg's enigmatic *Piano Sonata* (Opus 1)—a lofty undertaking indeed.

During this time I had been seriously contemplating transforming my original law review article on the Nuremberg Trials that I had just published in 2004 into a full-length book. Machiavelli (Che) then asked me what I would call this work? I told him that since it was basically on the same subject matter as my original law review article that I wanted to keep the original title, but use a different subtitle. Machiavelli thought for a moment and then looked upward and off to the side in an introspective manner, and immediately came up with the subtitle of this book—*The Last Tragedy of the Holocaust*. (He later changed his mind and preferred to substitute the word 'casualty' for 'tragedy.' I, however, preferred the tenor of the word, 'tragedy' and I thought the latter idiom to be more in line with the grand scheme and monumental scope I hope this book will have. Finally, since this work existed in prior abridged forms—first as a book chapter, secondly, as a law review article, I thought it prudent to change the subtitle to alert the reader that this was a very different work than its former incarnations and therefore took the author's initiative.

Exceeding gratitude also to my dear friend, mentor, surrogate father and professor, that eminent historian, musicologist, piano virtuoso, and scholar of aesthetics, Arthur R. LaBrew (1930 -). Professor LaBrew is the founder and editor-in-chief of the Michigan Music Research Center (Detroit, Michigan), for his proofreading early drafts of this manuscript, for typesetting the text, creating an index, and for his many suggestions on syntax, grammar, flow, and historical accuracy. And to Mr. John McClain, a retired U.S. Marine from Virginia and an avid reader of my weekly column for WorldNetDaily, for his invaluable and excellent editorial work which has given me a new slogan for this great branch of our military—Got a job? Get a Marine! Last but not least was Ms. Katie Smith, Customer Representative for Joe Christenson Printing Co. in Lincoln, Nebraska, for typesetting the entire manuscript numerous times and whose tireless efforts and dedication to this project (even when she was sick) literally almost brought me to tears. Most remarkably is that I never met this lady in person. Her efforts were totally altruistic—for the love of helping others.

The significance of this present work has already been recognized by many Holocaust scholars, museums, archives, educational institutions, religious institutions and Jewish scholars throughout the world, including—Elie Wiesel (Holocaust survivor and scholar, 1986 Nobel Laureate), The Elie Wiesel Foundation for Humanity, The United States Holocaust Memorial Museum, The Simon Wiesenthal Center, The Chambers Library of the Justices of the United States Supreme Court, particularly its two Jewish Justices—Ruth Bader Ginsburg and Stephen Breyer, also Justice Clarence Thomas, Justice David Souter, The Ronald Reagan Presidential Library, The George H.W. Bush Presidential Library, The Helene G. Simon Hillel Center at Indiana University, Dr. Robert Rozette, Director, Yad Vashem Library (Jerusalem), State Museum of Auschwitz-Birkenau, Leo Baeck Institute (New York), Israeli Ministry of Foreign Affairs (Jerusalem, Israel), The Jewish Agency, World Zionist Organization, and YIVO Institute for Jewish Research Today, The Bentley Historical Collection (University of Michigan), Strassler Family for Holocaust and Genocide Studies (Clark University), Harvard Law School, University of Cambridge, University of Cambridge Squire Law School, Oxford University Law School, University of Chicago Law School, State University of New York (Suffolk), Dr. Daniel Pipes (Middle East Scholar, analyst), Ward Connerly (fmr. Regent, UCLA, Founder of American Civil Rights Institute), Rabbi Daniel Lapin (Toward Tradition), Irene M. Rosenberg (University of Houston Law School), Dr. David Meltz (fmr. Dean, John Marshall Law School [Atlanta, GA]), Robert D' Agostino ([former Dean] Professor, John Marshall Law School), Guido Calebresi ([former Dean] Professor, Yale Law School, Dr. Anthony D'Amato (Law Professor, Northwestern University School of Law), Rabbi Charles H. Rosenzvieg (Founder, Holocaust Memorial Center, Farmington Hills, MI), Israeli Ministry of Foreign Affairs (Jerusalem), The Israeli Consulate of New England, World Jewish Congress, Anti-Defamation League, The Jewish Agency, Jerusalem Post, The Jerusalem Report, Jews for Judaism, New York Jewish Post, National Public Radio, Detroit Jewish News, Canadian Jewish News, numerous synagogues in addition to many other respected archives, academic institutions, and Holocaust scholars.

All passages and endnotes used from Professor Alan M. Dershowitz's book, *America on Trial: Inside the Legal Battles that Transformed Our Nation* (New York, Warner Books, 2004), have been granted expressed permission by the author and publisher.

All passages and endnotes used from Professor Daniel Goldhagen's book, *Hitler's Willing Executioners: Ordinary Germans and the Holocaust* (New York, Knopf Books, 1996), have been granted expressed permission by the author and publisher.

PROLOGUE

The rights of man come not from the generosity of the State, but from the mouth of God.

~ John F. Kennedy, Inaugural Address (1960)

The common men and women talked of him [Napoleon]; and in the intoxication of the words lost sight of their own cause, failed to realize the opportunities which democracy had open up for them, stumbled into the bypaths and dead-end roads of other ambitious and ruthless rulers. From which one may infer that it is not enough for the peoples of the world to destroy the militaristic dictator who threatens to enslave them; their task is not done when they have dealt with the man; it is not done until they have rooted out the legend through which he perpetuates his influence. [1]

~ Albert Carr, Napoleon Speaks (1944)

The principal ideas of this book put forward the proposition that the Framers of the United Nations and its international legal arm, the Nuremberg Tribunal, utilized a fundamentally defective jurisprudence and a diabolical legal philosophy over sixty years ago at the advent of the Nuremberg Trials called, *Positive law*. That the Allied Powers unquestioned allegiance to this twisted, perverted, ineffective and unconstitutional philosophy of law has virtually destroyed subsequent international war crimes cases which in modern times have devolved into utter farcical, symbolic, or show trials at The Hague, Tokyo, Dachau, Manila, Rwanda, Cambodia, the former Yugoslavia, Sierra Leone, Congo, Iraq, and other at other tribunals where the real perpetrators of genocide and war crimes seldom if ever are indicted let alone come to justice. This, in a nutshell, is the tragic paradox of positive law.

Another idea and purpose of this book is to present a case for a more ethical, substantive, and historically truthful, legally relevant philosophy and jurisprudence that the Framers of the UN and Nuremberg Tribunal *ought* to have relied on in judging the twenty-four Nazi defendants—Natural law. What is natural law? Natural law is the original philosophy out of the Judeo-Christian and Anglo-American legal traditions dating back thousands of years and served as the basis of virtually all laws in America and Europe prior to 1900. Writer and legal philosopher, David Adams, in his book, *Philosophical Problems in the Law*, defines natural law as—"principles and standards not simply made up by humans but rather part of an objective moral order, present in the universe and accessible to human reason." It is with Adams' definition of natural law where I launch my apologetic against the secular humanistic presuppositions of positive law and contend that natural law was the philosophy that the Framers of the United Nations and the Nuremberg Tribunal should have relied upon, but regrettably didn't. Moreover, that this reliance on this perverted, diabolical legal philosophy has sown the seeds of our present constitutional crisis, our present crisis in international law, and has pushed constitutional jurisprudence, the rule of law, and civilized humanity to the very brink of the abyss.

The impetus for this book developed out of a series of correspondences I had sent to an esteemed Israeli acquaintance of mine in October, 2003 about my original Nuremberg Trials article with Dr. Robert Rozette, Director of the Library Yad Vashem and The Holocaust Martyrs' & Heroes' Remembrance Authority in Jerusalem, Israel. Unbeknownst to him (I suppose) was how his previous encouraging comments about my Nuremberg Trials article was to me a truly epiphany experience which stirred a fire in my soul to broaden my original objectives in my article, to do more—to advance the cause of the Jewish people, both in Israel and the Diaspora, through my legal research and writings on the Holocaust and its aftermath, the infamous Nuremberg Trials, by conducting a substantive critique (at the micro-level) of the philosophical suppositions that formed its jurisprudence, legal, philosophical, political philosophy, and guided its legal investigation.

Other ideas of this book that eventually grew out of my examination of the philosophical theories and legal assumptions underlying the Nuremberg Trials are the following—

- Why did the Framers of the UN and it's international legal arm, the Nuremberg Tribunal, insist on using positive law—separating law from morals at the very start? Was there a surreptitious hidden agenda taken by this course? *Cui bono*?—To who's benefit or good? Who would gain from following this philosophy of law; this legal worldview? Who would loose?

- Why did the Framers of the UN and the Nuremberg Tribunal not include the former legal philosophy of natural law in their legal investigation and judgment of the Nazi defendants? After all, wasn't it the *moral* revulsion of Hitler's unbridled, savage genocide against the Jews and others a primary impetus in bringing the 24 high ranking Nazi officers to justice in the first place for their venal crimes against humanity?

- Did the UN's militant segregation of law and morals have an adverse effect on the Allies' case against the 24 Nazi defendants and in subsequent Nuremberg Trial cases? Did this dearth of philosophy and judicial impotence contributed to cases having over a 20 percent acquittal rate?

- Why were only 177 Germans and Austrians charged in the initial Nuremberg Trials and the dozen subsequent Nuremberg Trials out of the tens of millions of Nazi combatants and their supporters, enablers, and willing participants?

- Did the positive law legal philosophy of separating legality and morality started at Nuremberg in 1945 set a destructive precedent in subsequent international war crimes trials?—Tokyo, Dachau, Israel, Manila, as well as the most recent being Rwanda, the former Yugoslavia, Cambodia, Sierra Leone, Congo, and the present farcical trials in Iraq against the dictator, Saddam Hussein (Dujail, Anfal, etc…)

The variety of information I have used to manifest the ideas of this book principally originate from several sources including two previous writings of mine—(1) Chapter 4: "The Nuremberg Trials: Birth of the Death of the Rule of Law," from my second book, *The Inseparability of Law and Morality: The Constitution, Natural Law, and the Rule of Law* (Maryland: University Press of America, 2002);[2] (2) Law review article titled—*The Nuremberg Trials: The Birth of the Death of the Rule of Law (In International Law)*, 49 *Loyola Law Review* 101 (2003);[3] (3) various classical texts on jurisprudence, legal history, legal philosophy including Jean Bodin's essential work on the history of law titled—*Six Books of the Commonwealth* (1576), and SIR HENRY MAINE, *LECTURES ON THE EARLY HISTORY OF INSTITUTIONS*, (1875), who eloquently wrote about English sovereignty and empire during a period when both were at their height; JOHN W. SALMOND'S work, *THE FIRST PRINCIPLES OF JURISPRUDENCE* (1893), an encyclopedic exposition of definitions and essays on law by famous jurists, literary figures, scholars, from ancient times to the modern period and JAMES BRYCE, *STUDIES IN HISTORY AND JURISPRUDENCE*, (1901). For a modern treatment on legal history, Stanford University Professor of Law, Lawrence M. Friedman's two books: *A History of American Law* (3rd ed. 2005) and *American Law in the Twentieth Century* (2004), are the standard.

I also heavily relied on the actual Nuremberg Trials transcripts (*International Military Tribunal at Nuremberg Blue Series* [IMT]), particularly those excerpts of Robert Jackson, (Justice of the U.S. Supreme Court on leave to be the Chief Prosecutor for the U.S. at Nuremberg at the request of President Harry Truman), Hermann Jahrreiss (Professor of Cologne and Defense attorney for defendant Alfred Jodl),[4] Sir Hartley Shawcross (Chief Prosecutor for Britain), Judge Charles Wyzanski (Massachusetts Circuit Court Judge, who in 1946 wrote a series of popular articles in the Atlantic Monthly questioning the very existence and legality of the Nuremberg Tribunal who cynically characterized the entire proceedings as 'victor's justice'). I utilized a host of law review articles on the legal philosophical suppositions of the Nuremberg Trials and their correlation to the Holocaust by numerous scholars chief of which are—"The Myth of Is and Ought" by Arnold Brecht (Harvard Law Review [1941]), "Positivism and Separation" by H.L.A. Hart (Professor of Jurisprudence, Oxford University [1958]), "Positivism and Fidelity to Law: A Reply to Professor Hart," Lon Fuller (Professor of Jurisprudence, Harvard [1959]), "The Problematics of Moral Theory" (Judge Richard A. Posner, Harv. L. Rev., 1997), and my own comprehensive treatment of the history of American constitutional jurisprudence in, Ellis Washington, "Reply to Judge Richard A. Posner on the Inseparability of Law and Morality," Rutgers J. of Law & Relig., 1998.

Primary books referenced on the Nuremberg Trials and the Holocaust include—William Shirer, *The Rise and Fall of the Third Reich* (1949); Albert Speer, *Inside the Third Reich—Memoirs* (1969); Elie Wiesel, *Night* (1960), *Dawn* (1961), *The Accident* (1962); Daniel Goldhagen, *Hitler's Willing Executioners* (1996); Alan M. Dershowitz, *America on Trial* (2004); David M. Adams, *Philosophical Problems in the Law* (1992, 1996); David Barton, *The Myth of Separation* (1992), *Original Intent* (1997); H.L.A. Hart, *The Concept of Law* (1960); Lon Fuller, *The Anatomy of Law* (1968); R.A. Posner, *The Problems of Jurisprudence* (1990). The works by Professor Elie Wiesel I did not quote from verbatim, but relied on the magnanimous and ineffable "sprit" that wrote them to gain inspiration to write on my subject and to secure some measure of *entree* into the resplendent Jewish mind that birthed those works; narratives born in the duality of tragedy and redemption.

Some of the differences between my book and other books and articles on similar or related subjects on legal history, legal philosophy, constitutional law, international law, and the impact of law in shaping culture and society, include several particularly noteworthy sources—First, the interesting and engaging commentaries in the IMT trial transcripts and in his memoirs reflecting on his

Nuremberg Trial experience by Hermann Jahrreiss. Hermann Jahrreiss was Professor of Law at Cologne and Associate Defense counsel for defendant Alfred Jodl, leader of the Reichstag delegation, who skillfully and with some success utilized the "act of state" defense and the doctrine of absolute sovereignty. Both legal philosophies came directly out of John Austin's magnum opus, *The Province of Jurisprudence Determined* (1832), who along with Jeremy Bentham, are considered the founding fathers of Positive law.

Jahrreiss presented a lengthy apologetic on jurisprudential and historical considerations of the Nuremberg Trials. His eloquent discourses epitomize the most extensive efforts by defense counsel to elucidate a philosophical foundation for the case of the Nazi defendants. Secondly, is Jean Bodin's essential work on the history of law titled—*Six Books of the Commonwealth* (1576).[5] Bodin's work provides a comprehensive starting point for the study of a history of law out of the Western tradition of intellectual thought. The previous Western conception of law as subsequent and superior to man was by the late sixteenth century beginning to be replaced with the Machiavellian conception of law as a mere tool or servant of the state.

In Bodin's *Commonwealth*, "the Prince" though freed from the *law of man* and considered a law unto himself, medieval understanding of the law still constrained him to the ubiquitous *universal natural law* precepts that constrained all civil society, binding them to certain common ecumenical precepts of which all mankind were obliged to follow (i.e., Bible, natural law, common law, rule of law, theism, etc.). Nonetheless, the break with the medieval world of "the Law of Nature and of Nature's God" as Jefferson codified two hundred years later as natural law philosophy in America's Declaration of Independence (1776), was in the sixteenth century already being rent in two like the Temple veil as the Renaissance Period (and later, it's apotheosis, the Age of Enlightenment [1600-1830]) made their indelible mark on history. Jefferson's original title to this work—*A Declaration by the Representatives of United States of America, in General Congress Assembled* and are excerpted below. Jefferson's Declaration of Independence is a succinct, raw, sublime utterance of a free man that passionately wishes to secure that freedom and liberty for his country and for his people. Note the direct appeal to natural law which I italicized for clarity and emphasis:

> When, in the course of human events, it becomes necessary for a people to advance from that subordination in which they have hitherto remained, and to assume among the powers of the earth, the equal and independent station to which *the laws of nature and of nature's god* entitle them, a decent respect to the opinions of mankind requires that they should declare the causes which impel them to the change.[6]

Those eight seemingly benign words italicized above have done more to substantively delineate the original legal/political philosophy of America's Founding Fathers and the Framers of the U.S. Constitution in forming this democratic republic than any other source I've read which begs the question—In the history of American constitutional law, was law and morality (religion) originally irrevocably separated? Jefferson and the Framers of the Constitution certainly would not hold to this popular trend of segregating law from morals in modern times. Why then was law and morality separated by 1945, the year the UN and Nuremberg Tribunal were inaugurated? Was there some sinister, surreptitious motive afoot here by taking this course?

Unlike many other books on the Holocaust and the Nuremberg Trials, a number of authors and legal scholars fail to address the fundamental questions like I've proposed in my book; a position where I directly, unapologetically, and audaciously tackle many of the vexing paradoxes Hitler and his wicked henchmen unleashed in their hatred upon the world in World War II by doing an in depth comparative analysis of the foundational theories of Nazi ideology—positive law vs. natural law jurisprudence, as well as the many permutations these ideas spawned. Many authors I've read on the subject, if they say anything about the underlying philosophical speculations of the Nuremberg Trials, fail in any substantive way to delineate a proportional analysis of *why* the Nuremberg Trials were purposely established entirely on positive law grounds? Or why were natural law considerations were totally ignored by the UN?

Additionally, I propose the following prescient questions regarding the legal philosophical suppositions of the Nuremberg Trials—What is positive law? What was the philosophy or law or jurisprudence jurists relied on before positive law was enacted? What is natural law? Why did the UN and Nuremberg Trial Framers fail to expressly fail to mention natural law in their legal investigation against the 24 Nazi defendants? These are the difficult and intractable questions I address and wrestle with in this book on the shortcomings of the Nuremberg Trials; deficiencies that ironically became as I state in the subtitle of this book—*The Last Tragedy of the Holocaust.*

The methodological rigor I endeavor to bring to this opus analyzing positive law and it's failings as a viable legal philosophy and analytical jurisprudence are as follows—Positive law or Legal positivism (as it is often referred to in philosophical circles) is riddled with many flaws of which I cite in summary as follows—(1) Positive law fails to take account of sources of law that are independent of the state (i.e., indigenous sources like religion, tradition, values or culture); (2) Positive law fails to distinguish between *de jure* (by law, by right, legal) and *de facto* (by practice, quasi-legal, unofficially legal, or under the color of law) sovereignty; (3) Positive law fails to take account of functions of legal rules other than the "command" function; (4) Positive law fails to take account of legal obligations of the state. These and a variety of other defects of positive law inexorably lead many legal theorists and philosophers to erroneously examine law through the rose colored lens of the *letter* of the law at the expense of the *spirit* of the law. As we shall later see Secular Man's perverted and diabolical deconstruction of the rule of law and its mandated purpose of *Veritas* (truth) has, and will have monstrous and perverse consequences during the Holocaust, World War II, in the Nuremberg Trials and beyond.

Looking back sixty years ago, can it not be convincingly argued that what I refer to as the 'Nuremberg Trial philosophy' of separating law from morals has sown the seeds of tyranny and perpetuated the current chaos in international law? That adherence to humanistic principles called positive law and its antecedent philosophies—relativism, egalitarianism, empiricism, positivism, evolution, materialism, has caused a perversion of the rule of law in European and American foreign policy? In my book I make a concerted effort to give an answer to these most salient but intractable questions that have plagued international law, constitutional law, and war crimes tribunals ever since the advent of the Nuremberg Trials in November 1945.

The significance of my research and conclusions are linked to the encouragement found in Dr. Rozette's correspondences and were a critical catalyst toward motivating me to write this book. He showed me that there was a need in Holocaust literature of a book of this type and that my initial research and conclusions I had sent him on the Nuremberg Trials could indeed be further supplemented, elaborated, and expanded upon, and that I was in a perfect position to write such a book. For example, I recall during one correspondence in particular Dr. Rozette candidly telling me that there was a need in Holocaust scholarship for a unique book of this type that rather than looking at the Nuremberg Trials as a purely historical event (of which there are many), Holocaust scholarship needed a book that actually *analyzed* in a systematic and meticulous manner the underlying legal/philosophical suppositions and presumptions that even made the Nuremberg Trials a plausible entity in itself.

The relevant conclusions of this opus moreover provide a clear and present warning to the nations of the world in modern times, of the dire consequences for a people, a nation, a government, a legal system, or an international tribunal that follows the Nuremberg Trial philosophy—a perverse jurisprudence rooted in relativism, secularism, humanism, egalitarianism, materialism, and Progressive-era utopianism. That the analytical jurisprudence of positive law and logical positivism is a twisted, implacable legal theory that mandates a separation of the inseparable—that separates law from morality—the inevitable genocide of which such ideas as these have unleashed may tragically be apocalyptic and irrevocable. As I read Dr. Rozette's words I felt like the Old Testament prophet, Elisha, receiving the mantle from Elijah:

> Elijah went up by a whirlwind into heaven. He [Elisha] took up also the mantle of Elijah that fell from him.
>
> ~ 2 Kings 2:11-13[7]

To state in dispassionate terms that to reestablish the primacy and respect of the rule of law Congress, the Judiciary, the Executive, the academy and the legal community must radically change their reflexive bias against morality having *any* role in effecting or determining what the rule of law will be in formulating a law, an executive order, a legal opinion, in substantive jurisprudence, and to effect a practical constitutional interpretation, other wise society will continue to slide into the abyss of anarchy and nihilism because people in general will not obey or respect a rule of law absent a moral foundation.

I think that my book has the unique position in the voluminous volumes of Holocaust literature, to put forth an intelligent, succinct, trenchant legal and philosophical critique on the short comings of the Nuremberg Trials, and how impotent they were at vindicating the genocide against the Jewish people (and others) in the context of a micro-level analysis of this analytical jurisprudence (positive law) and its myriad of permutations — legal positivism, legal realism, humanism, liberalism, socialism, progressivism, which formed the ideas and the legal foundation of the UN as well as the legal machinery of Nuremberg Tribunal. Furthermore, to systematically analyze these other philosophies that played such a significant role in the ideas of the minds of the jurists and leaders like Presidents Woodrow Wilson, Franklin Delano Roosevelt, and Harry Truman, Justice Oliver Wendell Holmes, Justice Benjamin Cardozo, Justice Robert Jackson, Justice Felix Frankfurter, Judge Charles Wyzanski, Nuremberg Trial jurists like Hermann Jahrreiss and Hartley Shawcross, as well as contemporary jurists like my mentors Justice Clarence Thomas and Judge Richard A. Posner, but also law professors: Jonathan Turley (George Washington University), M. Cherif Bassiouni (DePaul), and Harvard Professors, Alan M. Dershowitz, Laurence Tribe, and Martha Minow—ideas like humanism, relativism, liberalism, secularism, egalitarianism, naturalism, emotivism, moral particularism, etc.

Finally and most notably is the final chapter (Epilogue) that seeks to put what I call the 'Nuremberg Trial Philosophy' in the context of modern international war crimes trials of contemporary times. Particularly, how the Nuremberg Trials slavish and ahistorical reliance on humanism, positive law, and analytical jurisprudence, a worldview and legal philosophy predicated on separating law from morals, impedes speedy and effective application of law to bring would-be international criminal defendants up on charges of war crimes, crimes against humanity, genocide, and conspiracy to commit war crimes.

In my book I try to systematically, lucidly and dispassionately chronicle that the precedent set by the Nuremberg Trials in 1945 has sent jurisprudence, international law and constitutional law, particularly in the area of war crimes trials, into the abyss of symbolic justice, bureaucratic ineptitude, too-little-justice-too-late, and legacy of farcical trials that have little effect in deterring evil men from committing genocide on the vulnerable. To show paradoxically, how the shameful legacy of the Nuremberg Trial Philosophy has emboldened more would-be tyrants to perpetrate more and more genocide across the world realizing there is little chance of them ever facing the bar of justice for their crimes.

The following letter accompanied my original law review article on the Nuremberg Trials as it was originally conceived as my personal gift to the Jewish people in exceeding appreciation for their contributions to humanity going back to earliest antiquity. I sent this letter and article out to many Jewish organizations, Holocaust scholars, Holocaust museums, synagogues, and other groups over a two year period many of whom I have gratefully acknowledged and received my original Nuremberg Trials law review article I wrote in 2004 into their archives—

Dear Elie Wiesel:

April 18, 2004

In memory of Holocaust Remembrance Day (April 18, 2004) and in exceeding gratitude and love for the contributions Jewish people have given humanity, please find attached an original copy of an article I would like your organization to add to its archives and to distribute to interested colleagues and groups. It is titled: *The Nuremberg Trials: The Death of the Rule of Law*. I am happy to report that I have recently had this work published, see *49 Loyola Law Review* (2003).

The response to this work has been tremendous. This article has been added to the following archives: The Supreme Court of the United States, The Ronald Reagan Presidential Library, The George Bush Presidential Library, The Simon Wiesenthal Center, The U.S. Holocaust Memorial Museum, The Helene G. Simon Hillel Center at Indiana University, The Bentley Historical Collection (University of Michigan), Yad Vashem Library (Jerusalem), State Museum of Auschwitz-Birkenau, Leo Baeck Institute (NY), World Zionist Organization, YIVO Institute for Jewish Research, Harvard Law School, University of Cambridge, University of Cambridge Squire Law School, Oxford University Law School, University of Chicago Law School, State University of New York (Suffolk), Dr. Daniel Pipes (Scholar, Middle East Terrorism), Ward Connerly (Fmr. Regent, UCLA), Rabbi Daniel Lapin (Toward Tradition), Israeli Ministry of Foreign Affairs (Jerusalem), The Israeli Consulate of New England, World Jewish Congress, Anti-Defamation League, The Jewish Agency, Jerusalem Post, The Jerusalem Report, Jews for Judaism, New York Jewish Post, National Public Radio, Detroit Jewish News, Canadian Jewish News, numerous synagogues in addition to many other respected archives, academic institutions, and Holocaust scholars.

As a Black man and a Christian, I have been a lover of Jewish culture and a friend of the Jewish people for many years. Long ago I made a vow to God to dedicate my legal career and writings to proclaiming truth to the law academy and to society based on the Judeo-Christian tradition of intellectual thought. I am honored to make this small contribution to bring the light of truth and Reason to a very dark and ignominious chapter of Jewish history.[8]

Shalom,

Ellis Washington, J.D.

26 November 2006
Grosse Pointe Park, Michigan

CHAPTER 1

HISTORICAL CONTEXT OF THE NUREMBERG TRIALS

PRESIDENT TRUMAN, LIBERAL UTOPIANISM, AND THE SEEDS OF TYRANNY

[President George Bush's speech] the "axis of evil" caused a sensation around the world because it established a new American foreign policy based on three distinctive principles: morality, preemption, and unilateralism.[1] ~ Charles Krauthammer

[W]ar. . . is an illegal thing.[2]

~ Henry Lous Stimson,
Secretary of War under FDR

As T. S. Eliot has said: "The last temptation is the greatest treason: To do the right deed for the wrong reason."[3]

~ Martin Luther King,
Letter from a Birmingham Jail (1963)

Like the moth to the flame, every world leader reflexively seeks to leave a "legacy"—Something for posterity, something that will outlive him in his elusive quest for divinity, for transcendence, yea, for the verity of eternal relevance, eternal life. This incessant, obsessive drive by many ambitious men who wield power to "do something"; "to be part of the solution, not part of the problem," to "make a contribution to humanity" sadly, even tragically, oftentimes harms humanity more than it helps them and if the political mechanisms are in place, oftentimes can approach genocidal proportions in the unintended circumstances unleashed upon civilization—a reckoning that must be paid unto the utmost farthing. For mortal man is in a dilemma, a paradox if you will—On the one hand within his soul is the spark of divinity that grants him eternal life, yet, on the other hand he is shackled to this mortal plane we call Earth with all of its wars, pestilence, wickedness, oppression, pride, ambition, and death. Like the moth, Man is attracted to the flame, here, and utopia on Earth, which in his pursuit of this ideal, plunges man and humanity into the abyss of Perdition. Thus are the pathological effects of Secular Man's quest for legacy which irrevocably and incessantly like the moth to the flame can (and has) devastated the world for generations to come. Such was President Woodrow Wilson's legacy—The League of Nations (1919), which twenty-six years later became established and greatly expanded by President Franklin Delano Roosevelt and renamed—The United Nations in 1945.

Positive law, the legal philosophy behind the creation of the U.N., despite its anti-religious pronouncements and biases is indeed a religion; a religion that the majority of my leftist colleagues in the courts, the legislature, the legal community, the law academy follow with unwavering allegiance. Let there be no doubt liberalism (or as I sometimes refer in this book, "liberal utopianism" is a religion.[4] It contains all of the vestments and symbolism of religion—priesthood, a holy text, disciples, sacraments, and most importantly a system of punishment for heretics. On this point, constitutional attorney and conservative writer, Ann Coulter has remarked in her recent bestseller, *Godless: The Church of Liberalism*:

> Liberals love to boast that they are not "religious," which is what one would expect to hear from the state-sanctioned religion. Of course liberalism is a religion. It has its own cosmology, its own miracles, its own beliefs in the supernatural, its own churches, its own high priests, its own saints, its own total worldview, and its own explanation of the existence of the universe. In other words, liberalism contains all the attributes of what is generally known as "religion."
>
> Under the guise of not favoring religion, liberals favor one cosmology over another and demand total indoctrination into theirs. The state religion of liberalism demands obeisance (to the National Organization for Women [NOW]), tithing (to teachers' unions), reverence (for abortion), and formulaic imprecations ("Bush lied, kids died!" "Keep your laws off my body!" "Arms for hostages!"). Everyone is taxed to support indoctrination into the state religion

> through the public schools, where innocent children are taught a specific belief system, . . .[5]

Since the advent of the Modern Age [1900 - present] liberalism has had a particular penchant for large, grandiose, geopolitical themes based exactingly on a secular ideal; a rigorous humanistic worldview that is followed with the fanatical zeal of the most ardent devotee of a cult. Wilson's League of Nations in 1919 was simply the apotheosis of liberalism great socialist vision for humanity that had finally come of age during the previous generation and the Progressive Era (1900-1915) as America and Europe prospered during the industrial revolution. British historian, Paul Johnson, elegantly narrated those times in his brilliant book, *A History of the American People*—

> The antibigness emotion so characteristic of the decades between the Civil War and World War One. . .[transfixed] Progressives, who tended to be highly educated intellectuals aiming at an urban audience. Historians have seen the . . . Progressive Era [from] 1900 up to America's entry into World War One. . . Progressivism was the hostile reaction of the educated middle class to the overwhelming power of Big Business, whose wealth and sale and lure elbowed them out of the political-economic picture entirely, or so they feared. Since the days of the Founding Fathers, the educated elite had guided, if they had not exactly run, the United States, and they felt their influence was being eroded by the sheer quantity of money now sloshing around in the bowels of America's great ship of state.[6]

A vision that history has proven, at the dawn of the Twenty First century, to have devolved into a terrible global nightmare of ceaseless wars and rumors of war amongst the nations. But was it supposed to happen this way? In the beginning it all began so innocently, so optimistically, so self-assured, so full of promise, so utopian, so full hope in man's self-redemption of Man. I refer to the year 1919 at the signing of the Treaty of Versailles on June 28 where that ubiquitous phrase, "The War to End All Wars" was coined which gave birth to an international "League of Nations." This leviathan, globalist organization was formed to give international oversight to guarantee the First World War really would be the war to end all wars—But was it?

A Brief History of the United Nations

The League of Nations, precursor to the United Nations, was the utopian dream of modern liberalism; the triumph of the Allied Powers following the conditions of a document known as "The Covenant." It set forth the League's mission—""To promote international cooperation and to achieve international peace and security." For the past sixty years since the advent of the United Nations in 1945, utopian liberalism has totally dominated international law and its first international case, the Nuremberg Trials, which in turn has set the paradigm for how subsequent international war crime cases would be handled as this new, bold "Nuremberg Trial philosophy" shaped and fashioned international war crime cases, international foreign policy and geopolitics until this day.

The League of Nations was the brainchild of U.S. President Woodrow Wilson, who because of his founding of this organization and the work of the League in securing Germany's compliance (at least extrinsically speaking) with the Versailles Treaty, was later that same year in 1919 awarded the Nobel Peace Prize. Ironically, however, the U.S. was never a member of the League because even though the Senate had a Republican minority, it was unified and along with some dissenting conservative Democrats, had enough votes to block ratification, rationally arguing that endorsing U.S. participation into League membership would subordinate the U. S. Constitution and America's independence as sovereign nation to the League's "Covenant" as the supreme law of the land and of the world. Thankfully in 1919 the two party system, a system of checks and balances, was still in effect, however, as we shall later see, just a few short years later with a new, bold, more visionary president at the helm, the two party system in America would for all intents and purposes merge into one.

From its inception the League has repeatedly demonstrated itself to be a bungling, corrupt, ineffectual political organization of the highest order given over to vile, perverse ideology under the guise of bringing unity among the nations. The litany of sins of omission and sins of commission have been noted by many other author's much more capable than I and therefore won't repeat them here. In 1919, the same year that the League of Nations was created, oversaw the Treaty of Versailles; a horrifically inept policy that saw the end of World War I and sowed the seeds for World War II by appeasing Germany and thus securing the rise of Hitler and the Nazis exactly twenty years later.

The following are merely some of the more egregious examples of the League's incompetence I cite for the sake of historical narrative—In 1931, Manchuria was invaded by Imperial Japan, where a puppet republic called Manchukuo was set up and fully controlled by Japan. When the League of Nations made token and superficial objections, Tokyo became indignant and immediately withdrew from the League. The League of Nations bitterly complained, remonstrated, and lodged numerous letters of protest, which Japan promptly mocked, disregarded, and ignored until the League realized that their efforts at diplomacy were all in vain. Coulter remarks on the vanity and historical paucity of diplomacy are instructive here:

> There are only two choices with savages: Fight or run. Democrats always want to run, but they dress it up in meaningless catchphrases like "diplomacy," "detente," "engagement," "multilateral engagement," "multilateral diplomacy," "containment" and "going to the UN"[7]

In 1935, Italy's brutal dictator, Benito Mussolini, noting the League's unproductive rejoinder to Japanese belligerence, took Japan's cue and wantonly and without provocation invaded Ethiopia utterly slaughtering the hapless Ethiopians who literally only had horses, swords, and spears against Mussolini's modern weaponry of machine guns, tanks, and bomber aircraft. Once again the

League followed their usual protocols repeatedly condemning Italy in the most vociferous rhetoric it could muster and even threatened diplomatic sanctions. And once again the League's impotence and its reflexive, impotent solution of diplomacy in the face of tyranny was once more rendered in vain while the world watched in horror as Mussolini's forces in 1936 occupied the Ethiopian capital, Addis Ababa, thus annexing Ethiopia as part of Italy.

As the League flittered and fluttered about powerless to respond to Imperial Japan or Mussolini's naked aggression, Hitler quietly took note of the League's impotence and incompetence and plotted his own diabolical designs of Aryan supremacy, German hegemony and European conquest. In 1933 Hitler's Nazi Socialist party finally consolidated its power ousting the corrupt, moribund, and irrelevant Weimar Republic of Paul von Hindenburg. Hitler then rapidly and in an unprecedented manner, rebuilt his military contrary to the expressed anti-armaments provisions in the Treaty of Versailles of 1919. What did the League do to stop Hitler's march to renewed militarism, his threats of global domination, bellicose rhetoric of Aryan supremacy, and European domination? It did the same thing the League of Nations is best at—appeasing and rewarding tyrants (beyond even their wildest dreams).

Far from punishing Hitler with sanctions or threatening Germany with a united military front, the UN awarded Germany to host the 1936 Olympic Games at Munich (although in fairness Germany had been chosen to host these games years before Hitler came to power). Nevertheless, the League, as a sanction for blatantly violating the anti-armament provisions of the Treaty of Versailles could have moved to have Germany removed as a venue to host the Olympic Games in 1936, but it didn't. This craven, pathetic response from the League further emboldened Hitler to press the League's resolve to the brink in 1938. That year Hitler decreed under the dual and diabolical pretext that the majority Czechs were oppressing the minority German population and that the German people need more *lebensraum* (living space), threatened to invade *all* of Czechoslovakia unless Britain and France agreed to German annexation of the so-called "Sudetenland" (the northern portion of Czechoslovakia that borders Germany). In retrospect it is arguable that World War II could have been averted had the West and the League of Nations not appeased and acceded to Hitler's outrageous demands, but instead met him with a strong united front and a cohesive warning to the effect—"Adolph Hitler, if you invade the Czechoslovakia, you will have crossed the Rubicon and will be at war with the world!" They could have, but they didn't. Once again the League failed to act at a critical juncture in geopolitical history with consequences that would later prove devastating to virtually all nations of the world.

Bolstered by his achievement at frightening the West and the League of Nations, Hitler, as a concession to his original claim on the Sudetenland, demanded that he be given a large part of Czechoslovakia in exchange for a promise to British Foreign Minister Neville Chamberlain that there would be no further demands and there would be peace. Amazingly, Chamberlain, who at that time was also the chief envoy of the incompetent League of Nations, shamefully and treacherously acceded to Hitler's outrageous demands giving Hitler Czechoslovakia without even the protocol of consulting the Czechs. This appalling act of appeasement by the League in effect guaranteed Hitler's next move and was tantamount to starting World War II when Hitler's Stormtroopers invaded the Rhineland and annexed the Ruhr as part of German territory. This time the League did not even posture with it's usual bureaucratic paper chase nor even lodge a formal vocal protest before the General Assembly, but merely watched in silent cowardice as Hitler finalized his plans for what historians would call, "World War II." Thus within two decades the world would witness a second "war to end all wars" between the Allied Forces of Britain and France against the Axis Powers of Japan, Italy, Austria, and Germany. Hitler's hubris, daring and bravado had the added effect of silencing every voice of reason left in Germany.

One of the very few and most eloquent voices of dissent to Hitler's genocidal madness was that great German minister, Reinhold Niebuhr, who wrote that "pacifism in the face of totalitarianism is a profoundly debilitating failure and can produce deeply immoral results." Niebuhr further developed these ideas against religious pacificism as a rational critique against Hitler's Nazi madness in his 1940 work, *Why the Church is Not Pacifist: Christianity and Power Politics*. Niebuhr wrote:

> The refusal to recognize that sin introduces an element of conflict into the world invariably means that a morally perverse preference is given to tyranny over anarchy (war). . . One of the most terrible consequences of a confused religious absolutism is that it is forced to condone such tyranny as that of Germany in the nations which it has conquered and now cruelly oppresses. It usually does this by insisting that the tyranny is no worse than that which is practised in the so-called democratic nations. Whatever may be the moral ambiguities of the so-called democratic nations, and however serious may be their failure to conform perfectly to the democratic ideals, it is a sheer moral perversity to equate the inconsistencies of a democratic civilization with the brutalities which modern tyrannical States practise. If we cannot make a distinction here, there are no historical distinction which have any value. All the distinctions upon which the fate of civilization has turned in the history of mankind have been just such relative distinctions.[8]

German Pastor Martin Niemoller, another courageous Christian who lived during those dark days, and paid the ultimate price for his courageous stand against the face of Nazi evil, stated the following words damning the pacifist doctrine of silent complicity or the sin of omission—doing nothing. The euphonious lyricism of Niemoller's prescient words are utterly transcendent when he wrote that—"In Germany they first came for the Communists, and I didn't speak up because I wasn't a Communist. Then they came for the Jews, and I didn't speak up because I wasn't a Jew. Then they came for the trade unionists, and I didn't speak up because I wasn't a trade unionist. Then they came for the Catholics, and I didn't speak up because I was a Protestant. Then they came for me - and by that time no one was left to speak up."[9]

World War II began with a vengeance on September 1, 1939, when Nazi Germany unleashed its demonic rage first by invading Poland with its famed *blitzkrieg*—lightening war. The colossal disaster of it all is that the war could almost certainly have been averted if the League of Nations had courageously stood in opposition to Hitler and backed him down at the ascendancy of his genocidal madness for world domination during that critical seven year period that Hitler consolidated his power—(1925-1932).[10]

Vice President Harry Truman became President of the United States on April 12, 1945 to replace the beloved Franklin Delano Roosevelt, who died at the ascent of his fourth term after years of ill health and ironically just prior to the fall of Germany, of which he spent a large part of his presidency either worried about or engaged in active war with. On May 7, 1945, less than a month after Truman's inauguration, V-E ("Victory") Day was celebrated and an international conference was hastily organized among the victorious Allies regarding how to deal with the vanquished Germany and to divide up the territory the Allies won back from Germany. Originally President Truman was resistant to appear at an international conference; however, postwar complications with the Soviet Union made it imperative that the President meet with the war Allies. Therefore, Truman, along with the Soviet leader, Joseph Stalin, and the British Prime Minister, Winston Churchill, met in Potsdam, Germany (July 17-August 2) to confer with other European leaders on the outcome of Europe after Germany's unconditional surrender. However, as fate would have it, shortly after the meeting in Potsdam, the capricious British public now wanted a "peace-time Prime Minister" and Churchill's conservative Tory party was unceremoniously swept out of office.

On July 26, in the middle of the Potsdam Conference, Churchill was forced to resign and was replaced as Prime Minister by Clement Attlee following the unforeseeable election victory by the British Labour Party in July 1945. This replacement in leadership at such a crucial time in history was both shocking and ironic. Shocking, because never in the history of British politics had a sitting wartime Prime Minister *not* been reelected by a large margin. Ironic, because Churchill, arguably the greatest statesman and political leader of his time, brought England from the brink of annihilation during the almost incessant bombings by Hitler's infamous Luftwaffe campaign against his nation, with his steely demeanor and the sheer moral force of his indomitable will.[11]

On August 2, 1945 at the Potsdam Conference, a document was drafted by the Allies called "The Potsdam Protocol." One particularly salient element of the Protocol was that each of the four Allied Powers would prosecute separate parts of the Nuremberg Trials. Nuremberg, a small industrial town in Bavaria, was chosen as the location for two reasons—first, symbolically, because in 1935 it was the city where Hitler's infamous discrimination laws were first drafted which deprived the Jews of all of their civil rights. Secondly, for pragmatic reasons, Nuremberg was chosen for it was at Nuremberg where one of the few prisons was still intact after the tremendous bombing campaign Germany suffered by the Allied Powers. However, episodes shortly preceding the Potsdam Conference were not favorable to those who wished for postwar solidarity among the Allies.

Later at the Yalta Conference held in the Crimea on February 4-11, 1945, the decision was made by the Allies to try German leaders as war criminals. It was also learned that the Soviet Union not only began consolidating its power and control over most of Eastern Europe, but in a patently Machiavellian manner, made accusations that the Western Allies had been clandestinely negotiating with Germany without its input. President Truman apparently naively believed (at least early on) that he could persuade Stalin to be less aggressive in his land grabs and to become more conciliatory and reasonable. This, even while as President Truman's chief foreign policy advisors, W. Averell Harriman and George Kennan, warned Truman that the Soviet Union was determined to expand its empire and spread its communist ideology to as many nations as possible despite objections from the Allies. Even more ominous was that once Russia's globalist, expansionist policy was enacted, it would be almost impossible to contain. Ironically, the ubiquitous public policy of *détente*, so embraced by subsequent administrations to address Soviet aggression particularly in the 1970s, was rightly condemned by Truman's advisors, (though it was formally called that), but regrettably their wise counsel was not heeded by Truman and the Allied Powers to stem the tide of Soviet communist hegemony. Indeed, Hitler was vanquished, but history would show that the world would face an even greater Hitler in Josef Stalin. For example, when Truman cancelled the Lend-Lease Act in May 1945, an act which would have facilitated a large loan to the Soviet Union, instead of conciliation, Stalin became enraged, defiant, and emboldened which only furthered his resolve toward communist expansionism over all of Eastern Europe, plunging the world into a forty-five year Cold War (1945-1990) between communist Soviet Union and the democratic United States.

On July 17, 1945, the opening of the Potsdam Conference was held as the war against the Japanese was raging at full force. During the conference, Truman briefed the Allies on the progress of the war in the Pacific theatre against Japan led by the colorful and irascible, General Douglas MacArthur. The Allies were resolute that the war would end only after an unconditional surrender. Fearful of a fruitless and bloody last defense of the home islands by the Japanese, the Allies accepted Stalin's renewed guarantee to join the war against Japan. President Truman contacted Stalin on July 24th after receiving word of the successful testing of an atomic bomb. However, the Soviet dictator appeared disinterested in the news. On July 26, 1945, the British and Americans, without consulting the Soviet Union, demanded in the Potsdam Declaration that Japan submit to an unconditional surrender. Other important agreements that came out of the Potsdam Conference were the creation of a Council of Foreign Ministers to work out the peace treaties for Italy, Austria, Hungary, Rumania, Bulgaria, and Finland. Meetings between July and August 1946 produced peace treaties with all these countries except Austria which was finally worked out in 1955, and only then were Soviet troops removed from German soil.[12]

THE GERMAN QUESTION

> There have been questions about what the American soldier is fighting for; now he knows what he is fighting against.
>
> ~ Gen. Dwight Eisenhower
> Upon his first visit to the Auschwitz Concentration Camp (April, 1945)

The Allies' main concern after Germany's surrender was determining the most effective way to disarm and de-Nazify Germany and bring charges against the remaining Nazi leaders for war crimes. During the London Conference from June 26 through August 8, 1945, the Allies formulated the idea of a Military Tribunal and a special international trial. However, negotiations were hindered by the Soviet's desire for collective retribution as opposed to the U.S. idea of prosecuting a clearly identifiable group of Nazi leaders for conspiracy to commit war crimes among other charges. History would deem that decision unfortunate; that the Allies chose the latter course of "symbolic justice" rather than the Soviet proposal to punish all of the guilty (officers, soldiers, and civilians alike) or the middle ground position of FDR's Jewish Secretary of the Treasury, Henry Morgenthau's proposal to summarily execute all of the German officers the Allies could catch. All of these ideas were considered by the Allies, but were eventually deemed unworkable in light of the Allies greater objective to rebuild Europe, which largely lay smoldering in ashes and destruction, as soon as possible. Administration of German businesses was to be assigned to an Allied Control Council in Berlin made up of British, French, Soviet, and American representatives of the four occupied zones. The Control Council's stated purpose was to preside over and administer the affairs of the defeated nation as a single economic entity. However, the precise nature of a future German government structure continued to be vague, and the verbal agreement on German unity militated against Stalin's persistence to maintain the Soviet zone under communist authority. The Soviet Union eventually relented on its more persistent claims for reparations from Germany when it was able to obtain industrial equipment from the western zones, which was facilitated by the United States in May 1946 (Lend-Lease).

More precarious for the future unity of Germany, however, was the Allies' agreement to divide Berlin into four sectors. Since the Allies did not condition a land corridor or access roads to guarantee freedom of movement between their respective zones, in 1961 the Soviet Union shrewdly erected the infamous "Berlin Wall," segregating East Germany from West Germany, which stood for the next two decades.

The London Agreement of August 1945, had a subsequent section called, *The Prosecution and Punishment of the Major War Criminals of the European Axis*. In this document the Allies outlined the scope, reasoning, and the necessity of creating a special International Military Tribunal whose central purpose would be to try the twenty-four designated Nazi leaders "whose offenses have no particular geographical location." The Agreement on the Prosecution and Punishment of Major War Criminals of the European Axis, was officially enacted by the Allies on August 8, 1945, and was popularly referred to as the Treaty of London.[13]

The Treaty of London followed the Moscow Declaration of October 30, 1943. The Charter of the Tribunal, detailed in the Treaty of London in articles 6(a), 6(b) and 6(c), listed three specific crimes with which the Nazi defendants were to be charged: (1) *Crimes Against Peace*, (2) *War Crimes,* and (3) *Crimes Against Humanity*. However, a fourth charge, *Common Plan or Conspiracy*, was integrated into the language of count one in the indictment and is generally regarded as applying to all three of the previously cited offenses.[14]

Birth of The United Nations

President Franklin Delano Roosevelt, liberals, socialists, and many European leaders, had long sought for an international globalist organization to supersede the modest efforts of the League of Nations. In their 1997 book on the Franklin Delano Roosevelt and the United Nations, Hoopes and Brinkley wrote of Franklin Roosevelt's role in the creation of the United Nations and his desire to build upon the efforts of Woodrow Wilson.[15] In David Golove's article on the history of the United Nations, the author wrote that Roosevelt "undertook the monumental task of vindicating Wilson's vision through the creation of a new league."[16] The League of Nations was the multinational globalist organization President Woodrow Wilson helped create to bring peace to the world after World War I.[17]

President Truman was elated that this utopian dream had finally come to fruition when he addressed the opening session of the San Francisco Conference in April 1945 to work out the details of the United Nation's Charter, and its subsequent signing on June 26, 1945.[18] Although passed by the United States Senate and ratified on July 28, 1945, neither the United States nor the Soviet Union approved the idea for an international police force. The United Nations Charter in Articles 39-51, provides that the UN will not have a standing army, however forces will be composed of member states—United States, Britain, France, Russia and China, if called upon by the Security Council.[19] Notwithstanding, the Charter allowed for police action against "an aggressor nation state." [20] To Truman and most European leaders, the United Nations was the most promising hope for world peace available, and Truman hailed the Charter as "a solid structure upon which we can build a better world."[21]

In its pursuit for peace through negotiation rather than war, the UN installed a General Assembly, a world forum for the deliberation of issues affecting all member states, and a Security Council consisting of six temporary and five permanent members–Britain, France, the Soviet Union, China, and the United States.[22] The Economic and Social Council, the Trusteeship Council, and the International Court of Justice were three of the more important organizations founded under the Charter.[23] A Secretariat, headed by a Secretary General, performed the administrative work of the organization.[24]

The UN's founding documents were signed by the Allied Powers in August 1945 at the close of the London Conference and completion of the Treaty of London.[25] This formalized the UN's Charter and its judicial arm, the Tribunal. Now all of the international globalist structures were in place to answer the German question and bring the Nazi leaders to justice. Or were they?

A Brief History Of War Crimes In The Context Of International Law

War Crimes are violations of the accepted rules of war. These rules, which outline the kind and extent of violence permissible in war, are to a degree delineated in written treaties (laws) and in part consist of de facto customs.[26]

Four compelling reasons are usually given for the necessity of rules of war. First, every despot has a self-seeking interest not to incite reprisals from the enemy, and not to incite neutrals to unite the enemy. Second, wars, however harsh, ironically, are used to lead in a new age of peace. Consequently, resolution should not be made too difficult: as the proverb goes—my enemy of yesterday may be my friend tomorrow. Third, nations do not want their military to become ungovernable; for as history has repeatedly demonstrated such a military force can easily turn against its own civilian government. Last, but not least, war has always been hated for humanitarian and many other reasons and generally taken only after diplomacy fails or an irretrievable act like an assassination has made war unavoidable (for example the assassination of Archduke Ferdinand that precipitated World War I). Having done all reasonable means, nations at least try to mitigate the damages—their brutality and destructiveness should to at least be constrained to some degree, if for no other reason than sheer self-preservation. These four points are the major reasons the law of war is the oldest and one of the most essential parts of international law. Particularly since the Middle Ages, the rules of war—as well as the conditions under which it is lawful to launch a war—have to a great extent occupied the resources of nations, of governments, jurists, and, undeniably, military men.

Rules of War

The rules of war are comprised of several categories: *Rules concerning the status of combatants*—these rules establish specifically if or when a person can lawfully engage in combat, in war, and other military actions. Regarding this point, trained and conscripted soldiers may kill enemy soldiers in battle, but it is against the rules of war for an individual civilian or a soldier disguised as a civilian to commit such acts of combat. *Rules concerning the conduct of hostilities*—these restrict and demarcate the manner and level of damage and misery that may be visited upon the people and country of the enemy, the treatment of prisoners of war, and so forth. *Rules dealing with the behavior of the occupying power in occupied enemy territory*—The more protracted a wartime occupation lasts (for example, at the end or World War II in 1945, Imperial Japan had occupied huge parts of China for over a decade), the more significant are these rules. Rules regarding such vital matters as the rights and duties of the aggressor nations and their citizens toward neutral nations and their citizens, particularly in regards to the behavior of the parties under a truce or during an armistice. The violations against any of these rules, whether mandated by treaties or by international law, are considered war crimes.

Historical Developments

Throughout various ages of history, the traditions, customs, and laws of war were very different; and for extended period of time, and in numerous regions of the world, customs were considered acceptable which during a different generation were regarded as entirely revolting and unacceptable. This aspect of war does not represent an unbroken course—a canon of the rules of warfare if you will. Warfare in one part of the world, or during a certain period of time, or under certain conditions showed signs of less brutality only to relapse again into a period or even an age savagery. For example, Mohammed sacking of Mecca (624) and Medina (630) and, again, of the Thirty Years' War (1618-1648), the bombing of Dresden, Hiroshima, Nagasaki (1945), were manifested by a violation of military customs which had been prevalent over in preceding periods and in other places.

Surveying the history of warfare, there are many examples demonstrating the "considered acceptable" status to pillage or even actually to destroy a conquered city, and to kill the populace, irrespective of sex and age. During other sieges or wars, at least certain places—Churches, Synagogues, Mosques, Temples—were considered safe havens from the ravages of war, particularly for women and children.

There is Biblical precedent here. The Old Testament (Deuteronomy 20:19, 20) forbids the destruction of fruit-bearing trees in enemy territory. In contrast, the ancient Greeks utilized very cruel aspects of war; thus, maladies were inflicted even on the corpse of a captured enemy leader—as vividly chronicled in Homer's *Iliad* regarding Achilles' maltreatment of Hector's body. However, during the Trojan Wars, one was allowed to give the enemy provisions during battle in exchange for a ransom.

The primeval code of *Manu*, the renowned legislator of India, operative long before the Trojan Wars, mandated that an enemy must not be harmed if he is asleep, or naked, or turning to flight, or defenseless, or folding his hands to ask for mercy. However, throughout the history of warfare, there are many examples where captured enemy soldiers were killed on the spot, or soldiers were allowed or ordered to summarily kill the enemy rather than risk reprisals from the enemy by taking them prisoner.

A comparative improvement in the law of war was the increasingly developed tradition not to kill prisoners but to conscript them into slavery (agricultural workers, household servants, soldiers for future battles and the like) or to barter them for one's individual soldiers who had been captured by the enemy. On this point, for example, Hemocratus, a Roman general in the service of Syracuse (on the island of Sicily), was punished by being exiled for commanding his troops to treat the invading Athenian armies with benevolence; while Julius Caesar was not like wise punished for having sold, rather than killed, 33,000 Belgian prisoners during his second campaign in Gaul.

Indeed, it was following the ancient laws of war that permitted the enslavement of conquered people that the Hebrews were taken in servitude to Egypt as chronicled in the Bible in the book of Exodus and again by the Babylonian King Nebuchadnezzar in the book of Kings (586 B.C.). The tradition of selling enemy prisoners at slave auction evolved into the custom of permitting the payment of ransom for their liberty. Of course there are examples in history of emancipating captives without ransom; while, conversely, in the sixteenth and seventeenth centuries it was again considered permissible to make slaves of prisoners.

Sectarian strife greatly influenced the rules of war as is evident with the current strife-war-strife between Israel and the terrorist group, Hezbollah, in Lebanon—a radical Muslim group whose mandate is to kill every Jew in the world (Book of Sirah: "Kill the enemy where you find him"). When the product of war was interpreted by a religious groups holy text to be the judgment of heaven, or the enemy nation or people were regarded as "infidels" or being forsaken by the gods, such doctrines were used as rationalization for the pitiless treatment of the vanquished. In contrast, the Stoics for example, Marcus Tullius Cicero (106-143 BC), taught that the defeated enemy must be summarily executed; and throughout history going back to antiquity, generals who conquered a town, city, or even a nation, in fact became their patrons. This was essentially done by General Douglass MacArthur, when the Pacific theatre defeated Imperial Japan in World War II which became a protectorate of America under his authority for several years until Japan was given a constitution that it still uses in large part until this day.

At various periods, more compassionate rules applied in wars between "equals (for example, conflicts between Christian princes or between Muslims) than in wars against "outsiders" or "infidels" (for example, between Christians and Muslims). Thus, in 1179, Pope Alexander III decreeing that only non-Christians could be enslaved during the Crusades is an example of this discriminatory use of warfare to particularly punish those who are of a different religion. Of course the Muslims were equally uncharitable when it came to its treatment of the "infidels" it captured during battle, most notably was the great Muslim leader Suleiman and French King Richard the Lionhearted (e.g., the sacking of Acre [1189-1191], the Battle of Jaffa [1192], the Battle of Aschalon [1099]).

Crucial to the development of international law was the existential cruel and barbaric the rules of war were *de jure* (by law) or *de facto* (by practice), the violations of such restrictions as did exist were considered as terrible atrocities; and during the course of time such "war crimes" were inflected with of sincere religious sentiments exacting punishments of a religious nature were threatened as the most powerful deterrent available—damning one's soul to eternal damnation for example. Accordingly, during the 11th century, church councils proclaimed the so-called "Truce of God," forbidding warfare on certain days and the harming during hostilities of certain categories of persons, especially priests, women, pilgrims, and merchants (and even extending to common beasts of burden), under penalty of excommunication. Likewise, in wars between peoples of different religions, "treachery—the violation of a treaty-created or customarily sacrosanct rule, such as the molestation of heralds of truce, or the breach of a promise of free conduct—would be punished by severest reprisals." Although Nuremberg holds the distinction in this history of law as being the first "international" war crimes trial, technically speaking, punishment of violations of the rules of war via judicial procedure occurred in an English court in 1305 in the noted case against the Scotland hero, Sir William Wallace, for "waging a war of extermination against the English population," "sparing neither age nor sex, monk nor nun." Since the latter part of the Middle Ages, traditions and practices have developed which ultimately led to the modern law of war; and, in the opinion of a foremost British jurist, Lord Wright of Durley (Robert Alderson Wright), chairman of the United Nations War Crimes Commission, "there have been hundreds of cases in which national military tribunals have tried and convicted enemy nationals of breaches of the laws of war." To demonstrate this point, throughout the Franco-Prussian War of 1870-1871, the Germans executed many French *francs-tireurs* (irregular combatants) for violations of the laws of war.

During the Age of Enlightenment, the tradition of jurists and philosophers of the seventeenth and eighteenth centuries greatly humanized the behavior of potential war criminals during.. For example, Montesquieu (1689-1755) held that to murder prisoners of war is contrary to all law, and Jean Jacques Rousseau (1712-1778) furthered that prisoners of war ought not to be held in dungeons or prisons, or put in shackles, but should be placed in comfortable accommodations and liberated after the end of the war. Customs of war to such effect were decided upon in the *Treaty of Amity and Commerce* between the United States and Prussia (1785), signed by Benjamin Franklin and King Frederick the Great.

GENEVA AND THE HAGUE

Crucial development in the advancement of the laws of war was made after the 1860's to a certain extent due to the effects of the horrors of the Crimean War (1853-1856) and the American Civil War (1861-1864), through international treaties concluded between states. The Geneva Conventions of 1864 and 1906, for example, were treaties specifically designed to improve the conditions of wounded soldiers during existing warfare. The most significant among the treaties codified before World War I were the diverse conventions and regulations accepted at international conferences held at The Hague in 1899 and 1907, and particularly the "Convention respecting the Laws and Customs of War on Land" and the "Regulations respecting the Laws and Customs of War on Land," annexed to the convention of 1907. The rules and principles laid down therein comprise the most determined effort at the time of the Nuremberg Trials to "define with greater precision the rules and customs of war on land."

The Hague Regulations of 1907 have generally formed the foundation of the law of war of the twentieth century. Although subsequently further distinguished by a variety of international conventions—e.g., "the Geneva Prisoner of War Convention of 1929" and "the Geneva Conventions of 1949"—The Hague Regulations of 1907 (as they are often referred to) have continued to form the center of the law of war of the twentieth century. These international treaties have been so universally accepted by the majority of nations that, as numerous tribunals have stated, they are compulsory upon all states, persons, and leaders, which means that breach of these ubiquitous treaties would constitute war crimes.

Several of the articles of the 1907 regulations, cited here at random, may specify their scope and meaning: "Volunteer corps" (now often referred to as organized partisans, guerrillas, or terrorists), if fulfilling definite circumstances designated in these regulations, have the same rights and duties as would a standing army. Humane treatment of prisoners of war is mandated. For example, their board, lodging, and clothing must be "on the same footing as furnished to the troops who captured them." It is particularly prohibited to utilize poison or poisoned weapons (i.e., "weapons of mass destruction" [WMDs]) "to kill or wound an enemy who has surrendered" or "to declare that no quarter will be given."

Furthermore the wanton attack or destruction, by whatever means, of cities, towns, villages, dwellings, or buildings which are undefended is expressly prohibited. "Escaped prisoners who are retaken before being able to rejoin their own army are liable only to disciplinary punishment. Prisoners, who, after succeeding in escaping, are again taken prisoner, are not liable to any punishment on account of the previous flight." Where one country unlawfully invades or occupies another country, "family honor and rights, the lives of persons, and private property, as well as religious convictions and practices, must be respected." Private property cannot be indiscriminately taken. Looting and plundering are formally prohibited. Mass punishment is forbidden in that in warfare there can be no general penalty, pecuniary or otherwise, that shall be inflicted upon the civilian population due to the acts of individuals for which they cannot be regarded as jointly and severally responsible. "The property of municipalities, that of institutions dedicated to religion, charity and education, the arts and sciences, even when State property, shall be treated as private property—that is, must be "respected and cannot be confiscated by the occupant."

Basic Principles Regarding War Crimes

In view of the fact that the rules of war are a major element of international law, it is axiomatic that no nation can unilaterally amend them. No legislature, government, monarch, or general can by any pronouncement, declaration or judgment, decree that something which is a war crime is permitted to their own forces. In 1842, Daniel Webster, United States secretary of state, declared: "The law of war forbids the wounding, killing, impressing into the troops of the country, or enslaving or otherwise maltreating the prisoners of war unless they have been guilty of some grave crime, and from the obligations of this law no civilized state can discharge itself." War crimes can be punished, not only by the institutions of the country of which the offender is a citizen—for example, a soldier who rapes a civilian, or an officer who orders the torturing of prisoners of war will in a civilized country be court-martialed by his country—but also will be subjected to criminal charges by the country of his enemy.

It was long been considered settled law dating back to the Middle Ages respecting the right of the enemy to try enemy combatants for war crimes and has been uncontested throughout the centuries. Indeed, given that the rules of war are *international* law, such enemy combatants may have charges brought against them, and, if found guilty, punished despite the fact that there is no existing laws in that country sanctioning such measures. For this reason, Gen. George Washington acted properly when in 1780, during the American Revolutionary War, he had Maj. John Andre brought up on charges of spying by a Board of General Officers. Andre was fittingly convicted by this Board as a spy "under the laws of war" namely, under the *international* rules of war at that time there existed no controlling legal authority in *American* law in 1780 that expressly predetermined the criminality of Andre's actions. The case was cited as precedent by United States Attorney General James Speed in 1865 regarding the trial of President Abraham Lincoln's assassins:

> The laws of war exist and are of binding force upon the departments and citizens of the government though not defined by any law of Congress . . . when war comes, the laws and customs of war come also, and during the war are part of the law of the land.[27]

Similarly, the United States Supreme Court stated shortly after the Civil

War (in *Dew* v. *Johnson*): "What is the law which governs an army invading an enemy's country? It is not the civil law of the invaded country; it is not the civil law of the conquering country; it is the law of war." War crimes are very severe offenses. On this point the United States basic field manual really places emphasis when it reads: "All war crimes are subject to the death penalty, although a lesser penalty may be imposed. Not only military personnel are bound by the law of war." Consequently, any civilian can be found guilty of a war crime—for example, a physician, like the infamous Nazi doctor, Josef Mengele, who subjected thousand of innocent Jewish civilians, prisoners of war, the mentally ill and the infirm to ghastly and inhuman medical experiments, or the German businessmen that actively participated in the confiscation of civilian (and enemy) property, is expressly prohibited under the laws of war.

Actual battle conditions, however, do not presume guilt even for persons alleged to have committed war crimes, and such persons may not be punished without their guilt being well established beyond a reasonable doubt by a military tribunal. Summary executions of enemy combatants may amount to a war crime in and of itself; however, international law has not established what exact rules should be. There have been circumstances in extreme wartime conditions where summary procedure may suffice, nevertheless, if it should grant the accused the basic rights of a fair trial according to the general principles of law as accepted by the international community of nations. In a broader sense, the expression "war crimes" define two other forms of behavior violating international law, namely "crimes against peace" and "crimes against humanity"—these were the expressed charges brought against the twenty-four Nazi defendants in the Nuremberg Trials of November 1945.

Crimes Against Peace

These consist in "planning, preparing, initiating, or waging of war of aggression." Following World War II, the International Military Tribunal at Nuremberg (composed of one each American, British, French, and Russian judge), limited criminal culpability to the top leaders of Adolf Hitler's Germany. Likewise the International Military Tribunal for the 16 Japanese officers at the so-called "Tokyo Trials" (composed of one judge each from Australia, Canada, pre-Communist China, France, Great Britain, India, the Netherlands, New Zealand, the Philippines, the USSR, and the United States), convicted high military officers of Japan (although ironically Emperor Hirohito was given immunity from all criminal prosecutions). Mutually these tribunals stated in their judgments that to initiate a war of aggression "is not only an international crime; it is the supreme international crime." But both tribunals stressed those only persons actually formulating or influencing governmental policy can be charged with "crimes against peace." Prosecutor Robert Jackson referred in his Opening Address at the Nuremberg Trials that: "We want to reach the planners and designers, the inciters and leaders . . ." Furthermore, at the Tokyo Trials, judgment toward the Japanese defendants was further rationalized that "the duty of an army is to be loyal." For this reason, neither privates, captains, nor generals of an antagonist nation can be culpable for war crimes provided them "merely performed their military duties of fighting a war waged by their government, and did not personally participate in the making of the policy of aggression."

The idea that "aggression" is a crime is closely related with the distinction between "just and "unjust war. "Unjust war" basically denotes in UN-speak, "aggressive war", and includes particularly, aggression committed in violation of expressed provisions in the treaty *not* to attack. The difference between just and unjust war goes back for more than 2,000 years. Roman statesmen and jurists from antiquity insisted upon this point made by the two most prominent "doctors of the Catholic Church; St. Augustine in the 5th century, and St. Thomas Aquinas in the 13th century. This was also upheld by the father of the modern law of nations, Hugo Grotius (1583-1645), and other famous Dutch jurists; and by Spanish scholastics and French and German thinkers of the "Age of Enlightenment." Actual judicial precedents for the contention that crimes against peace are punishable also exist. Thus, the Senate of Rome requested the extradition for trial of Hannibal for inciting nations to make war upon Rome, and of Brutulus Papius of Samnium for attacking Rome in breach of treaty. (Both committed suicide). In 1474, Sir Peter of Hagenbach, governor of Breisach, was tried by a court composed of Austrian and Swiss judges and executed for having waged a "terroristic war."

During the era of tyranny and autocracy in Europe, the distinction between just and unjust war was in the eyes of the "divine" monarch or despot. But when in 1815, Napoleon Bonaparte, violating his word of honor, escaped from Elba to France, regathered some of his old forces, and reignited the war, the Allied Powers of Europe declared him a criminal fugitive and "an enemy and disturber of the tranquility of the world who has incurred public vengeance." Subsequently, Britain, with the permission of the other Great Powers, punished Napoleon by banishing him to the desolate island of St. Helena.

Ironically, a cursory review of war crimes cases under international law even prior to Nuremberg demonstrate that more often than not, the guiltiest went free. Take the case of the German Emperor William II. He was to be tried by an international tribunal Under the Versailles Treaty (1919) "for a supreme offence against international morality and the sanctity of treaties (especially including the violation of the German-guaranteed neutrality of Belgium and Luxembourg)." However, jurisdictional wrangling prevented his day of reckoning because the Netherlands, where William had fled, refused to extradite him, thus, he was never brought to trial for the numerous atrocities he committed by plunging Europe (and the world) into the abyss of World War I.

The interim period between the two great World Wars witnessed several international pronouncements and formal treaties which condemned "wars of aggression" as unlawful and subject to criminal prosecution. Thus, in February 1928, the sixth Pan American Conference of 21 American republics resolved that "war of aggression constitutes an international crime against the human species all aggression is illicit."

The Nuremberg and Tokyo international tribunals attached special importance to the "General Treaty for the Renunciation of War (Kellogg-Briand Pact) of August 27, 1928, because it was ratified before World War II by virtually all countries of the world." However, the treaty does not specifically state that unleashing a war of aggression is criminal act, on the other hand, the Nuremberg International Tribunal seemingly tried to make a more definite statement on whether or not starting a "war of aggression" violates international law when it declared:

> The solemn renunciation of war as an instrument of national policy pledged in the Kellogg-Briand Pact involves the proposition that such a war is illegal in international law; and that those who plan and wage such a war, with its inevitable and terrible consequences, are committing a crime in so doing.[28]

The Kellogg-Briand Pact, in addition to several other pronouncements, further enumerated in international law, the principles codified by the Nuremberg international tribunal. Furthermore, these laws received additional weight due to the fact that the General Assembly of the United Nations, by a unanimous resolution of December 11, 1946, ratified and incorporated these principles into its own charter, as did subsequently, the eleven-nation Tokyo tribunal.

Ironically, It should be mentioned, that for all of the progressive ideas and ideals inculcated into international law since the twentieth century from the establishment of the League of Nations and the Versailles Treaty (1919) through the establishment of the United Nations (1945) that presently consists of over 190 member nations, that after World War II, only thirty-six leaders (twelve German and twenty-four Japanese), out of the many thousands of war crime suspects tried, were executed for "war crimes." This is indeed the tragic and sad legacy of the impotence of Secular Man to rule himself, and the utter failure of positive law, rooted in humanism, to provide a viable moral framework in defense of justice and the rule of law.

Crimes Against Humanity

Crimes Against Humanity are war crimes—murder, extermination, deportation, torture, and other mass atrocities like "ethnic cleansing and persecutions of entire racial, class, religious, and political groups, all fall under this principle. If the victims are enemy citizens, such acts constitute "war crimes" in the narrow sense of the term. However, if the victims were, for instance, German nationals, such deeds were considered punishable under international law (that is, also by non-German courts), *provided* they were committed in connection with "crimes against peace," or "war crimes."

The Nuremberg international tribunal interpreted these crimes carefully. Its articles hold that "revolting and horrible" as was "the policy of persecution, repression and murder of civilians in Germany before the war of 1939," the tribunal was not capable to address these circumstances. It did, on the other hand, find certain defendants guilty of wartime atrocities, regardless of the nationality or jurisdiction of the victims, for the reason that they were committed "in execution of or in connection with the aggressive war." In other words, when, for instance, mentally or physically deficient persons were methodically exterminated and regarded as "useless eaters in occupied territories as well as in Germany," or when German Jews and gypsies were deported to concentration camps, summarily executed, and sent to the gas chambers just as were foreign Jews, gypsies, Christians, religious minorities, political dissenters, the mentally ill, and other "undesirables" pursuant to the Nazi master race theory, all this was a fundamental part of a comprehensive criminal war policy. Subsequent war crimes tribunals, particularly the Tokyo trials, which had to deal with indictments for "crimes against humanity" utilized case law precedent and understanding of the Nuremberg international tribunal.

While the Nuremberg and Tokyo tribunals addressed war crimes of an international nature, it should be noted that since World War II, war crimes trials left unanswered or ambiguous the vital question as to whether atrocities committed en masse by or with the collusion of a government *in peacetime* against entire groups of its *own* population (i.e., Tokyo, Dachau, Manila, Cambodia, Rwanda, and the former Yugoslavia), constitute international crimes; that is to say, whether the culprits can be brought to justice before an international criminal tribunal or court outside of the legal system of the countries where the criminal acts originated.

THE IMPOTENCE OF WAR CRIMES TRIALS AFTER WORLD WAR I

The infamous war strategies of "terror in violation of the laws of war," which Germany utilized in World War I, were the primary catalyst to a resolute demand to bring to justice the perpetrators responsible for those war crimes. The Versailles Treaty, ratified in 1919, provided that Germany should surrender to the Allies the most egregious war criminals for trial. Nevertheless when in February 1920 the first version of that list of infamy included some 900 names—including the former imperial crown prince, Field Marshal Paul von Hindenburg, and General Erich F. W. Ludendorff—was offered, German resentment was so vociferous that the Allies were forced into a compromise posture—specifically, that all aspects of the legal proceedings—from conducting the preliminary investigations, appointing the judges and attorneys, to running the trials, would be wholly administered by the German Supreme Court! Of course the result was a total charade and a mockery of justice. Illustrative of this fact was that of the 901 persons grievously incriminated by evidence furnished by the Allies (mainly Great Britain, France, and Belgium), 888 (over 98 percent) were either acquitted or not indicted at all. To add insult to injury, the entire self-judgment by the German Supreme Court gave rise to fanatical and extreme demonstrations and riots, which directly lead to the rise of numerous fascist and anarchist groups most notabaly the virtually anonymous Hitler and his Nazi Socialist Party. Of the thirteen who were deemed guilty by the Court, none received significant prison sentences, but on the contrary were distinguished inside and outside the Court as national heroes—So much for the progressive-era experiment of allowing the vanquished nations the honor of judging themselves. One can see the German experiment of World War I shows that intention to be contrary to human nature, and powerless to prevent genocidal war.

War Crimes Trials in Connection with World War II

The most celebrated trial held during World War I, was the theatrical production by the Germans at Riom (France), of French statesmen, for alleged "crimes against peace." The objective was to provide evidence that the accused, and particularly Leon Blum, the former French prime minister who was of Jewish ancestry, had been implicated in a Jewish plot to start a world war against Germany, but the evidence right away pointed in the contradictory direction. The scapegoat trial quickly collapsed, and the defendants unjustly put in concentration camps. The first trial of an officer of the infamous "Nazi Elite Guard extermination troops", was held in Kharkov, USSR, in 1943.

With the examination of the incomparable mass atrocities systematically carried out by Germany from the inception of World War II on September 1, 1939, many declarations were issued by the League of Nations, as well as formal warnings sent by the Allies, for the duration of the war, demanding that Hitler and his chief henchmen be brought to justice. The United Nations Charter of 1945 explicitly outlawed "wars of aggression." Indeed, the UN Charter admits only two circumstances in which one country is allowed to use military force against another:

1. When a country must defend itself against an attack from another country;
2. When the Security Council authorizes the use of military force against a country that is in violation of the principles of the UN Charter.

Determination was also strong to punish Japanese atrocities perpetrated in the distant Asian and Pacific theaters of war. In 1943, a body was organized to achieve this result. It was called the "United Nations Commission for the Investigation of War Crimes," and was composed of representatives of seventeen nations. This group was established with its headquarters in London and was to serve as a repository of information and evidence compiled by the Allies against German and Japanese war atrocities. In May 1944, at the appeal of China, the commission organized a Far Eastern subcommission.

The Nuremberg Trials were convened from November 20, 1945, to October 1, 1946 before the International Military Tribunal against twenty-four Nazi leaders including Hermann Goering, Hess, Speer, and other principal officers of the Third Reich. Nuremberg was chosen as the venue for convenient and symbolic reasons—practically speaking, Nuremberg was one the few cities after the war that still had an intact courthouse to conduct the trial and a prison to hold the Nazi defendants. Symbolically, Nuremberg had significance because this city served as the stronghold of National Socialism where Hitler had held his colossal annual rallies. The infamous "Nuremberg Laws of 1935"—denaturalization laws enacted in Nazi Germany that used pseudoscience as a basis for discrimination against the Jews, were enacted in this city. British member of the tribunal, Lord Justice Geoffrey Lawrence, was chosen to serve as Chief Justice over the tribunal which was established and administered pursuant to the London Treaty signed by all the Allied Powers—United States, USSR, Britain, France, in August 1945, as well as ratified and formally recognized by representatives from nineteen other member states of the United Nations.

Of the twenty-four former leading Nazis indicted, twenty-two were tried, including Martin Bormann *in absentia*; one of the defendants (Goering) committed suicide before pronouncement of execution could be rendered against him. Another (von Pappen) was not tried for medical reasons. Twelve of the defendants received death sentence, three were given life imprisonment, four given lesser prison sentences, and three were acquitted of all charges against them. In subsequent Nuremberg trials, a total of 185 other leading German personalities—cabinet ministers, field marshals and admirals, industrialists, ambassadors, jurists, physicians, and so on, were brought up to face various war crimes charges before twelve tribunals, composed entirely of United States judges, at Nuremberg between December 1946 and March 1949 under the legal authority issued by the Allied Control Council for Germany. Of these, four defendants committed suicide, and four were excused from the proceedings for health reasons. Of the remaining 177, these United States tribunals sentenced twenty-five to death, twenty to life imprisonment, ninety-seven to lesser prison terms, and acquitted thirty-five. Thus the Nuremberg Trials had an amazingly high 20 percent acquittal rate (1 out of 5). This is an astonishing figure considering Nazis and Nazism has historically been a synonym, (a byword if your will) for the most unrestrained, intractable form of evil perpetrated by man against his fellow man in modern times. How then could anyone (save a person indicted due to mistaken identity) have not received some sort of punishment? The impotence of the Nuremberg Trials on this point is simply beyond the pale and one of the darkest stains in all of human history and therefore why I unequivocally stated in my Prologue that the Jews got a raw deal at Nuremberg.

On January 19, 1946, the Tokyo International Tribunal was convened by General of the Army, Douglas MacArthur, as Supreme Commander of the Allied Powers (SCAP). The substantive and procedural law utilized in this trial was identical to that relied upon by the Nuremberg international tribunal. Conversely, there were four chief prosecutors (represented on the bench by each of the Allied Powers) at Nuremberg, and only one chief prosecutor (an American, Joseph B. Keenan, former assistant to the United States attorney general) at Tokyo. The trial lasted (including a seven-month recess to prepare the 1,200-page judgment) from May 3, 1946, to November 4, 1948.

The Tokyo trial was presided over by the Australian member, William Flood Webb, Chief Justice of the Supreme Court of Queensland. General Hideki Tojo was the most recognized of the defendants and Japan's prime minister from 1941-1944, was hanged as a war criminal in 1948. Of the original twenty-five defendants brought to trial, seven were given the death sentence, sixteen were sentenced to life imprisonment, and two to other prison terms.

Thankfully the Tokyo Tribunal did not follow the acquittal rate of the Nuremberg Trials (20 percent). On the other hand, hundreds of thousands of Japanese troops were sworn to fight to the death by the command of the god, Emperor Hirohito (who ironically escaped judgment by the Tokyo Tribunal), caused the death of tens of thousands of Allied troops and perpetrated legendary episodes of wanton savagery and war crimes against prisoners of war (the Bataan Death March [1942]) as well as the atrocities against the Chinese civilians in 1931, and against the Philippine civilians from 1943-1945) represent one of the darkest chapters in the annals of the history of warfare, particularly in the twentieth century.

In addition to the Nuremberg and Tokyo Trials, many other trials were convened from 1945 forward by American, British, French, Australian, Belgian, Dutch, Polish, Norwegian, Soviet, Czechoslovak, Israeli, and other courts in various parts of Europe and the Far East. The defendants were largely citizens of former enemy countries, but many nationals of the individual countries moreover, were tried as willing participants, collaborators, enablers and abettors in the war crimes of the enemy.[29] Harvard University historian, Daniel Jonah Goldhagen, wrote an excellent book ten years ago regarding the necessity of comprehensive complicity of ordinary German citizens for Hitler's Third Reich and his war against Europe and America to have remotely succeeded. Goldhagen makes the following prescient remarks to this end—for what developments would a comprehensive explanation of the Holocaust have to account? For the extermination of the Jews to occur, four principal things were necessary according to Dr. Goldhagen's analysis:

1. The Nazis - that is, the leadership, specifically Hitler - had to decide to undertake the extermination.
2. They had to gain control over the Jews, namely over the territory in which they resided.
3. They had to organize the extermination and devote to it sufficient resources.
4. They had to induce a large number of people to carry out the killings.

> The vast literature on Nazism and the Holocaust treats in great depth the first three elements as well as others, such as the origins and character of Hitler's genocidal beliefs, and the Nazis' ascendancy to power. Yet, as I have already indicated, it has treated the last element, the focus of this book, perfunctorily and mainly by assumption. It is therefore important to discuss here some analytical and interpretive issues that are central to studying the perpetrators. Owing to the neglect of the perpetrators in the study of the Holocaust, it is no surprise that the existing interpretations of them have been generally produced in a near empirical vacuum. Until recently, virtually no research has been done on the perpetrators, save on the leaders of the Nazi regime. In the last few years, some publications have appeared that treat one group or another, yet the state of our knowledge about the perpetrators remains deficient. We know little about many of the institutions of killing, little about many aspects of the perpetration of the genocide, and still less about the perpetrators themselves.[30]

Because of this lack of focus, most of what has been written or passed around as "facts" are misconceptions and myths regarding the actual perpetrators of this slaughter. One of the ideas passed as history is that most of those "exterminated" the Jews, Gypsies and others, were killed in the gas chambers, and the idea that it was the technological aspect of this efficient killing method that substantially supported the ability to commit this genocide, and the implication that it would not have taken place absent this technology, or at a substantially reduced expanse. Attached to this is the modern transportation available and the modern data processing that "kept the line moving." It is broadly believed that it was innovations that made possible this wholesale slaughter, as if it were the first of its type. This is far from the truth as history proves in every era. It has been stated many times that the determination of necessity in dealing with the "cleaning house" was a determining factor in the Third Reich's choosing of "gas chambers" as if such widespread slaughter could not be accomplished absent it.

At the same time, the standard story of "who ran these genocide machines" puts the operation of not only the gas chambers, but the dozens of other systematic ways of killing large masses, almost exclusively by the hands of the notorious SS men, devoted to the Nazi ideal and willing to do the brutal work of killing. The facts have been unquestioned on this issue until recently, and it has been suggested to such an extent that people recoil at the idea of "ordinary Germans" being willing participants. Those few "ordinary Germans" who have been personally identified as taking part, have been assumed to have made the choice of cooperating and doing the killing, or becoming one of "those" victims themselves.

These aspects of the whole of the actual Genocide, have been taken as fact on faith, and have been paraded about as if there were no issue to be questioned in this, and with the underlying implication that anyone would do the same if put in that position. This understanding has been arrived at, not by questioning and pursuing the facts on the ground, as we arrived at the scenes of horror, but by accepting the input supporting this myth as "the whole cloth", even though it has been primarily anecdotal.

This was accepted by the allies as reasons and excuses for not having refused to participate, and the people of the Allied Nations, accepted this primarily because discarding it out of hand would suggest any people would be capable of the same, were they put in the same position. However, when the accounting is done, it is simply impossible to place it all in the hands of the select few who achieved stature in the SS, and the distortion has become the reality, in spite of the facts.

CHAPTER 2

THE SHAMEFUL LEGACY OF THE NUREMBERG TRIALS IN CONTEMPORARY JURISPRUDENCE

WHY LEGAL POSITIVISM IS AN INTRACTABLY FLAWED LEGAL PHILOSOPHY

History, the final judge of our deeds.

~ John F. Kennedy
Inaugural Address (1960)

Thus, you must know that there are two kinds of combat: one with laws, the other with force. The first is proper to man, the second to beasts; but because the first is often not enough, one must have recourse to the second. [1]

~ Niccolo Machiavelli,
The Prince (1513)

Let me write with particular clarity and candor here; I have never been comfortable with the entire premise, the utter necessity, moral authority, or the legal legitimacy of the Nuremberg Trials; with its philosophical underpinnings of positive law and legal positivism, its judicial outcomes that look askance at moral and legal constructs such as vengeance, the unity of legality and morality, right and wrong, good and evil, absolute truth, yea, even God. But most importantly, I have the continued inimical effects of positive law upon our present-day legal system in America and the West, particularly in international law, but also the diabolical effects of positive law throughout the legal system of America.

The Nuremberg Trials was purposely established entirely on positive law grounds by the Framers of the UN. Positive law or legal positivism (as it is often referred to in philosophical circles) is riddled with many flaws of which I cite in summary as follows—(1) Positive law fails to take account of sources of law that are independent of the state (i.e., indigenous sources like religion, tradition, or culture); (2) Positive law fails to distinguish between *de jure* (by right; legal) and *de facto* (quasi-legal; acting as legal or under the color of law) sovereignty; (3) Positive law fails to take account of functions of legal rules other than the "command" function; (4) Positive law fails to take account of legal obligations of the state. These and a variety of other defects of positive law inexorably lead many legal theorists and philosophers to erroneously examine law through the rose colored lens of the *letter* of the law at the expense of the *spirit* of the law. As we shall later see, this perverted understanding of the law and its mandated purpose, will have disastrous consequences in the Holocaust and in the Nuremberg Trials.

Before I go further into my critique on the failings of positive law and its applications in the Nuremberg Trials, allow me to cite some of my favorite classics on the subject of legal philosophy and the history of law including such works as *SIR HENRY MAINE, LECTURES ON THE EARLY HISTORY OF INSTITUTIONS*, who eloquently wrote on English sovereignty and empire during a period when both were at their height. JOHN W. SALMOND'S work on JURISPRUDENCE, is an encyclopedic account of definitions and essays on law by famous jurists, literary figures, scholars from ancient times to the late nineteenth century. In his writings Salmond protested against "the creed of what is termed the English school of jurisprudence" because it "attempted to deprive the idea of law of that ethical significance which is one of its most essential elements." (Salmond's words above are in essence, the thesis, if you will,, of this book which will be elaborated upon throughout). Then there is a two volume work by James Bryce—*STUDIES IN HISTORY AND JURISPRUDENCE*, which systematically explains the nature of legal and practical sovereignty.

Of course I would be remiss not to mention H. L. A. HART'S pioneering work, *THE CONCEPT OF LAW*, a work that addresses the variety of laws and commands in society. Other recent but still classic articles on jurisprudence or legal philosophy include—Roger Fisher, *Bringing Law to Bear on Governments*, who suggested that a realistic approach to international law should understand motivations for domestic governmental compliance, Ronald M.

Dworkin, in his work, *The Model of Rules*, called legal positivism the form of law "accepted in one form or another by most working and academic lawyers who hold views on jurisprudence." This rather broad definition of positive law has been rather helpful to me formulating my ideas regarding what I refer to as the "Nuremberg Trial philosophy" [2] — a worldview of international law where the rule of law has for the past century been utterly secularized and stripped of most of it's moral, ethical, rational, and religious content.

This book is intended to be a through examination of the jurisprudential presuppositions underlying the Nuremberg Trials. As stated in the Prologue, a principle aim in writing this book is merely seeking to uphold the common sense principles of the rule of law on what proper philosophy of law the Nuremberg trials *ought* to have been established under and to consciously avoid the pitfalls of many other books and articles on the subject befell—getting bogged down in the minutiae of conflicting statutes of different countries, jurisdictional speculations, and sovereignty issues.[3] The broad, generalized, and objective principles of natural law grounded in the Judeo-Christian intellectual tradition of legal thought would be more than enough to convince any reasonable person of the Nazi defendants' guilt and the requisite imperative for any legitimate legal system that justice, and the imperative that the law upholding it, be rooted in the inseparability of legality and morality. The best evidence of such a legal system being natural law, the very jurisprudence that the American colonists adhered to. The rule of law that the Founding Fathers of America held sacred, the philosophy of law that virtually all of the Framers of the Constitution, the Bill of Rights and the Declaration of Independence, pledged their life, liberty and their sacred honor to uphold and defend.

My opinions regarding the Nuremberg Trials are in many ways markedly different from those of mainstream academic thought, the law academy, and from conformist historians and legal theorists I have read who by in large take the positive law analytical jurisprudence of the UN and its organs as self-evident, particularly the Nuremberg Tribunal unreservedly and virtually without any substantive critique. Unlike the conventional view, which holds that the Nuremberg Trials were a vindication of the rule of law and a triumph of justice over the Nazi empire,[4] I view the Nuremberg Trials as a colossal triumph of positive law over America's original natural law jurisprudence which was strongly rooted in the Judeo-Christian tradition of intellectual thought—an act entrenched in the doctrine of secular humanism, that I argue has not only totally perverted international law over the past sixty years, but has so misrepresented the moral underpinnings of the common law traditions of Anglo-American jurisprudence and the original natural law legal philosophy which mandated a unity between law and morality, that in contemporary times there is little evidence acknowledging even the necessity of morality in law. Thus, the difficulty in modern times of the utter impotency of the law academy in condemning such colossal examples of human depravity and evil as Saddam Hussein, Osama bin Laden, Nasrallah, etc., but on the contrary these same scholars write voluminously against President George W. Bush and his efforts to use the rule of law to protect American citizens in a post-9/11 world by wiretapping international calls of suspected Islamic terrorists.

I also contend that the Nuremberg Trials contributed greatly to the death of the common law (e.g., the rule of law), which codified those natural law principles in Anglo-American jurisprudence dating back in English law to the Magna Carta. For definitional purposes a general explanation of the common law would be instructive here:

> *Common law*: the system of jurisprudence, which originated in England and was later applied in the United States, which is based on judicial precedent rather than statutory laws. . . the Common law is generally derived from *principles* rather than *rules*; it does not consist of absolute, fixed, and inflexible rules, but rather of broad and comprehensive principles based on justice, reason, and common sense. It is of judicial origin and promulgation. Its principles have been determined by the social needs of the community. . .[5]

Furthermore, the natural law tradition in the Western canon includes preeminent natural law natural rights philosophers such as Socrates, Plato, Aristotle, Cicero, Marcus Aurellius, St. Augustine, St. Thomas Aquinas, Hobbes, Sir Thomas More, Locke, Montesquieu, Blackstone, and virtually all of the Framers of the United States Constitution including such men as—Washington, Franklin, Jefferson, Madison, Adams (Samuel, John & John Quincy), Hamilton, Witherspoon, George Mason, John Hancock, and many others.

Natural Law and the Exclusionary Rule

Writer and legal philosopher, David Adams, in his book, *Philosophical Problems in the Law*, defines natural law as "principles and standards not simply made up by humans but rather part of an objective moral order, present in the universe and accessible to human reason." [6] Natural law is *normative* and *censorial* and knowing the folly and intractable nature of humankind, America's constitutional Framers were prescient enough to include built-in exclusionary clause which holds that where human practices and institutions (i.e., statutes, laws, rules, judicial opinions, executive orders, constitutions, local ordinances) fail to measure up to natural law they are *not* considered to be legitimate law. Under these proscribed circumstances where the legislature, the executive, or the Court enacts or decrees a law, a statue, an executive order that does not have the moral foundation of the rule of the rule of law, the people are not obliged to follow such laws. Harvard Professor of Jurisprudence, Lon Fuller, referred to this moral conception of law as "fidelity to law."

For example, in the nineteenth century America had a system of discriminatory laws based on race called "Jim Crow" laws or *de jure* (by law) discrimination statutes. From the time of America's Founding by the Pilgrims landing at Jamestown in 1607 to the passage under the Lyndon Johnson administration of the Voting Rights Act (1964) and the Civil Rights Act (1965, 1968), Black people by in large were not able to access or enjoy those certain "inalienable rights" that Jefferson spoke of in the lofty language of the Declaration of Independence when he penned these immortal words in 1776: "We hold these truths to be self evident that all men are created equal that they are endowed by their creator with certain inalienable rights: life, liberty and the pursuit of happiness. . ." These "laws" were written into local ordinances, statutes (*de jure* = by law), but also taken for granted as social and cultural benefit ("White privilege") by your average American citizen (*de facto* = by practice). So entrenched, systematic, and institutionalized was slavery and racial discrimination, that it took a four year-long bloody civil war and 100 years of de facto discrimination laws (Black codes) to be ruled unconstitutional by the Court and subsequent legislative acts, to finally give Blacks and other minorities any semblance of justice and "equality under the law." During the early 1960s leading figures of the civil rights movement like James Farmer, Dr. Martin Luther King, Jr.'s, Roy Innis, and numerous other civil rights leaders (many members of the clergy) vociferously protested against racism and discrimination courageously enacted the natural law exclusionary rule principle in their fight for equality. On this point recall what I consider Dr. King's most impressive work—*Letter from a Birmingham Jail* (1963)—

> Now, what is the difference between the two? How does one determine whether a law is just or unjust? A just law is a man-made code that squares with the moral law or the law of God. An unjust law is a code that is out of harmony with the moral law. To put it in the terms of St. Thomas Aquinas: An unjust law is a human law that is not rooted in eternal law and natural law. Any law that uplifts human personality is just. Any law that degrades human personality is unjust. All segregation statutes are unjust because segregation distort the soul and damages the personality. It gives the segregator a false sense of superiority and the segregated a false sense of inferiority. . . .
>
> We should never forget that everything Adolf Hitler did in Germany was "legal" and everything the Hungarian freedom fighters did in Hungary was "illegal." It was "illegal" to aid and comfort a Jew in Hitler's Germany. Even so, I am sure that, had I lived in Germany at the time, I would have aided and comforted my Jewish brothers. If today I lived in a Communist country where certain principles dear to the Christian faith are suppressed, I would openly advocate disobeying that country's antireligious laws.[7]

A second example of natural law's exclusionary rule was from a well-known precept of English Common law with origins dating back to natural law which held that if an official abused the power of his office, he would lose the protection of his office and become liable to the citizen right-holder whose rights would be upheld by the sovereign (the Tribunal, court, etc.).

> When a wrong has been done by the King's officer to a British subject, the person wronged has no legal remedy against the Sovereign, for "the King can do no wrong"; but he may sue the King's officer for the tortious act, and the latter cannot plead the authority of the Sovereign, for from the maxim that the King

cannot do wrong it follows, as a necessary consequence, that the King cannot authorize wrong.[8]

Regarding how foundational natural law was viewed by all of America's constitutional Framers and was embodied in its founding documents, David Barton, writes—

> The philosophers embraced by the Founders all expounded a similar theme: the importance of Natural law and the Bible as the foundation for any government established by men. Natural law and the Bible formed the heart of our Founder's political theories and was incorporated as part of their new government.[9]

David Adams defines positive law as law that is posited or dictated by man.[10] It is *expository* and *analytical.* It is a system of orders, commands or rules as opposed to principles, made by man for man, apart from any supernatural source, to be enforced by the raw, naked power of what English philosopher John Hobbes referred to in his writings as the Leviathan state.[11] Positive law, by being solely of human origin, is "artificial" as opposed to "natural." On this point, Hagerstrom wrote:

> [T]he whole theory of subjective rights of private individuals. . . is incompatible with the imperative theory. The description of them [claims to legal protection] as rights is wholly derived from the idea that the law which is concerned with them is a true expression of rights and duties in the sense in which the popular notion of justice understands these terms.[12]

Oxford professor and legal philosopher, H. L. A. Hart, further expounding upon above affirmed that: "[Hagerstrom] insisted that if laws were merely commands the notion of an individual's right was really inexplicable, for commands are, as he said, something which we either obey or we do not obey; they do not confer rights."[13] That follows ipso facto if laws are commands that do not confer rights, under a positive law construct we have no rights but those given to us by the ubiquitous, omnipotent State. That follows logically if the state gives you your rights (rather than under a natural law paradigm protects them) then what the State giveth, the State taketh away. Therefore, it follows logically that if one holds to a purely positive law (secular) idea of law with no higher authority than the state, then your conception of law mirrors Orwell's apocalyptic visions of a leviathan globalist State devoid of morality as so prophetically, vividly, and interestingly delineated in his classic treatises on the apotheosis of the modern State—*Animal Farm* (1945), and *1984* (1949):

> *1984 - Chapter 2*: "Nearly all children nowadays were horrible. What was worst of all was that by means of such organizations as the Spies they were systematically turned into ungovernable little savages, and yet this produced in

them no tendency whatever to rebel against the discipline of the Party. On the contrary, they adored the Party and everything connected with it… All their ferocity was turned outwards, against the enemies of the State, against foreigners, traitors, saboteurs, thought-criminals. It was almost normal for people over thirty to be frightened of their own children."

1984 - Chapter 3: "If the Party could thrust its hand into the past and say this or that even, *it never happened*—that, surely, was more terrifying than mere torture and death."

"And if all others accepted the lie which the Party imposed—if all records told the same tale—then the lie passed into history and became truth. 'Who controls the past' ran the Party slogan, 'controls the future: who controls the present controls the past.'"

"Day by day and almost minute by minute the past was brought up to date. In this way every prediction made by the Party could be shown by documentary evidence to have been correct; nor was any item of news, or any expression of opinion, which conflicted with the needs of the moment, ever allowed to remain on record. All history was a palimpsest, scraped clean and reinscribed exactly as often as was necessary."

Animal Farm—Old Major warns, "Your resolution must never falter. No argument must lead you astray. Never listen when they tell you that Man and the animals have a common interest....we must not come to resemble him...No animal must ever live in a house or sleep in a bed, or wear clothes, or drink alcohol, or smoke tobacco, or touch money, or engage in trade."

The 7 Commandments are abridged for the last time, simply reading, "All animals are equal but some animals are more equal than others."[14]

It is difficult not to accord Orwell prophetic status in rereading his works especially in light of the creation of the two contemporary globalist entities—the United Nations (1945) and the Nuremberg Tribunal (1945)—two glaring examples of socialist utopianism, the former in politics, the latter, in law. Orwell's works foreshadowed in brilliant relief the utterly devastating consequences visited upon subsequent generations, even until this day, as once provisional problems that are now the domain of the ubiquitous, global, oppressive Leviathan State.

HOLMES, POSITIVE LAW AND ITS PHILOSOPHICAL CONNECTIONS TO NAZISM

We now come to the portion of the book that endeavors to make the case of the inevitable result of any legal system based on positive law to devolve into the repeated refrain of political expediency—democracy, socialism, totalitarianism, anarchy, nihilism, death. The notion of positive law is as Justice Oliver Wendell Holmes (1841-1935) understood it, law stripped of any morality, content, influence, or reliance.[15] Richard A. Posner, an appeals court judge and lecturer at the University of Chicago Law School, referred to positive law as absent of any "metaphysical commitments." Posner, like Holmes a century before, viewed law as stark, foreboding, and anti-emotive—*law as it is*. This as opposed to those whom Posner viewed as "moralists" and "moral entrepreneurs", who view *law as it should be*.[16] In my lengthy apologetic to Judge Richard Posner's 1997 Oliver Wendell Holmes Lecture delivered at Harvard Law School ("Reply to Judge Posner . . ."), I opened with the following synopsis of Posner's majestic exegesis on the separation of legality and morality:

> This article is a formal Reply to Judge Richard A. Posner's article published in the Harvard Law Review. Posner's article was actually an amalgamation of lectures he gave as the speaker of the annual Oliver Wendell Holmes Lecture series celebrating the 100th anniversary of Holmes's famous essay, *The Path of Law*.[17] In these lectures, Posner addresses his aversion to what he calls "academic moralism," moral philosophy, legal theory, moral theory and "moral entrepreneurs" because moral theory lacks the "intellectual cogency or the emotional power to change people's beliefs or behavior." By academic moralism, Posner means the propensity by certain legal philosophers and legal theorists in using moral or political arguments to defend an intellectual or legal end. Posner holds to the idea of a strong separation of legality and morality and has a "visceral dislike" towards academic moralism.[18]

This brings me to some of the writings of Justice Holmes and how his ideas on law, jurisprudence and law's influence on public policy both nationally and internationally, greatly influenced the philosophical presumptions relied on in the Nuremberg trials. Let me state unequivocally at the onset of my apologetic that I will try to be fair in delineating his views on the subject despite that fact that Justice Holmes was in my opinion, one of the most virulent and influential anti-Natural law jurists of this past century. Nevertheless, Holmes is almost without peer in the succinct, prudent, logical and colorful way he addresses the law, history, philosophy, as well as his sweeping knowledge of virtually any academic subject which he expresses with his unique élan.

Holmes held to the idea outlined in his famous 1897 article, *The Path of Law,* that law should be viewed through the utilitarian lens as a tool of social control, experience, and raw, statist power of a sovereign over the people.[19] One of the most notable remarks Holmes made on the law was in his seminal work, *The Common Law* (1881), where he stated—"The life of law has not been *logic*; it has been *experience*." By "logic" Judge Holmes' meant:

> The formalistic, religion-based logic that reasoned downward syllogistically from assumed truths about the universe; the proposed counter-system was "experience," the changing "felt necessities" that reflected current social values and were altered by time and circumstances. . . [This was] merely a fatalistic acceptance that law was not so much the embodiment of reason as a manifestation of dominant beliefs at a given time.[20]

Moreover, Holmes, in his letter to his friend, Sir Frederick Pollock, sounded a social Darwinist view of the law as "simply an embodiment of the ends and purposes of a society at a given point in its history."[21] A contrasting position of Holmes was made by Albert W. Alschuler in his book, *Law Without Values: The Life, Work, and Legacy of Justice Holmes.* Alschuler gave a scathing but truthful assessment of his subject when he characterizes Justice Holmes as a distasteful man who, among other things, espoused Social Darwinism, favored eugenics, and as he himself acknowledged, came "devilish near to believing that might makes right." Alschuler's debunking of Holmes and his derisive critique of contemporary legal scholarship will be a lightning rod for discussion and debate.[22]

Holmes reduced law to its lowest (and most brutal) common denominator to simply mean, "beliefs that have triumphed."[23] It is with pungent irony that the litany of twentieth century dictators—Lenin, Stalin, Mao, Mussolini, Hitler, Castro, Idi Amin, Pol Pot, Saddam Hussein, the Saudi Sheiks, the Iranian Mullahs, Osama bin Laden would take Holmes humanist conceptions of the law and use it to create some of the most egregious and infamous examples of genocide the world had ever known—butchering tens of millions in the name of some tyrannical ideology which that particular despot wanted to impose onto the masses. Furthermore, Holmes conception of law (within a generation—1897-1937) purposely and explicitly divorced law from morality—a unity and synthesis presumed in the Anglo-American legal systems going back centuries. Holmes further remarked, "[t]ruth [is] the majority vote of that nation that could lick all others."[24] He also stressed that "when it comes to the development of a *corpus juris* the ultimate question is what do the dominant forces of the community want and do they want it hard enough to disregard whatever inhibitions [i.e., morality, Christianity] may stand in the way."[25] Regarding the arbitrary nature of law as he understood it, Holmes remarked:

> I see no reason for attributing to man a significance different in kind from that which belongs to a baboon or a grain of sand. I believe that our personality is a cosmic ganglion, just as when certain rays meet and cross there is a white light at the meeting point, but the rays go on after the meeting as they did before, so, when certain other streams of energy cross at the meeting point, the cosmic ganglion can frame a syllogism or wag its tail.[26]

It is these views *against* natural law (affirming an inseparable synthesis between law and morality) and *for* positive law (insisting that a wall be erected between law and morals) that logically and inexorably lead Holmes's legal philosophy to be adopted by Hitler, Nazism, and the jurisprudence of the Nuremberg trials. Let me be clear here; of course I am not calling Holmes a Nazi sympathizer for history has deemed him a jurist of the highest order, and ironically Holmes died the year Hitler consolidated his power in 1932, however I wish to show to the reader how what I consider some of Holmes' perverse ideas on law can be further perverted by despots in high authority—truly wicked men like Lenin, Stalin, Mao, Mussolini, and Hitler, who can transform a positive law paradigm, which mandates a separation between legality and morality, to then push to the abyss the logical ends of a positive law legal system—totalitarianism, anti-Christianity, anarchy, nihilism, death.

On the contrary, natural law is, as America's constitutional Framers understood it, law as it *ought* to be.[27] Many noted scholars of law of past generations understood this including Edward S. Corwin, who in his great work, *The "Higher Law" Background of American Constitutional Law*, discusses the evolution of the philosophy of law; Arnold Brecht, *The Myth of Is and Ought*, contending that the separation of "is" and "ought" is artificial. Hart, in his article, *Positivism and Separation*, advocated that there is a division of the law *as it is* from the law as it *ought to be*. Famed Harvard professor of philosophy, Lon Fuller, in his work, *Positivism and Fidelity to Law: A Reply to Professor Hart*, argued convincingly that Hart's is/ought position is contradictory. Thus, at the dawn of the twenty-first century we revisit the age-old battle between *is* and *ought*.[28]

POSITIVE LAW IN MODERN TIMES

FULLER IN THE GAP

How did we get here? How did America devolve from a legal system that presumed an irrevocable bond between law and morality to our present secular-based legal, positive law—a legal system that mandates a strict separation between legality and morality? The roots of our current humanistic conception of law in modern times were planted by the seeds of positive law in the nineteenth century by English legal theorists, Jeremy Bentham[29] (1748-1832) and John Austin[30] (1790-1859). Oxford Professor of Philosophy, H. L. A. Hart, in his classical work, *Positivism and Separation,* ably discusses the positive and negative aspects of legal positivism as infused into Anglo-American jurisprudence by works of Bentham and Austin. Hart's model writing is still superior to all other attempts on this subject. I am exceedingly indebted to Hart's pioneering work in legal philosophy and this article is heavily reliant on his tremendous contributions to the field, particularly his detailed and copious notes, many of his primary and secondary sources are referenced in this book.

Regarding the writings of Jeremy Bentham on positive law and legal positivism, Hart noted an exclusionary element in one of the Founding Fathers of positive law; that Bentham, as a personal observer of the anarchy of the French Revolution, sought in his theory of law to expound that certain laws were too morally outrageous and evil to obey and that fighting against such laws had to be seriously considered in any legitimate system of laws.[31] Critical questions to consider regarding the separation of law and morals include: (1) If the law is not what it ought to be; if it openly combats what Fuller refers to as the "principle of utility," ought we as a society to obey it?; (2) Ought we to violate it?; (3) Ought we to remain neutral between the law which commands evil and morality which forbids it?[32] These are salient questions of which philosophers, law academics, legislators, lawyers, judges, politicians, activists, and interested laymen grapple with daily and of which even in modern times, there appear no ready-made answers, however, in this book I will pose what I hope will be some solutions based on recent historical evidence and events.

With the publication of John Austin's *magnum opus*, *The Province of Jurisprudence Determined*, natural law was now systematically replaced with what he deemed a new and superior legal philosophy—positive law, or law that is posited or delegated by human authority to human subjects, as opposed to the former legal philosophy—natural law, which views law as inseparable from God's universal principles of nature.[33] Austin's work is actually a series of six lectures that he gave on jurisprudence which were first published in 1832. In Austin's *Province of Jurisprudence Determined*, when he writes of law he refers only to positive law. Natural law, by its omission, is rendered in Austin's work to be obsolete and irrelevant in a coherent analysis of the substantive principles of law. *Province* also originates the dual positive law principles of the *command doctrine* (law as a command of a sovereign to its subject that must obey at fear of punishment) and *superior orders doctrine* (an order from the sovereign or state must be obeyed at fear of punishment).[34]

One hundred thirteen years after Austin's apologetic on positive law was published, defense attorneys for the Nazi defendants in the Nuremberg Trials in 1945 shrewdly borrowed Austin's command and superior orders doctrines as a major part of their defense and was so convincing to the Nuremberg Trial Justices that when you combine the dozen or so trials together that made up "the Nuremberg Trials," was successful in securing the freedom for about thirty percent of the defendants not to mention avoiding the hangman's noose.[35]

FDR, THE SUPREME COURT, AND A SWITCH IN TIME SAVES NINE

A key event in the history of American constitutional law jurist, Oliver Wendell Holmes (1841-1935) was in my opinion, one of the most virulent and influential anti-Natural law jurists of this past century. Nevertheless, Holmes was almost without peer the prudent, outspoken sage of Progressive-era jurisprudence and constitutional thought. This monopoly of public opinion which controlled the marketplace of ideas was further dominated by the ruling liberal elites primarily from the northeastern states along the Atlantic coast. Flush with confidence from his unprecedented four term reign president of the United States, Franklin Delano Roosevelt (1933-1945) thought he had the majority of the public confidence to secure the political mandate to pack the U. S. Supreme Court with liberal or left-of-center judges to facilitate the passage of his vast expansion of government programs euphemistically referred to at his "New Deal." Although Roosevelt died in office in 1945, several months into his fourth term and shortly before the Allies forced Germany's unconditional surrender, during his tenure as President FDR personally appointed eight (8) Supreme Court Justices–1 Chief Justice and 7 Associate Justices. Here they are named followed by the year of appointment to the Court—

- Chief Justice, Harlan Stone (1941);

Associate Justices

- Hugo Black (1937),
- Stanley F. Reed (1938),
- Felix Frankfurter (1939),
- William O. Douglas (1939),
- James F. Byrnes (1941),
- Robert H. Jackson (1941)
- Wiley B. Rutledge (1943),
- Harold H. Burton (1945).[36]

Roosevelt's bold, ambitious, and comprehensive expansion of government through radical socialism as his remedy to pull America out of the economic malaise of the former detached, conservative Herbert Hoover administration, (which Roosevelt and others were fond of saying that Hoover's policies actually percipitated stock market collapse of 1929 and the Great Depression), formally launched his New Deal government programs during the first 100 days of his administration in 1933. However, for our purposes in this book, the single most familiar New Deal story is that of the contest between the New Deal and the so-called "Nine Old Men"—

> According to this story, the stodgy majority of the Supreme Court, held hostage by the doctrine of laissez-faire, repeatedly shot down New Deal legislation until President Roosevelt, goaded beyond endurance and emboldened by his 1936 landslide majority, challenged the Court directly. Roosevelt proposed that because the Justices were elderly and tired and needed help, he would call for legislation permitting him to appoint new Justices to aid the incumbents with their work. His foes called the plan "Court-packing," and a titanic struggle ensued for the soul of the American Constitution. Finally, the Justices carried out an abrupt "switch in time" that took the steam out of the push to pack the Court. The story ends, as do many great American historical dramas, by giving everybody something. Roosevelt lost his plan but gained a more cooperative Court. The Justices saved the institution of the Court, but gave in to Roosevelt and began upholding New Deal measures. And the people got both a more cooperative Court and a renewed appreciation of their beloved Constitution.[37]

Professor Barry Cushman of St. Louis University Law School, has completed a constitutional history of the New Deal,which characterizes as myth the unflinching laissez-faire Court, is coming under fire. First, Cushman rejects as overblown, the traditional characterization of the Court as unflinchingly "laissez-faire" until the 1937 "switch in time" that defused the Court-packing plan. Secondly, many of the New Deal measures that the Court struck down deserved to be struck down—they were badly drafted, violating central constitutional principles, (e.g., [the void for] vagueness and mootness doctrines, regarding statutory construction) and the draftsmen knew or should have known what they were doing. Third, the so-called "switch in time" apparently was not a response to the Court-packing controversy; it represented two Justices' sincere belief that the specific law before them (the National Labor Relations Act) was free of constitutional defect and thus different from the laws they previously had struck down. Cushman's analysis of the actual doctrinal history of the Supreme Court is persuasive, but, nonetheless, the "conventional" story of the battle between creative uses of government power and laissez-faire constitutional theory shaped both American constitutional law and the American people's understanding of how that law has developed over time.[38]

My question is this—Is it rational to believe on the one hand that time and time again the Court ruled FDR's New Deal programs as an unconstitutional usurpation of the executive branch over the legislative branch, to now treat the Court's apparent unity and favorable view toward the National Labor Relations Act and subsequent New Deal programs as "constitutional"? This is beyond the pale. Cushman's analysis is simply a case of historical revisionism. Historically speaking, the conventional view of Roosevelt's 1937 Court Reform Bill against the Court were a Machiavellian power grab. Human nature being intractable the way it is, Roosevelt wanted his New Deal programs enacted by executive decree (bypassing normal legislative procedures), but was kept in check by the Court telling Roosevelt to follow the constitutional process and avoid separation of powers violations in his present willful course of action. Roosevelt responded with patent hubris that I am the President (capital "P") and I can do what I want. Have I not been elected by the People? Herein was Roosevelt's paradox. How could Roosevelt get around the inconvenient truth called the Constitution that was blocking his New Deal programs from being enacted into law? Easy, to paraphrase Admiral Nimitz, the famed War World II Navy commander—"Damn the Constitution, full steam ahead!"

Accordingly, it should be clear to any objective observer of history that first, FDR's leviathan New Deal programs were clearly an unconstitutional usurpation of the executive branch over the legislative branch, and secondly, FDR, under America's constitutional scheme, should have worked with the Senate and the House of Representatives to draft and properly enact the New Deal programs through Congress. Not following these explicit procedures was an express violation of the constitutional separation of powers doctrine, whereby it is unconstitutional for any of the three branches of government—executive, legislative, judicial, to intrude in the function in the enumerated powers of the other branches.

Secondly, FDR's growing frustration at having virtually all of his New

Deal programs struck down as unconstitutional by the Court provoked him to launch his second shameful power grab—by executive order, whereby he sought to add four more liberal Justices to the Court who would tip the balance of power to approve his New Deal programs. This act, had it been enacted, would have clearly been an unconstitutional usurpation of power of the executive branch over the judicial branch of government in addition to an expressed violation of the constitutional separation of powers doctrine.

Thirdly, FDR and the Supreme Court, which at the time was equally culpable for their cowardice, treachery and complicity in this most shameful episode of the entire Court packing ordeal, historically has gotten a pass. This infamous compromise, the so-called "switch in time saves nine," contrary to what Cushman calls the "conventional" story of the battle between creative uses of government power and laissez-faire constitutional theory, distorted both American constitutional law and the American people's understanding of how that law was to properly develop over time under the common law system of jurisprudence.

Roosevelt and the Court's "switch in time saves nine" compromise gutted and perverted the Constitution in such a way as to forever alter the balance of power that the constitutional Framers were so scrupulous to uphold—opening the floodgates of executive, legislative, and judicial excesses as to render the constitution essentially obsolete and dead and the new, de facto, shadow constitution was born, thus Holmes' cynical words cited before have now become prophetic—"Truth [i.e., political power] is the majority vote of that nation that could lick all others." [39] FDR's sad and cynical legacy of acquisition of power through social Darwinism's "survival of the fittest" philosophy and the contemptuous patronizing by doling out governmental largess, spawned new, rapacious and ever-creative actions by politicians in modern times.[40] With the U.S. Constitution now neutralized and rendered a mere tool, FDR could wield his executive authority to coerce the legislative and judicial branches to bow to his will. FDR withdrew his court packing bill of 1937 from Congress because he had bribed two unscrupulous members of the Supreme Court (Chief Justice Charles Evan Hughes and Justice Owen Josephus Roberts) to now vote yes on his New Deal legislation. The fix was in and the stage was now set for Roosevelt's final act to this grand tragic opera—The United Nations and the Nuremberg Tribunal.

THE NUREMBERG TRIALS AND THE UNITED NATIONS

1945 was a critical year for America and the world. FDR died in April, 1945. Vice President Truman was appointed to replace him. America breaks Japanese hegemony in the Pacific in such monumental battles as Midway, Leyet, and D-Day. V-J Day ("Victory over Japan Day") occurred on August 15,

1945, solidifying the Allied Powers victory and enshrining for eternity the Axis powers ignoble defeat. The Potsdam and London and Conferences were convened securing Germany's unconditional surrender and formalized judicial proceedings to punish the Nazi leaders and planners of World War II. 1945 was also the year that the United Nations was formerly created at the San Francisco Conference which subsequently gave the world its first truly international court cases–the Nuremberg Trials (1945-1948) and the Tokyo Trials (1946-1948).

Historically speaking these were the first two international trials to unreservedly rely on positive law—the separation of law from morals—in a legal proceeding of this magnitude. Recall that positive law at that time was an obscure, exotic philosophy of law known mostly by jurists and constitutional law professors, but which had at that time been largely inconspicuous to the American public. After all, it would be just two more short years before the Court "found" a separation of church and state in the infamous *Everson v. U.S.* (1947)[41] case, which opened the flood gates to the Court finding a right of privacy to do things that only a few years before would be lewd, lascivious, and at minimum a violation local decency ordinances (i.e., *Griswold v. Connecticut, Miranda v. Arizona, Roe v. Wade, Mapp v. Ohio, Lawrence v. Texas*, etc.).

I want to clearly and unequivocally state that the positive law philosophy of Bentham and Austin of Langdell and Pound, of Holmes and Cardozo, of Wilson, Roosevelt and Kennedy, and the legal and philosophical foundation of international law was now the controlling legal authority of the Nuremberg Tribunal. Furthermore, this "Nuremberg Trial philosophy" with its globalist, secular humanist worldview, has by extension, further denigrated America's constitutional republic and has placed the moral precepts and presuppositions foundational to natural law and to America's constitutional ideals rooted in the Judeo-Christian tradition, in great jeopardy to such an extent that we are presently witnessing the death of the rule of law not only in international law but in Anglo-American law, Anglo-American culture—the death of Western civilization.[42]

Beginning in the late 1800s, the academy had become increasingly more liberal, secular, and humanistic in their worldview and in their approach to teaching law to law students. This was primarily due to the slavish acceptance by the academy of the ideas of four infinitely famous and influential men—Karl Marx (1818-1883), Charles Darwin (1809-1882), Oliver Wendell Holmes (1841-1935), and Sigmund Freud (1856-1939). I choose these four preeminent thinkers of the late nineteenth century as not wholly responsible for the devolution of the moral content of the rule of law, culture, and society, but because particularly the ideas of these men are representative models to answer the questions—who, when, and how Anglo-American law went from a natural law paradigm to a positive law paradigm in less than a generation. Moreover, critical to the thesis of this book, how the diabolical (and now largely disproved) ideal and ideals of these giants of the academy have utterly perverted not only law, but science, religion, politics, economics, culture, and society. Regarding Darwin and by extension—Marx, Holmes and Freud, upon whose theories and philosophy is heavily indebted, cultural writer, Ann Coulter wrote in her unique vociferous style of the synthesis between social Darwinism and Hitler's Aryan supremacy ideology:

> On Darwinism and Nazism: Hitler's embrace of Darwinism is not a random fact, unrelated to the reason we know his name. It is impossible to understand Hitler's monstrous views apart from his belief in natural selection applied to races. He believed Darwin's theory of natural selection showed that "science" justified the extermination of the Jews. On Darwinism's appeal to liberals: Liberals subscribe to Darwinism not because it's "science," which they hate, but out of wishful thinking. Darwinism lets them off the hook morally. Do whatever you feel like doing - screw your secretary, kill Grandma, abort your defective child - Darwin says it will benefit humanity! Nothing is ever wrong as long as you follow your instincts. Just do it - and let Mother Earth sort out the winners and losers.[43]

Applying Darwinian evolution to all fields of study in the liberal arts academy occurred within two generations after the establishment of one of America's first law schools—Harvard Law School (1817) and the subsequent appointment of Christopher Columbus Langdell as dean of the law school (1870-1895). Langdell's creation of the case method of study was expressly modeled after Darwin's "scientific" evolutionary approach to the law explicitly to show the law student, through the study of cases, how the law "evolved" to become what it is today. Langdell believed like many legal scholars of his day that the law evolved from cases and cases evolved from judge's opinions. After all when Langdell became the dean at Harvard Law School 1870, the first edition of Charles Darwin's *Origin of the Species* was only eleven years from its creation.

By the early 1900s applying Darwinism to all aspects of the liberal academy had been codified, solidified and regarded as beyond debate by most of the leading academics, scientists, philosophers, judges, and politicians both here in America and throughout Europe and the West. In modern times, justices, judges, law professors, law philosophers, lawyers, jurists, intellectuals, civil liberties groups and legislators for the past century have used positive law and legal positivism philosophy in virtually all of America's law related and law making institutions (i.e., constitutions, courts, Congress, executive agencies, etc.) In my view this has likewise contributed to and perpetuated the erosion of the rule of law in existing times to such a degree that sophistic propaganda and societal acquiescence to the legal fiction of the separation of law and morality is now viewed by the majority of law professors, legal philosophers, judges and even the mainstream media, and the general public, as conventional thinking, a sound philosophy of law, and an enlightened, secular worldview that is beyond all rational argument. Thus, the current constitutional crisis in times, along with the seemingly impotency of the rule of law to remedy social and cultural pathology, particularly in relation to how law affects society, has denigrated and perverted America's legal system to such a degree as to not only rob it of a stable moral foundation, but to leave in its wake, a legal system that few people feel consciously or morally obligated to follow.

By separating laws from morals, we have also separated reason from sanity and have opened the floodgates to a public contempt for the rule of law, which, with regards to international law, reached its apotheosis in the Nuremberg Trials, whereby in 1945 the United Nations Framers the gave the world the UN, the Nuremberg Tribunal, and it's attendant leviathan bureaucracy, proudly trumpeted the contention that unlike anachronistic, moral-based legal systems of the past, a new age had dawn upon humanity whereby humanistic positive law would be the controlling jurisprudence of the Nuremberg Tribunal. Given the results of this legal perversion—the Nuremberg Trial philosophy has disseminated into all aspects of American's law-related institutions, particularly the courts and the legislature. As humanity moves into the twenty first century, the downward spiral of increasing societal instability, bad public policy, socialism, democracy (= mob rule), anarchy, and eventually civilization nihilism, will become America's and the West's ignominious demise to a 2,500 year by-in-large sterling contribution to world civilization.

THE NUREMBERG TRIALS AND INTERNATIONAL LAW

The shameful legacy of the Nuremberg trials did not happen in a vacuum or out of thin air, but was a conscious means to punish the vanquished nations of Japan and Germany and to eventually bring them back into the Pantheon of civilized nations. The Nuremberg Trials, at least in part, resulted from several rather utopian, naïve, and dangerous treaties signed by the participants of World War I including America, Britain and France, namely: (1) The Briand-Kellogg Pact of 1928 "by which Germany, Italy, and Japan, in common with practically all the nations of the world, renounced war as an instrument of national policy";[44] (2) The Geneva Protocol of 1924 for the Pacific Settlement of International Disputes (the so-called Geneva Convention) signed by the representatives of forty-eight governments, "declared that a war of aggression constitutes . . . an international crime";[45] (3) The Eighth Assembly of the League of Nations in 1927, "on unanimous resolution of the representatives of forty-eight member nations, including Germany, declared that a war of aggression constitutes an international crime";[46] (4) The Sixth Pan-American Conference of 1928, held that "[a] war of aggression constitutes an international crime against the human species";[47] and, (5) Articles Forty-Six and Forty-Seven of The Hague Convention of 1907 in which the United States and many other countries accepted the rules that in an occupied territory of a hostile state "family honor and rights, the lives of persons, and private property, as well as religious conviction and practice, must be respected."[48]

It is evident, at least by 1907 at the ratification of the first Hague Convention, that the illegality of aggressive war was one of the "generally accepted rules of international law."[49] Furthermore, The Hague Convention "prohibited resort to certain methods of waging war"[50] methods no doubt Nazi Germany and Imperial Japan were in flagrant violation of during World War II. However, it must be noted that neither The Hague Convention, nor subsequent treaties before 1945, made provisions for a legal or judicial system to try and punish people who had violated this law, thus neglecting to provide a workable remedy in the event of a violation. The Hague Convention also did not provide a specific remedy for a violation of this aspect of international law.[51] Therefore it was evident that for almost forty years—from 1907 at the ratification of the first Hague Convention, up until the San Francisco Convention, formally establishing the United Nations in 1945, that the illegality of "aggressive war" was one of the "generally accepted rules of international law."

Although natural law presumes an integration of legality and morality, notwithstanding, even from a positive law viewpoint, these excerpts of past international treaties ratified by dozens of nations prior to World War II, should have put Germany, the German people and the world on notice on the illegality of waging an "aggressive war" against another nation, yet Germany and the Axis powers waged a genocidal war against the world twice in the twentieth century.[48]

The ignominious legacy of a hundred years of positive law legal theory (1900-2000) and legal positivism as the philosophical basis for international law and international treaties, has lead to positive law jurisprudence in local, federal, and Supreme Court rulings, both in America and the Occident, leading to the pathetically limited and largely ineffective show trials in Nuremberg–the apotheosis of positive law jurisprudence, liberal judicial activism, progressivism, and secular humanistic reasoning of the grandest scale.

How did the Nuremberg Trials come about? How could such a tragic abrogation of the rule of law come to be in modern times? Furthermore, following the legacy of the Nuremberg Trials, just how effective and relevant are contemporary international trials such as those currently being conducted by the United Nations at The Hague for Rwanda, Yugoslavia, and Iraq? And regarding Iraq (a country in which America has been at war longer that it was during World Wars I and II) how effective and relevant will the upcoming international trials be against the infamous Iraqi dictator, Saddam Hussein, and his brutal Baathist (Sunni) Party regime? According to recent reports, the Rwanda and former Yugoslavia trials cost over $100 million a year to operate and to date for all of that money spent in pursuit of "justice", very few of the leaders, or in the rhetoric of the Nuremberg Trials, the "plotters, and planners" of these horrific episodes of savagery, have been brought to justice and the rank and file "soldiers", in the spirit of Nuremberg, have virtually gotten away with war crimes in some respects surpassing the atrocities of Hitler in its brutal savageness against innocent victims.

Following the symbolic punishment paradigm of Nuremberg a Washington Times columnist cites the pathetically dismal tally of convictions by The Hague, writing that:

> [A]t the International Criminal Tribunal for the Former Yugoslavia, 117 have been indicted, sixty-seven persons have been brought into custody, twenty-six

have been convicted, five acquitted, eleven are currently standing trial, and one is awaiting the judgment of the court. At the International Criminal Tribunal for Rwanda, seventy-six have been indicted, fifty-seven have been brought into custody, eight have been convicted, one acquitted and seventeen are currently on trial.[52]

On 11 March 2006, Prime Minister Slobodan Milosevic died under mysterious circumstances in his prison cell at The Hague, allegedly from chronic heart ailments and high blood pressure, but others, close to the investigation into the death of the former leader, believe that he was poisoned by his jailers at the behest of high level UN officials to avoid his public testimony that could really bring embarrassment regarding the UN's policy in the Balkans. Slobodan Milosevic had been on trial since February 2002, defending himself against sixty-six counts of crimes, including genocide, in Croatia, Bosnia and Kosovo. He was the first sitting head of state ever to be indicted for such crimes.[52A]

Should we expect that the number and proportion of indictments and convictions for the war crimes trials for Rwanda or the Former Yugoslavia be any different from those achieved at Nuremberg sixty years before? Could we expect any different results? The ubiquitous definition of a crazy person is someone who does the same thing the same way, time after time, and expects different results. The same judicial precedents, trial techniques, acquisition and presentation of the evidence established at Nuremberg have been followed in the subsequent trials in Rwanda, the Former Yugoslavia and in many other venues throughout the world. Why then is the general consensus among legal scholars as well as the general public, that such "symbolic justice" of punishing the leaders or the so-called, "plotters and planners" of the war crimes, left very few observers satisfied with the results? Consider especially, the poor victims of their savage atrocities. A more thorough treatment of these salient questions will be addressed in the book's Epilogue.

Similarities between previous international treaties cited above and the legal philosophy of positive law utilized as defenses in the Nuremberg Trials are startling. First of all, it was the Nuremberg Trials that six decades ago legitimized and presented on an international stage and televised to the world the now popular Austinian legal philosophy of the separation of legality from morality—his separability thesis. This is a fundamental tenet of positive law. Furthermore, the then newly discovered "separability thesis" was a radical and revolutionary invention in the fields of legal philosophy and constitutional law at the time. Since then, as these ideas secured wider acceptance in the academic world, it has so greatly influenced jurisprudence, international law, and judicial decision making so much so that by 1960 British legal philosopher, H.L.A. Hart could confidently write,

> [I]n each of them [Austin and Bentham] the utilitarian separation of law and morals is treated as something that enables lawyers to attain a new clarity. Austin was said by one of his English successors, Amos, 'to have delivered the law from the dead body of morality that still clung to it.'[53]

Was there a "new clarity" achieved in the establishment Nuremberg Trials? Did the Nuremberg Trials' utilization of positive law cause to occur in the words of Hart to be "delivered the law from the dead body of morality that still clung to it"? I think not. It appears to me to be counterintuitive to indict and convict certain Nazi leaders of war crimes, crimes against humanity, genocide, and other very serious charges which are morally reprehensible, to then turn around a say that we are not going to judge you on *moral* grounds, but will bend over backwards to judge the Nazi defendants on purely *legal* grounds. This is indeed a quite untenable position of Nuremberg, and one of the major reasons the legacy of Nuremberg or what I refer to as the "Nuremberg Trial philosophy" has been utterly impotent to achieve any reasonable level of comprehensive justice against those convicted of war crimes, even until this day.

William Markby, in his book, *Elements of Law*, noted that by establishing a distinction between positive law and morals Austin created the foundation for a science of law) stating that "[p]ositive laws, as Austin has shown, must be legally binding, and yet a law may be unjust." [54] Like Blackstone before him and Fuller after him, Austin, under his positive law paradigm, held to a type of exclusionary rule. In his writings according to Markby Austin has admitted that law itself may be immoral, in which case it may be our moral duty to disobey it.[55]

Second, it was this sophistic legal defense, Austin's superior orders doctrine that their Nazi defense attorneys relied on so heavily to achieve substantial success in the defense. Surprisingly, out of the twenty-four major Nazi leaders and 153 lesser Nazi leaders tried at the dozen Nuremberg Trials, almost thirty percent of all Nazi defendants were acquitted, and only 18 percent received the death penalty. The overwhelming majority of the Nazi defendants in all of the Nuremberg Trials received only token prison sentences. On this point, British historian Paul Johnson writes:

> [T]he ardour to punish lasted longer but was eventually damped by the march of history. By the time the I.G. Farben executives were sentenced at Nuremberg (29 July 1948), the Berlin blockade had started . . . Karl Krauch, the man who Nazified the firm and personally selected Auschwitz for the *Buna* plant, got only six years. Eleven other executives got prison terms from eight years to eighteen months – "light enough to please a chicken-thief," as the prosecutor Josiah DuBois, angrily put it.[56]

It cannot be overstated that the Nuremberg trials were merely show trials concocted by the Allied Powers for political expediency. The Jews got a raw deal at Nuremberg. Adding insult to injury, Nuremberg was so extremely limited in scope regarding what Nazi businesses and Nazi-supported companies would ultimately be brought to justice that it failed to produce anything but token convictions. For example, only four of the seven prominent Nazi organizations were even considered to be tried as criminal organizations. (The actual number of Nazi organizations would have had to number in the thousands)—

> Businessmen behaved in a decidedly unheroic manner during the Nazi era," said Jonathan Wiesen in his article "Fifty Years of Forgetting and Remembering" (*Dimensions,* undated). "Most of them, especially leaders of larger companies, not only refrained from risking their lives to save Jews, but actually profited from the use of forced and slave labor, the "Aryanization" of Jewish property, and the plundering of companies in Nazi-Occupied Europe... Greed drove all too many 'apolitical businessmen' to engage in odious conduct.
> Companies that were actively participating in holocaust atrocities and their association with specific concentration camps are found including AEG, BMW, Shell, Daimler-Benz, Siemens, Ford, Heinkel, I.G. Farben Industries, Krupp, Telefunken, and Volkswagen. . . . Insurance companies turned over life, property and other forms of insurance to the Nazi regime, which cashed them in. A long list of insurance companies is detailed. Germany's Alliance, Italy's Generali, Switzerlands's Winterthur are just a few who succumbed to the Nazi regime's demands. "...dignified professionals were Hitler's advance troops. Police officials disregarded their duty," says Edwin Black in his book "IBM and the Holocaust." . . . . Black continues, "Lawyers perverted concepts of justice to create anti-Jewish laws. Doctors defiled the art of medicine... Scientists and engineers debased their higher calling to devise the instruments and rationales of destruction.
> The world's media and governments remained silent and companies hid behind a mantle of corporate lawyers, accepting little or no guilt. . . . The world was horrified once the full truth became known and the world's citizens swore that another Holocaust would never happen again. . . . Companies that participated in the Holocaust were called to task after World War II (WWII). The price was heavy for some, but not for all. In any case, the price was not high enough.[57]

How could I. G. Farben CEO, Karl Krauch, the Nazi businessman who not only chose the location of Auschwitz as site for the central clearinghouse so to speak, of all the death camps, but knowingly and willingly transformed a former respected German business into a ghoulish and perverse Nazi enterprise directly responsible for the death by poisonous gas of millions of Jews, in addition to other "undesireables" (e.g., the crippled, the mentally ill, Catholics and other Christians, Jehovah Witnesses, Gypsies, and German citizens caught helping any of these people).

According to the research of Karen Friedman, I.G. Farben employed 35,000 people in pharmaceuticals and chemicals) as slave laborers at Auschwitz, with 25,000 dying there. Out of the paucity of only seven [7] German businesses and corporations tried in the Nuremberg Trials, how in the name of reason, could only four [4] businesses actually be tried for specific war crimes at the Nuremberg Trials? These statistics are woefully inadequate in light of recent materials released for public view from Nazi archives. How can an entire country as large and as technologically superior as Germany was in the 1930s and 1940s, have only four organizations out of doubtless tens of thousands of organizations, corporations, and businesses—generating hundreds of millions of dollars in revenue annually (in 1930s dollars), be determined to have been complicit in these "war crime defined" criminal enterprises? At the least the corporate heads should have been brought to trial by the enlightened humanistic jurists of the Nuremberg Trials on charges of being aiders and abettors of Nazi war crimes. That this was not done by the Nuremberg Tribunal is truly beyond the pale, and an affront to all logic, reason, justice, and truth.[58]

NUREMBERG TRIALS— FOR THE JEWS, JUSTICE DENIED

Was justice achieved at the Nuremberg Trials for the six million Jews, mercilessly murdered in Hitler's death camps along with the millions of other Allied soldiers and civilians who suffered unspeakable pain and death? Based on the evidence, the answer is a categorical NO. Therefore, I must ask the essential question—in modern times, how is the legal philosophy of positive law and legal positivism manifested today? In contemporary American society, the Nuremberg philosophy of separating morality from legality is alive and well in a truly Orwellian allegiance to a worldview that separates one's personal life from one's private life. A recent popular example of this is the case of America's former President, William Jefferson Clinton (1993-2000). During the midst of President Clinton's legal battles regarding the Paula Jones and Monica Lewinsky affairs, his approval rating remained at or near 70 percent.[59]

How could William Clinton, a president of such unquestionably low moral character enjoy such high poll numbers and popular notoriety during his term as President, even as evidence of his personal conduct (i.e., obstruction of justice, perjury, lying to a federal judge under oath, jury tampering, etc.) became irrefutable even by his most loyal apologists? The answer reaches the deepest, darkest recesses of the human condition. Like the erudite, secular, smug German public of the 1920s, Americans of the 1990s were convinced that since everything seemed to be going well economically, they did not care about the President's "private life" as long as he ran the country well. Evidence that this perspective has descended to the level of the private citizen's perspective is the fact that President Clinton's transgressions, though legion, made the average citizen comfortable with their own personal short-comings.

Hitler and his henchmen would be pleased, for had they been tried in an American court of law today they would have a good chance of being exonerated for their genocidal acts against humanity, because the positive law philosophy that separates law and morals, for the past 100 years has become the standard jurisprudence in American courts as well as in the Occident. Additionally, these Nazi defendants would be given lucrative book, movie, and speaking engagements as the liberal media and "the experts" try to "understand" why the Nazis were so misunderstood by the world. This same naïve, exploitable, and short-sighted mentality was evident seven decades ago when in 1933, Hitler and his small, zealous band—the National Socialist Party, ascended to power replacing the enfeebled, promiscuous, and impotent Weimar Republic, which by the early 1930s was intractably mired in nineteenth century Victorian provincialism, excess, and irrelevance.

Once Hitler had consolidated his power via a comprehensive, omnipotent statute titled—Enabling Act of March 24, 1933, he was able to, in effect, commit a bloodless *coup d'etat* over the previous German government, The Weimar Republic, and nullify the Weimar Constitution. Hitler's "Enabling Act" granted him sweeping executive, legislative and judicial powers. Hitler alone had authority to change statutory and constitutional law by decree, which thus gave legal validity to his termination of the separation of powers doctrine previously held under the Weimar Republic. Hitler alone could summarily pronounce judgment and the sentence of death on his enemies, which he famously did against his number two man, Ernst Julius Rohm, a German military officer and the commander and co-founder of the Nazi Sturmabteilung or the SA, in the infamous purge of June 1934 called, "The Night of the Long Knives." In a word Hitler was now the "god" (little "g") of Germany and lord over the German people. To get an idea of the grandeur of his new power, one can review a Nazi law titled—*Gesetz zur Behebung der not von Volk und Reich* [Law for Eliminating the Distress of People and Reich]. Article One provides in part: "Apart from the procedure provided in the Reich Constitution, laws of the Reich can also be decreed by the Reich Government"; and Article Two provides in part, "Laws decreed by the Reich Government may depart from the Reich Constitution as long as they do not have as their object, the institutions of the Reich Parliament [*Reichstag*] and the Reich Council [*Reichsrat*] as such." [60]

To most German citizens of the early 1930s, Hitler and his Nazi party were radical, fresh, energetic, ostentatious, bold–promising a better life for all German people both in Germany and an ever-expanding greater Germany beginning with Hitler's annexation of the *Sudetenland* (Czechoslovakia), extending even to encompass most of Russia.

William L. Shirer, in his classic work, *The Rise and Fall of the Third Reich*, expressed the exceedingly dour sentiments that affected the mind set of the German people and their receptiveness to the Nazi government, when he wrote:

> The response of the German people, after fifteen years of frustration and of resentment against the consequences of a lost war, was almost unanimous. Some 96 percent of the registered voters cast their ballots and 95 percent of these approved Germany's withdrawal from Geneva. The vote for the single Nazi list for the Reichstag (which included Hugenberg and a half-dozen other non-Nazis) was 92 percent. Even at the Dachau concentration camp 2,154 out of 2,242 inmates voted for the government which had incarcerated them! It is true that in many communities threats were made against those who failed to vote or who voted the wrong way; and in some cases there was fear that anyone who cast his vote against the regime might be detected and punished. Yet even with these reservations the election, whose count at least was honest, was a staggering victory for Adolf Hitler. There was no doubt that in defying the outside would as he had done, he had the overwhelming support of the German people.[61]

Furthermore, it became imperative to Hitler and those in Germany that held extreme nationalist views, that a restoration of Germany's military supremacy from the humiliating and harsh limitations imposed on them by the victorious Allied Powers after World War I in the Treaty of Versailles in 1919 was of first priority. After their crushing defeat in World War I failed to even bring charges against the former imperial crown prince, Field Marshal Paul von Hindenburg, General Erich F. W. Ludendorff, and other senior military officers; the Allies left Germany's military virtually intact, and turned a blind eye when Hitler became the only European power to rebuild his military forces, while America and other European nations allowed their forces to languish.[62]

German public opinion in the 1930s rationalized Hitler's despot ambitions contending that his Nazi party made Germany a much better place to live and greatly improved the quality of life. The truth is that under the Nazi regime the German people temporarily enjoyed a higher standard of living. Hitler's Nazi party built schools, hospitals, nursing homes, and provided food, shelter, and generally speaking, a more comfortable way of life for the average German citizen. However, this idyllic lifestyle ended abruptly on September 1, 1939, when Hitler broke the Munich Pact with Britain and Prime Minister Neville Chamberlain, within a year of its signing. As the Nazi *blitzkrieg* swept across Poland in just three weeks, England and France promptly declared war against Germany.[63] America declared war on Germany and Japan the day after the Japanese bombed Pearl Harbor on December 7, 1941.[64]

By 1945, twelve years after Adolph Hitler boasted that his Third Reich would endure for a millennium, Berlin and all of Germany was brought to economic ruin and existed only as a smoldering heap of twisted metal, destroyed buildings, and ashes intermingled with a multitude of disfigured corpses. Hitler and most of his generals were either killed, captured by the Allies, or in hiding, either within Germany or in South America; principally Argentina, which was an ally of Germany. The German people gave up their liberty, and freely elected a madman who promised that Germany would be a great country again. The lessons here are demonstrable–one should never sacrifice moral principles for political expediency and economic gain; to do so is to engage in the folly of Goethe's *Faust* who sold his soul to the devil for a promise to be young again, only to be tricked by that same devil, ruining his life and that of many others.[65]

CHAPTER 3

EXPOSITION

We can never forget that everything Hitler did in Germany was "legal" and everything the Hungarian freedom fighters did in Hungary was "illegal." It was "illegal" to aid and comfort a Jew in Hitler's Germany. But I am sure that, if I had lived in Germany during that time, I would have aided and comforted my Jewish brothers even though it was illegal. If I lived in a communist country today where certain principles dear in the Christian faith are suppressed, I believe I would openly advocate disobeying these anti-religious laws.[1]

~ Dr. Martin Luther King,
Letter from a Birmingham Jail (1963)

In the Nuremberg Trials (1945-1949), a series of thirteen separate trials, Nazi high officials, officers, and industrialists were tried by an International Military Tribunal for war crimes and other atrocities committed during World War II that violated the accepted laws of war. The charges brought against the Nazi defendants accused them of originating, plotting and waging aggressive war, using slave labor, looting occupied countries, and abusing and murdering civilians (especially the Jews) as well as prisoners of war. As early as October 1943, the Allied Powers had decided to try major Nazi officials for war crimes at the conclusion of the war when the American, British and Soviet foreign ministers met in Moscow.

Planning for the trials began soon after V-J Day (September 2, 1945), and the Tribunal opened in Nuremberg, Germany on November 20, 1945, before a board of distinguished judges representing each of the Allied countries. By the time the Nuremburg Trials were held, three of the highest Nazi officers, Adolph Hitler, Heinrich Himmler, and Josef Goebbels had committed suicide.

Hermann Goering (founder of the Gestapo), Joachim Ribbentrop (Nazi foreign minister), Wilhelm Keitel, Alfred Jodl, Ernst Kaltenbrunner, Julius Streicher, Hjalmar Schacht, Martin Bormann (in *absentia*), Karl Doenitz, Hans Frank, Wilhelm Frick, Hans Fritzsche, Walther Funk, Rudolf Hess, Erich Raeder, Alfred Rosenberg (chief Nazi racial theorist), Fritz Sauckel, Arthur Seyss-Inquart, Albert Speer, Konstantin von Neurath, Franz von Papen, and Baldur von Schirach were tried one by one for individually specified crimes. Popple, in his work, *The Right to Protection from Retroactive Criminal Law*, noted that a total of 177 Germans and Austrians were indicted.[2] The actual number was 185, but four Nazis were acquitted for medical reasons and four for committed suicide. Of the twenty-four Nazi defendants, twenty-one were convicted; of these, nine were sentenced to prison terms (most were freed within seven years) and the remaining twelve were executed by hanging. Regarding the actual sentences handed down by the Nuremberg Tribunal, Popple further states:

> Thirteen separate trials of war criminals were held in Nuremberg between 1945 and 1947. These trials were presided over by judges from all four major victorious Allied Powers: America, Britain, France and the Soviet Union. A total of 177 Germans and Austrians were indicted. All but thirty-five were found guilty: twenty-five were executed, twenty were sentenced to life imprisonment and ninety-seven were sentenced to shorter prison terms.[3]

These sparse numbers are even more pathetic and stark when shown in percentages. The thirteen separate Nuremberg Trials freed almost one in five Nazi defendants (19 percent); Only 14 percent were executed; 11 percent were given life sentences; 54 percent were given short prison sentences of seven years or shorter. "Light enough to please a chicken thief" as Nuremberg prosecutor from France, Dubois sarcastically framed it.

The general consensus among World War II statisticians and historians is that roughly eighteen million [18,000,000] people were killed by Hitler and his

Nazis either directly, like the six million Jews he sent to the death camps, the millions of soldiers killed in battle, or the millions of innocent civilians, like the English, who suffered greatly from the nightly bombing raids of Hitler's infamous Luftwaffe. That said, what of Hitler and the German people, who were largely complicit and willing participants of Hitler's Nazi dreams of 1,000 Reich? Roughtly 20 percent (1 out of 5) of the Nazi defendants were found not guilty for one of three reasons: for medical reasons, because the charges against them couldn't be proven, or they committed suicide before they could be hanged.

Goering and Bormann both escaped hanging; the former by suicide and the latter by remaining at large. Robert Ley hanged himself in his cell, Gustav Krupp was too ill to stand trial, and due to a mix-up with another defendant, Krupp's empire was left intact. Three were acquitted—banker Schacht, Fritzsche (substitute for boss Goebbels), and Franz von Papen (the "Silver Fox"). The rest were hanged on October 16, 1946. Also, other lower level officials were tried, including officers and guards from the Dachau prison camp and civilians who had murdered American aviators.

In the later Tokyo Trials, (1946-1948) given the precedent of the Nuremberg Trials, one would have expected even more indictments ending in executions and life prison sentences, however, they yielded even fewer guilty defendants than the pathetic few Nazi's of Nuremberg—with only sixteen Japanese leaders imprisoned and only seven hanged. This dismally low numbers of already miniscule low proportion of Japanese war criminals works out to the following percentages—70 percent imprisoned; 30 percent executed; 30 percent acquitted.

It is indeed a tragic paradox of the biblical proportions that for the millions of Jewish people and other innocents who died at the hands of the Nazis in World War II, why were only 177 people brought to judgment by the Nuremberg Trials? Likewise, regarding Japanese aggression leading to the death of tens of thousands of Americans at Pearl Harbor, Leyet, Midway, Iwo Jima and in other battles with Japan, why were only twenty-three Japanese leaders tried and not one Japanese soldier who willingly fulfilled the commands of their superior officers? Why were no Italian leaders charged? Italy, led by Mussolini, was Germany's most ardent ally during the war and a vital partner of the Axis Powers, was Mussolini (and his mistress's) death by hanging, as accomplished by the mob in the central square, considered adequate symbolic punishment? Was the fact that after the war Italy was a very important anti-communist ally, the reason? Why was no mention made, in the Nuremberg Trials, of the 1939 Nazi-Soviet Pact? This was an unholy alliance between two of the 20th century most unmerciful tyrants—Hitler and Stalin, whereby Stalin sought to dissuade Hitler from his Eastern conquests toward Russia, and where Hitler used Stalin to gain time and leverage to mount his blitzkrieg, first into Poland, but eventually up to the very gates of Moscow itself, much to the astonishment and chagrin of Stalin.

Therefore a seminal question regarding the efficacy of the Nuremberg Trials is this—Were the Nuremberg Trials and Tokyo Trials resplendent examples of justice and triumph of the rule of law over notoriously wicked men, or were these trials a colossal sham, and a cover up of historical proportions representing the denigration of the rule of law? In this book, I hold that in large part, the Nuremberg Trials were indeed a monumental fraud; an insult to the millions of Jews who perished in Hitler's ovens, and undeniably the last tragedy of the Holocaust.

Critics of the Nuremberg Trials contend that the trials retroactively criminalized actions that under German law had been legal, and the disobedience of such was punishable by death. Vengeance rather than impartial justice was also a familiar refrain as the critics of the Nuremberg Trials claimed that the Tribunal had no recognized legal authority to try the Nazi defendants. The most noted critic holding this view was Charles Wyzanski, Jr., a young, ambitious judge at the district court in Massachusetts. He wrote a series of respected articles outlining his views on the Nuremberg Trials that were published in the popular magazine, Atlantic Monthly.[4]

Supporting the legal philosophy used to judge the Nazi defendants in the Nuremberg trials was Supreme Court Justice Robert Jackson, whom President Harry Truman personally chose to be the chief prosecutor representing the United States in the Nuremberg Trials. Jackson argued that such ubiquitous international treaties as the Kellogg-Briand Pact of 1928, which was called a Treaty for the Renunciation of War as an Instrument of National Policy, dated August 27, 1928,[5] and signed by sixty-two nations (including Germany); as along with several other international treaties that renounced war as a solution for international disputes, made aggressive warfare a capital offense and subject to trial.[6] These treaties were made and ratified specifically to deter war atrocities identical to the ones for which the Nazi defendants were being tried.[7]

The conclusion of World War II in April of 1945 witnessed the Allied Powers of the United States, Britain, the Soviet Union, and France summarily defeat the Axis powers of Hitler's Germany, Hirohito's Japan, and Mussolini's Italy. While the end of World War II signaled the end of the largest and deadliest World War in the history of mankind, it ushered in the beginning of another paradox regarding questions of morality and legality. The question arose among the Allies as to how to adjudicate the senior Nazi officials, and other high ranking officers of the Nazi regime, who were now under international scrutiny for "war crimes." How could these men be judged for their heinous crimes? How could justice be meted out and the rule of law be effectively applied to these wicked Nazi war criminals?

BIBILCAL PRECEDENT AND THE UNITED NATIONS

Prior to the Nuremberg Trials, under the United Nations, governments and nation states were seeking to formulate a one–world government where all international borders would become a thing of the past. While many leaders and representatives characterized this attempt as poorly formulated, some writers like Melvin Sickler and Myron Fagan, went even further to characterize mankind's attempt to unify himself under a single government as a "satanic plot."[8] This comprehensive globalist quest for unity among the nations of the world is not without precedent. In biblical and secular histories, world rulers such Nebuchadnezzar, Ramsees, Alexander the Great, and Genghis Kahn notwithstanding, such a wide-spread effort to unify the nations of the world had not been attempted since biblical times.

It was Nimrod, the first titular world ruler, who tried in vain to build a giant ziggurat (a pagan astrological tower) called the "Tower of Babel" in ancient Babylon—the ruins of which still stand today in modern Iraq. This event is chronicled in *Genesis* 11:4 ("And they said, Go to, let us build us a city and a tower, whose top may reach unto heaven; and let us make us a name, lest we be scattered abroad upon the face of the whole earth"). This arrogant rebellion by Nimrod and the Babylonians was in direct defiance of God's prior commandment in *Genesis* 9:1—"And God blessed Noah and his sons, and said unto them, be fruitful, and multiply, and replenish the earth." Nimrod's defiance and arrogance against God's explicit commands that the people of the earth spread out throughout the earth is further underscored by Nimrod's arrogant, anti-God leadership—(". . . let us build us a city and a tower, whose top may reach unto heaven; and let us make us a name, lest we be scattered abroad upon the face of the whole earth").[9] The UN is the Tower of Babel Redux in modern times.

The concept and public policy implications of a United Nations was revolutionary and unique in international law for two reasons: (1) The size and scope of both the number of member nations and its ultimate objectives of a singular World nation with its own World Court, The International Court of Justice as the judicial arm of the United Nations which regularly reports to the General Assembly,[10] the World Bank,[11] World Currency, and World Military, dwarfing all previous attempts to form a so-called "one world government"; (2) the League of Nations (which later became the United Nations) was purposely formed under several unprecedented philosophies, namely *humanism* (man is the center of all things), *secularism* (there is no God but man and the state), *radical liberalism* (freedom without morality or conscience), *positive law* and *logical positivism* (separation of legality and morality), *relativism* (moral equivalence of all things, or the idea that no person, place, or thing is superior to another), *egalitarianism* (the equality of results rather than opportunities), and *individualism* (the severe reduction of restraints to pleasure).[12] Prior to positive law, natural law was not only the controlling philosophy of international law but of American constitutional law. Furthermore, natural law was the originating philosophy of all of American law and its founding documents–the Declaration of Independence, the Constitution, and the Bill of Rights.

Regarding the foundational position natural law played as the controlling philosophy of American constitutional law, international law as well as all of its law related institutions from the rulings of local magistrates to the leading opinion handed down by the United States Supreme Court, Professor Burnham wrote: "The scholars have traced the ideas of the [Founding] Fathers back not only to Locke, Montesquieu, but Aristotle and Cicero and Plutarch, Hobbes, Burlamaqui, Milton, Hooker, Bolingbroke, Blackstone, Burke, Shaftesbury and a score of collateral branches."[13] "The Fathers were the masters, not the victims, of these inherited ideas, and sometimes it is the rhetoric more than the ideas that is taken over."[14]

Christian writer, Rousas John Rushdoony, noted that John Witherspoon, one of the Framers of the Constitution was a Presbyterian minister educated at Edinburgh University. Witherspoon later became the first president of Princeton University, bringing the principles of Samuel Rutherford's *Lex Rex* (1644) (*The Law and the Prince*) into in spirit and in letter in the writing of the Constitution.[15] Witherspoon was the only clergyman to sign the Declaration of Independence. He served two terms on the Continental Congress and was a key member on several influential committees of the first Congress. His students included a president (James Madison), a vice president (Aaron Burr), ten cabinet officers, twenty-one senators, thirty-nine congressmen, twelve governors, as well as other public figures.[16] Witherspoon's influence on James Madison was great. He was president of Princeton when Madison attended. The so-called 'Ivy-League' schools were in the early years very serious about the inseparability of law and morality to such a degree that some of the requirements at the time included that every student shall attend worship each morning and evening, every student shall attend public worship on Sabbath, and every student shall complete various religious assignments.[17]

In America and Europe, positive law and legal positivism had been growing steadily and concurrently with the advent of the modern Industrial Age of the mid-nineteenth century. This took place concurrently with the rise of the secular humanist movement of the mid-1850s up through the Progressive Era (1900-1915).

Liberals, progressives, socialists, elites, intellectuals, secularists, and radicals of all stripes, the press, and most notably, the academy, all wholehearted welcomed this bold new legal theory that brazenly, and by definition, prided itself on being anti-religious and 'scientific' (it was neither). Positive law would pay no tithe to the so-called "Judeo-Christian tradition." Consequently, a hundred years later when the United Nations Charter and Tribunal were drafted, its Framers naturally chose a legal philosophy devoid of any moral pretense—a legal theory that explicitly and scrupulously separated legality from morality, based solely on the analytical jurisprudence of legal positivism. In contemporary jurisprudence, Oxford University professor of jurisprudence, H. L. A. Hart, citing John Gray's work regarding legal positivism, divided it into five categories:

> (1) The contention that laws are commands of human beings,
> (2) The contention that there is no necessary connection between law and morals or law as it is and ought to be,
> (3) The contention that the analysis (or study of the meaning) of legal concepts is (a) worth pursuing and (b) to be distinguished from historical inquiries into the causes or origins of laws, from sociological inquiries into the relation of law and other social phenomena, and from the criticism or appraisal of law whether in terms of morals, social aims, "functions," or otherwise,
> (4) The contention that a legal system is a "closed logical system" in which correct legal decisions can be deduced by logical means from predetermined legal rules without reference to social aims, policies, moral standards, and
> (5) The contention that moral judgments cannot be established or defended, as statements of facts can, by rational argument, evidence, or proof ("noncongnitivism" in ethics).[18]

Hart further noted that "Bentham and Austin held the views described in (1), (2), and (3) but not those in (4) and (5). Opinion (4) is often ascribed to analytical jurists, but I know of no 'analyst' who held this view."[19]

At the creation of the legal machinery that spawned the Nuremberg Court, very few voices were heard in opposition to this radical new legal philosophy as fifteen centuries of natural law philosophy in international law became obsolete by the institution of the UN's Charter and the establishment of the Nuremberg Trials Tribunal.[20] The fallout from the Allies' unworkable foreign policy of positive law over natural law as the new philosophical basis and controlling authority of international law would affect the world in unintended ways in apocalyptic proportions just a few years after all of the Nuremberg Trials and the Tokyo Trials were concluded by 1949. Directly linked to the tentative, naïve, utopian, and pathetically limited scope of the Nuremberg Trials, were several pivotal events; the collapse of the American-backed government in China of Chang Kei Sheik and the rise of the communist despot, Mao Tse-Tung; the Korean War (1952-1955); and the Cold War between the United States and the Soviet Union (1945-1989/90).

With a radically expansionist mindset, our Soviet and Chinese allies learned well from their American and European partners, that the liberal appeasement politics of the Neville Chamberlain school of public policy would be their most effective primary foreign policy with few exceptions. Even to this day, as Israel belatedly fights a battle for its very survival on two fronts; the Palestinian terrorist group Hamas in the Gaza strip, and at Israel's northern border, the terrorist group Hezbollah in Lebanon.[21]

Another fundamental problem with the Nuremberg Trials was that for the first time, a major trial was conducted on an international stage based solely on the newly created, naturalistic philosophy based on the principle of the separation of legality from morality. This unprecedented attempt by the Nuremberg Tribunal Framers to remove moral considerations from the law would ironically prove to be a boon to the very war criminals they were trying. The Nazi defendants, led by Hermann Jahrreiss, the capable associate defense counsel and law professor at Cologne, and associate defense counsel for defendant Alfred Jodl, seized upon this obvious loophole and mounted a viable defense. Jahrreiss and all of the Nazi defense attorneys skillfully and with some success utilized many positive law concepts including Austin's "act of state" defense and the doctrine of absolute sovereign. Both legal philosophies came directly out of John Austin's *Providence*.

- "Commands" involve an expressed wish that something be done, and "an evil" to be imposed if that wish is not complied with.

- Rules are general commands (applying generally to a class), as contrasted with specific or individual commands ("drink wine today" or "John Major must drink wine").

- Positive law consists of those commands laid down by a sovereign (or its agents), to be contrasted to other law-givers, like God's general commands, and the general commands of an employer to an employee.

- The "sovereign" is defined as a person (or determinate body of persons) who receives habitual obedience from the bulk of the population, but who does not habitually obey any other (earthly) person or institution. Austin thought that all independent political societies, by their nature, have a sovereign.

- Positive law should also be contrasted with "laws by a close analogy" (which includes positive morality, laws of honor, international law, customary law, and constitutional law) and "laws by remote analogy" (e.g., the laws of physics).[22]

At the Nuremberg Trial, Jahrreiss presented a lengthy but brilliant apologetic on Austin's analytical jurisprudence, in his opening statement. His discourses epitomize the most extensive attempt by defense counsel to specify a philosophical foundation for the defense's case.[23] The Nazi defendants cynically asked—Can we as German citizens of the sovereign nation of Germany, be judged by the Allied Powers (i.e., other sovereign nations) under a higher law called international law? If so, then neither Germany nor any of the Allied Powers are sovereign powers in the Austinian sense of the word. John Austin, in his *Providence*, outlined his superior sovereign analysis consisting of three components: (1) the sovereign's *intention* that the subject act or not act in particular situations; (2) the sovereign's *expression* of such intention to the subject; (3) the sovereign's *power* to enact or impose obedience to his commands by the subject.[24]

Law professor, Doug Linder in an article titled, *A Commentary on the Jus-*

tice Case, cited the following prescient description regarding Defense attorney Jahrreise's noteworthy legal skills particularly in analytical jurisprudence:

> We pass now from the forgoing incomplete summary of Nazi legislation to a consideration of the law inaction, and of the influence of the "Fuehrer principle" as it affected the officials of the Ministry of Justice, prosecutor, and judges. Two basic principles controlled conduct within the Ministry of Justice. The first concerned the absolute power of Hitler in person or by delegated authority to enact, enforce, and adjudicate law. The second concerned the incontestability of such law. Both principles were expounded by the learned Professor Jahrreiss, a witness for all of the defendants. Concerning this first principle, Dr. Jahrreiss said: "If now in the European meaning one asks about legal restrictions, and first of all one asks about restrictions of the German law, one will have to say that restrictions under German law did not exist for Hitler. He was legibus solutus in the same meaning in which Louis XIV claimed that for himself in France. Anybody who said something different expresses a wish that does not describe the actual legal facts."
>
> Concerning the second principle, Jahrreiss supported the opinion of Gerhard Anschuetz, "Crown Jurist of the Weimar Republic", who holds that if German laws were enacted by regular procedure, judicial authorities were without power to challenge them on Constitutional or ethical grounds. Under the Nazi system, and even prior thereto, German judges were also bound to apply German law even when in violation of the principles of international law, As stated by Professor Jahrreiss:
>
> "To express it differently, whether the law has been passed by the State in such a way that it was inconsistent with international law on purpose or not, that could not play any part at all; and that was the legal state of affairs, regrettable as it may be."
>
> This, however, is not to deny the superior authority of international law. Again we quote a statement of extraordinary candor by Professor Jahrreiss:
>
> "On the other hand, certainly there were local restrictions for Hitler under international law. He was bound by international law. Therefore, he could commit acts violating international law. Therefore, he could issue orders violating international law to the Germans."
>
> The conclusion to be drawn from the evidence, presented by the defendants themselves is clear: In German legal theory Hitler's law was a shield to those who acted under it, but before a Tribunal authorized to enforce international law, Hitler's decrees were a protection neither to the Fuehrer himself nor to his subordinates, if in violation of the law of the community of nations.
>
> In German legal theory, Hitler was not only the Supreme Legislator, he was also the Supreme Judge. On 26 April 1942 Hitler addressed the Reichstag in part as follows:
>
> "I do expect one thing: that the nation gives me the right to intervene immediately and to take action myself whenever a person has failed to render unqualified obedience...."
>
> "I therefore ask the German Reichstag to confirm expressly that I have the legal right to keep everybody to his duty and to cashier or remove from office or position without regard for his person or his established rights, whoever, in my view and according to my considered opinion, has failed to do his duty...."

"From now on, I shall intervene in these cases and remove from office those judges who evidently do not understand the demand of the hour."

On the same day the Greater German Reichstag resolved in part as follows:
". . . the Fuehrer must have all the rights postulated by him which serve to further or achieve victory. Therefore—without being bound by existing legal regulations—in his capacity as leader of the nation, Supreme Commander of the Armed Forces, governmental chief and supreme executive chief, as supreme justice, and leader of the Party—the Fuehrer must be in a position to force with all means at his disposal every German, if necessary, whether he be common soldier or officer, low or high official or judge, leading or subordinate official of the Party, worker or employee, to fulfill his duties. In case of violation of these duties, the Fuehrer is entitled after conscientious examination, regardless of so-called well-deserved rights, to mete out due punishment, and to remove the offender from his post, rank and position, without introducing prescribed procedures."

The assumption by Hitler of supreme governmental power in all departments did not represent a new development based on the emergency of war. The declaration of the Reichstag was only an echo of Hitler's declaration of 13 July 1934. After the mass murders of that date (the Roehm purge) which were committed by Hitler's express orders, he said:
"Whenever someone reproaches me with not having used ordinary court for their sentencing, I can only say: 'In this hour I am responsible for the fate of the German nation and hence the supreme law lord of the German people'."

The conception of Hitler as the Supreme Judge was supported by the defendant Rothenberger. We quote:
"However, something entirely different has occurred; with the Fuehrer a man has risen within the German people who awakens the oldest, long forgotten times. Here is a man who in his position represents the ideal of the judge in its perfect sense, and the German people elected him for their judge—first of all, of course, as 'judge' over their fate in general, but also as 'supreme magistrate and judge'."

In the same document the defendant Rothenberger expounded the National Socialist theory of judicial independence. He said:
"Upon the fact that the judge can use his own discretion is founded the magic of the word 'judge'."
He asserted that "every private and Party office must abstain from all interference or influence upon the judgment", but this statement appears to be mere window-dressing, for after his assertion that a judge "must judge like the Fuehrer", he said:
"In order to guarantee this, a direct liaison officer without any intermediate agency must be established between the Fuehrer and the German judge, that is, also in the form of a judge, the supreme judge in Germany, the 'Judge of the Fuehrer'. He is to convey to the German judge the will of the Fuehrer by authentic explanation of the laws and regulations. At the same time he must upon the request of the judge give binding information in current trials concerning fundamental political, economic, or legal problems which cannot be surveyed by the individual judge."

Thus it becomes clear that the Nazi theory of the judicial independence was based upon the supreme independence of the Fuehrer, which was to be channelized through the proposed liaison officer from Fuehrer to judge.[25]

To the substantive question of positive law: "who has the right in a society to be sovereign?", James Bryce makes the following comments: "The person or body to whom, in the last resort, the law attributes this right, is the legally supreme power or Sovereign, in the State."[21] During the Nuremberg Trials, it was no doubt difficult for the Allied Justices and Prosecution team, (Russia notwithstanding, since it was concurrently living under a supreme sovereign—Stalin), to fully comprehend the supreme sovereign, and the supreme sovereign state principles that the Nazi defendants held paramount. Under these principles, Hitler, as the Chancellor of Germany and its "Furher" (i.e., leader), was the ultimate sovereign of Germany and the German people, and he sought to expand his sphere of domination to encompass the entire of Europe.

> The Nazi defendant's appeal to superior orders, and the doctrine of the sovereign, was a calculated and risky strategy for they deceitfully, and with some degree of success, shifted the focus from universal, objective principles—morality, the rule of law, legality, and justice, by which they would clearly been condemned as guilty—to the amorphous, subjective area of philosophy and the legal labyrinth of criminal jurisdiction, superior orders, supreme sovereign, act of state, *ex post facto*, *nullum crimen*, legal positivism, analytical jurisprudence, etc, whereby the Nazi defendants could have a fighting chance to mitigate the grave charges against them. To get a glimpse of the mindset of the Nazi defendants during the trial, and the utter moral bankruptcy, sociopathic tendencies, and perverse mindset they all shared, the eyewitness and Nuremberg Trial psychologist, G. M. Gilbert, in his important work, *Nuremberg Diary*, recounted the following conversation between two Nazi defendants during the Nuremberg Trials— Ribbentrop was arguing with Hess but getting nowhere, since Hess has no recollection of the world events recounted in the Indictment. Ribbentrop then remarked to me [G.M. Gilbert] "Why all this fuss about breaking treaties? Did you ever read about the history of the British Empire? Why, it's full of broken treaties, oppression of minorities, mass murder, aggressive wars, and everything."[26]

Conversely, Nazi defendant, Albert Speer, who was Hitler's chief architect and in 1942 was promoted to become his minister for armaments, (due in large part to Hitler's dissatisfaction with Goering's inability to secure German's airspace), chronicled in his *Memoirs* an encounter with G.M. Gilbert stating:

> At this time the prison psychologist, G.M. Gilbert, was going from cell to cell with a copy of the indictment, asking the defendants to write their comments on it. When I read the partially evasive, partially disdainful words of many of my fellow defendants, I wrote, to Gilbert's astonishment: 'The trial is necessary. There is a shared responsibility for such horrible crimes even in an authoritarian state. I still regard it as my greatest feat of psychic courage to have held to this view throughout the ten months of the trial.'[27]

Ribbentrop's outrageously immoral sentiments to Hess and his perverted moral equivalence speculations about the British Empire in comparison to the Nazi's Third Reich cannot be dismissed as unique or an aberration among the ideas Nazi defendants held sacred, but to the contrary, was reflective and indicative of a common Nazi worldview that in their minds, justified their atrocities against humanity in general, and against the Jews in particular as a necessary requirement of Darwin's "survival of the fittest" principle—whereby a stronger race and nation dominates the weaker races and nations.

To the typical German citizen living in the early 1930s, Hitler and the Nazi party's bellicose rhetoric seeking to redeem Germany from the shame of the Versailles Treaty and the moribund, decadent Weimar Republic, by expanding German lebensraum (living space) and purging the Germany of the Jews (the scapegoat and embodiment of all that afflicted Germany) and other inferior races and peoples, was it's manifest destiny.

Ribbentrop's view that the stronger nation has always dominated the weaker nations was not only revisionist history, but more importantly, the popular philosophy (especially in academic and intellectual circles) of social Darwinian evolution which, as stated early in this book played a critical part in formulating and indoctrinating the German people to have undivided allegiance to the Nazi worldview of Aryan supremacy. From Hitler's rise to power, Germany's credo became—RACE IS DESTINY. DESTINY IS INEXORABLE. Speer's seemingly contrite confession to Dr. Gilbert regarding the necessity and justness of the Nuremberg Trials and his explicit guilt was indeed an exception and may have been uttered during a rare moment of genuine introspection, but certainly was not the majority view shared by his fellow Nazi defendants. To this day Albert Speer has the distinction of being the only one of the original twenty-four Nazi defendants to publicly express remorse for his crimes.

In addition, the Nazi defendants wrongly assumed that because law and morality had been separated, they could (primarily through Austin's separability and superior sovereign theses) escape the hangman's noose. Fortunately, justice had not yet become totally separated from reason and common sense and sanity. By purposely removing the presumption of legality integrated with morality, God, and morality from the rule of law, by the creation of the United Nations and the UN Tribunal, the Allied Powers unwittingly (I assume) set the stage for other defendants to challenge the rule of law under purely legal terms. During all of the legal proceedings of the Nuremberg Trials, moral considerations did not impose any effect on legal outcomes. The entire legal proceedings to this extent were quite bizarre.

The Nuremberg Tribunal was given the mandate to symbolically bring to trial twenty-two chief Nazi leaders, but had from its inception, removed the one element that gives law it's ethical force—Morality rooted in ethical principles that transcend time and the laws of mere mortal man. This was a legal and public relations coup for the Nazi defendants and they exploited the moral ambiguities of positive law to the furthest extent that they could.[28] For the remainder of the Nuremberg Trial proceedings, the Nazi defendants could take on the cloak of moral equivalency that their Nazi cause backed by the "Sovereign Nation of Germany", imbuing them within a sophistic sense of legal (and paradoxically moral) legitimacy.

Now that it was mandated that the Nuremberg Trials would follow the analytical jurisprudence of positive law—a secular paradigm that erected a wall of separation between law and morality that had been infused in the Nuremberg trial proceedings, the Nuremberg Tribunal gave the Nazi defendants a key to their own jail cells. Strangely enough, the Allies, by their reflexive bias against the Judeo-Christian tradition in the rule of law in the history of Anglo-American jurisprudence, had, not only made this possible, but made it almost inevitable. Despite the fact that 50 percent of the original twenty-two Nazi defendants were executed, the others were to a more or less degree, given a chance at a "pass" and the chance of acquittal. The more Nuremberg Trials the United Nations put on (remember there were thirteen in all lasting from 1945-1949), the better the chances of the Nazi defendant's were at not only escaping the hangman's noose, but had a 20-25 percent chance of obtaining a full acquittal!

On the other hand, under a natural law paradigm, with its strong principle foundations in the Judeo-Christian tradition, public/private morality, American society, and constitutional law, lamentably, no longer played a vital role of undergirding justice as it did in former generations. By 1945, the year of the Nuremberg Trials, Anglo-American jurisprudence as well as continental jurisprudence of Western Europe had become intractably secularized and virtually all aspects of the law's original Judeo-Christian traditions had been purposely and systematically purged. Law now stripped of his moral authority and its relevance based on religion and the inscrutable will of God as delineated in the Bible, was now under a positive law paradigm. Law, to the secular academic, legislator or judge, was a cold dead letter given life by the omnipotent sovereign State imposing it's own will over another—"Jefferson's 'inalienable rights' of the people" as endowed. This was in essence the apotheosis of Darwin's worldview applied to law and legal philosophy—"Survival of the fittest!"

The pivotal question has thus become almost rhetorical in it's complexity and scope—How did America change from a nation founded "under God" whose national motto is "In God we Trust," to a nation that has lost sight of the foundational structure which undergirds its laws? As well as how did the Supreme Court move from a judicial body that was supposed to *interpret* the Constitution, to one that *creates* a Constitution by legislating from the bench?

These questions aren't easily answered, however an argument could be convincingly made that the demise of America's legal foundations occurred when society, in increasingly influential and affluent circles, impugned and rejected laws that were based on solid, irrevocable, moral, universal, absolute values, and embraced and even championed laws based on an arbitrary system of synthetic laws based on positivism, relativism, situation ethics, materialism, individualism, hedonism, paganism, or any litany of other secularist ideologies that above all presuppose a separation of law and morality, a purge of all religious, moral and ethical content from legal and political considerations.

Furthermore, this synthetic approach to law has transcended all branches of knowledge in the academy–law, the humanities, medicine, education, science, the arts, and mass media. These sentiments were echoed by Emory law professor Harold Berman, who said: "One major symptom of this threatened [nervous] breakdown is the massive loss of confidence in the law, not only on the part of "law-consumers", but also on the part of law-makers and law distributors." [29] That "there is an enormous chasm between what incoming students think the law is–an organized set of facts–and what it really is—uncertainties."[30] America, as the creator of the League of Nations and it's successor organization, the United Nations; America, the leading nation of the triumphant Allied Powers that fought a war on two fronts summarily defeating both the fascistic empires of Imperial Japan and Nazi Germany; America, that greatest nation of the history of nations, that created all of the legal machinery (Nuremberg Tribunal, Nuremberg Trials, UN Charter) even selecting the prosecutors, Justices and venue where Nazi and Japanese aggression, would face grim judgment for its faults in this arena.

America, from the onset of the Nuremberg Trials when drafting the UN Charter, the document that created and defined the purpose and scope of the Nuremberg Tribunal, could have insisted on a unity of law and morals, and excluding all legal philosophies that held to a separation of law and morality when debating which rule of law to be followed at Nuremberg. Tragically, America did just the opposite, and President Truman, Justice Jackson and other influential liberal jurists, legislators, and those entrusted in this monumental task, not only failed in their duties to delineate the atrocities committed by the Nazis against the Jews and others, but added insult to injury by perversely limiting the number of Nazis that would ever face the bar of justice, and giving those called to judgment, every opportunity for mitigation or acquittal, by infusing the Nuremberg Tribunal with a jurisprudence that insisted on separating legality from morality in the creation of the Nuremberg Trials Tribunal, instead of following the precedent of "natural law." This leaves the cogent question: why this treachery against the rule of law and the Jewish people?

Under the newly created UN Tribunal paradigm, the machinery of law was left in the hands of a purely secular, humanist bureaucracy for the first time in history of Western civilization. The separation of law from morality doctrine, which limited the Nuremberg Trials to purely legal issues, and largely relegated moral charges to superficial, perfunctory rhetoric (on both sides), with no real consequences to either the lawyers or the judges, gave the Nazi defendants a plethora of new defenses that were of dubious legal or moral foundation in Anglo-American jurisprudence, international law, or in constitutional law. A reading of the transcripts of the International Military Tribunal at Nuremberg, particularly of Nazi defendants Goering, Hess, Ribbentrop and Keitel, reveal an exceedingly perverse, myopic, craven, even surreal tone which the Nazi defendants used to rationalize Nazi genocide extends exceedingly beyond the pale. [31]

The Treaty of London was signed by the Allied Powers on August 8, 1945 which became the legal basis of the Charter for the International Military Tribunal at Nuremberg.[32] The Charter specified three categories of criminal activity and each of the twenty-four Nazi defendants were charged with several counts:

> (1) *Crimes Against Peace*: namely, planning, preparation, initiation or waging a war of aggression, or a war in violation of international treaties, agreements, or assurances, or participation in a Common Plan or Conspiracy for the accomplishment of the fore-going;
>
> (2) *War Crimes*: namely, violations of the laws or customs of war. Such violations shall include . . . murder, ill-treatment or deportation to slave labor or for any other purpose of civilian population or in occupied territory, murder or ill-treatment of prisoners of war . . . wanton destruction of cities, towns, or villages, or devastation not justified by military necessity;
>
> (3) *Crimes Against Humanity*: namely, murder, extermination, enslavement, deportation, and other inhumane acts committed against any civilian population, before or during the war, or persecutions on political, racial, or religious grounds . . . whether or not in violation of domestic law of the country where perpetrated.[33]

Stanley Paulson contends that the rejection of the primary defenses of the Nuremberg Trials: (1) Act of State; (2) Superior orders; and, (3) *Ex Post Facto*, could not "be justified on either legal or philosophical grounds" but was derisively referred by him as "Allied policy."[34] However, had the United Nations Tribunal enacted its legal authority under the universal precepts of natural law, no such questions of justification over the legality of the Tribunal could have been logically sustained because in a civilized society, murder is murder whether or not a statute makes it illegal. Chief Prosecutor Robert H. Jackson, concurred with this view in his Opening Statement when he sarcastically asked, "Does it surprise these men that murder is a crime?" Academics, intellectuals, liberal politicians, secular-minded judges, lawyers and jurists, however, have long been aware of the underlying philosophical disputes between natural law and positive law and now had a perfect forum to exploit these differences on an international stage at the Nuremberg Trials.[35]

The prosecutors of the Allied countries used the above terminology from the Charter at the Tribunal to indict the Nazi defendants on essentially four counts: (1) conspiracy to wage aggressive war, (2) waging an aggressive war, (3) commission of war crimes, and (4) perpetration of crimes against humanity.[36] The Charter set punishment at death, determining that neither official position nor the orders of a superior were legitimate defenses.[37] The fact that membership in the SS, Gestapo, or leadership in the Nazi party was criminal in itself invalidated the principle of individual responsibility for crimes and invalidated the superior orders document as well as given the Tribunal the legal authority to declare a group organization a criminal entity.[38]

In the next chapter I will examine the underlying philosophy of law utilized try the Nazi defendant's in the Nuremberg Trials. I have chosen to systematically analyze two representative opposing views and two different conceptions regarding the Nuremberg Trials. The first by Charles Wyzanski, Jr., a well-known and respected judge of the U.S. District Court for the District of Massachusetts from 1941-1986. The second view is by Justice Robert H. Jackson, lead prosecutor for the United States at Nuremberg, who was at the time, on leave from his post as an Associate Justice of the United States Supreme Court.[39]

CHAPTER 4

JUDGE CHARLES WYZANSKI'S VIEWS ON THE NUREMBERG TRIALS

You will now pay the penalty for conduct which was contrary to law and a crime when you executed it, although, owing to the imperfection of the international machinery, there was at that time no court competent to pronounce judgment against.[1]

~ Sir Hartley Shawcross, Chief Prosecutor for Great Britain at Nuremberg

In April of 1946, Judge Charles E. Wyzanski, Jr., Senior District Judge of the United States District Court in Boston, wrote an article titled, *Nuremberg: a Fair Trial?*, in which he addressed his concerns about the upcoming Nuremberg Trials.[2] Judge Wyzanski voiced his apprehensions (and no doubt the sentiments of many academics, politicians, and American's at that time) about the hazards of attempting to administer international justice in a vacuum without the benefit of guiding precedent, especially given that the judiciary panel was to be composed not of disinterested legal experts, but of political leaders from the very countries against which the defendants were said to have committed their crimes.[3] Wyzanski warned that if the UN Tribunal judges succumbed to (justifiable) feelings of outrage, and indulged an urge to punish without granting the defendants a fair trial, it would establish a dangerous precedent for war crimes retribution.[4] However, seven months later, after the verdicts had been reached against the Nazi defendant's in the first set of Nuremberg trials, Wyzanski explained that the exemplary manner in which the trial had been conducted dispelled his skepticism about the feasibility of forging an international legal system.[5] He wrote,

> [T]he Nuremberg proceedings were a model of forensic fairness . . . . But the outstanding accomplishment of the trial . . . is that it has crystallized the concept that there already is inherent in the international community a machinery both for the expression of international criminal law and for its enforcement.[6]

Besides a large proportion of the general public, Wyzanski views against the legal legitimacy of the Nuremberg Trials struck a chord with many professors in the academy, the largely liberal press, and with the Democratic party which under FDR and recently, Harry Truman, had dominated political public opinion in America for decades. This monopoly in the 'marketplace of ideas,' as Holmes phrased it, became particularly acute when Wyzanski criticized the legal validity of the Charter of the International Military Tribunal at Nuremberg, asserting that the Charter in essence created *ex post facto* law (i.e., after the fact or "new law").[7]

Wyzanski also questions three other basic characteristics of the Charter and the Tribunal: (1) The Charter and Tribunal as legal fictions in that they did not and could not exist in any viable legal sense as a system of laws to judge the Nazi defendants; (2) The Tribunal's power was omnipotent, becoming prosecutor, judge, jury, and executioner; and, (3) The Charter tried to reconcile two very different legal systems—the Continental system of most European countries and the common law system of the United States and Britain, particularly in regards to criminal procedure and substantive law.[8]

A Brief History of the Superior Orders Doctrine

One of the more intractable problems of the law to be faced in trying war criminals is deciding the culpability of men who maintain, that in the throws of war, they were merely following the chain of command or orders of their superiors—that any unlawful acts committed on their part were not done unilaterally, intentionally, willfully, or wantonly. This basically is the so-called "superior orders" defense. And it was a primary defense frequently brought up by the Nazi defense attorneys throughout the Nuremberg trials. The law of superior orders is found in the rule book, *Rules of Land Warfare*, (paragraph 347) and reads as follows—

> Individuals of the armed forces will not be punished for these offenses [*violations of the customs and laws of war*] in case they are committed under the orders or sanction of their government or commanders. The commanders ordering the commission of such acts, or under whose authority they are committed by their troops, may be punished by the belligerent into whose hands they may fall."[9]

Observe that in this rule the regular soldier is excused but his commander or government is legally responsible. As in the Nuremberg trials, following this rule did not make it straightforward to get at the guilty "leaders and planners." The central question then is this—is it the lieutenant who orders a squad of soldiers to blow up a house filled with women and children? Or is it the captain who issued the order to the lieutenant, or the major, or the colonel, or the general from whom the original command came? This was the paradox that the Allies tried to avoid with their symbolic "show trials" at Nuremberg.

The Framers of the UN Tribunal avoided these vexing legalities by only indicting the "planners and designers, the inciters and leaders" of Nazi genocide, but as one ascends higher and higher until only the chief of state—Hitler or Tojo—is reached, and he, according to many legal theorists (i.e., Charles Wyzanski, Jr., Laurence Tribe, Richard Posner, Alan Dershowitz, Cass Sunstein, Richard Epstein, Akhil Reed Amar, Tony Kushner, Jonathan Turley, and many modern-day liberal law academics that hold views on the Holocaust and the Nuremberg Trials), is immune to prosecution on the principle of "Sovereign head of state," and can lead to the belief that the Nuremberg Tribunal did not have the legitimate legal authority to try the Nazi defendants for war crimes in the first place, based on the principles of "positive law" as delineated in the original statement of principles to be followed in this unique tribunal.

The issue being raised in these modern times is whether the superior orders doctrine should be changed. Historically speaking, the superior orders rule did not enter the American *Rules* until 1914—the start of World War I. Prior to that, the *Rules* failed to mention "superior orders," and American military law upheld the principle that a soldier following his commander's orders is *not* protected if the order is unlawful. Admittedly, the regular soldier is in a precarious predicament. Commanded to commit a detestable act, he may be unaware that under the current international laws of civilized warfare descended from the Nuremberg Trials, it is unlawful. Despite the fact that he is committing an act of violence (or even murder), it seems difficult to hold him guilty, since in the words of radio commentator Rush Limbaugh, 'killing people and breaking things' is all that his military training has molded him to do on command and with reflexive compliance.

Applying the superior orders doctrine to the Nuremberg and Tokyo Trials, the defense attorney would postulate—What is the ordinary Nazi or Japanese soldier's choice? Either he can disobey an appalling command and be punished—perhaps shot on the spot—or follow orders and later be charged by the United Nations with murder or even worse, "war crimes" in contravention of the recognized rules and international laws of war. This scenario is illustrated by a German officer of World War II. Accused of war crimes in a Belgian village, he replied, "Yes, I know it was contrary to the law of nations, for I am a doctor of law. I did not wish to do it, but I did it in obedience to the formal order of the Governor General of Brussels." On the other hand, the American Articles of War defended a soldier or officer who refused to follow a clearly illegal command.

Thus it follows that Nazi soldiers, SS Stormtroopers, or members of the Gestapo knew that when ordered to torture or gas civilians or prisoners of war, that he is perpetrating an evil act. If he is true believer of Nazi propaganda of Aryan supremacy and the innate preeminence of Germany over all other nations of the world, he may even commit the crime of his own free will. Therefore, would it follow logically that this Nazi soldier should he be protected by claiming submission to his commander's superior order? In order to understand the paradox of the Nuremberg Trials it is imperative to examine American British, and German thinking on the subject, as delineated in noted cases developed in international law long before the Nuremberg Trials were established in 1945.

SUPERIOR ORDER DOCTRINE: EARLY PRECEDENT

The so-called "Maxwell Case" was one of the most noted precedents on the subject of a superior's orders originating to the Napoleonic Wars. [10] French prisoners in a Scottish jail had refused to snuff out a light in their cell window when ordered to do so by a guard. This guard, under the express command of Ensign Maxwell, fired at the light, killing one of the prisoners. Maxwell was tried and convicted of murder by the High Court of Justiciary of Scotland. His petition that he was acting under orders of higher officers was rejected. The court affirmed that "every officer has discretion to *disobey* order against the known laws of the land." [11]

THE AMERICAN VIEW

Another well-known American case regarding international war crimes are that of *Mitchell v. Harmony* (1851)[12] which involved a civil suit arising out of the Mexican War. An American Army officer in Mexico illegally confiscated the cargo of a trader in occupied territory. When the officer was later sued for the value of the supplies, he defended to have acted under orders of a superior officer. The court dismissed the defendant's plea. Chief Justice Taney of the United States Supreme Court ruled: "It can never be maintained that a military officer can justify himself for doing an *unlawful* act by producing the order of his superior. The order may *palliate*, but it cannot justify [the act].".

The case, *The United States v. John Jones* (1813),[13] was likewise a famous American case regarding the superior orders rule. The facts were that some members of the crew of an American privateer were brought up on charges because during the War of 1812, they stopped and searched a neutral Portuguese vessel on the high seas, badly mistreated the captain and crew, and confiscated their valuables. The court found all of the defendants guilty of the acts charged. With regard to the defense of Jones and the others that they had only obeyed their captain's orders, the justice said:

> This doctrine . . . alarming and unfounded, is repugnant to reason, and to the positive law of the land. No military or civil officer can command an inferior to violate the laws of his country; nor will such command excuse, much less justify the act. Can it be for a moment pretended, that the general of an army, or the commander of a ship of war, can order one of his men to commit murder or felony? Certainly not.[14]

Despite these early cases that seem to set the precedent against a superior orders defense, in subsequent American cases on superior orders, however, there developed a line of judicial precedent that gave the benefit of the doubt to the military point of view. The courts reasoning was especially discerning since in most cases, the act in question was performed during wartime conditions where those soldiers and officers charged with wartime atrocities were under a tremendous amount of great stress that required in some cases split-second decisionmaking in order to save their life or the lives of the soldiers under their command. Nevertheless, the unconditional rule which deems the soldier guilty if the order turns out in fact to have been unlawful is indeed qualified in these decisions.

Under These cases that arose since *U.S. v. John Jones, et al.,* have a tendency to grant exemption if the soldier followed an order which was not "palpably" illegal. Despite the court's trends in military tribunals, to date it cannot be said with certitude, that the American judicial rule regarding superior orders is settled law.

THE ENGLISH VIEW

Under English law, a soldier accused of war crimes, which used a "superior orders defense", has, to some extent, a more sympathetic position than he would under most American legal precedent. The foremost case in English legal history regarding superior orders is that of *Regina v. Smith* (1900).[15] During the Boer War, a guard of British soldiers, sent out on a perilous mission, had an argument with a South African native who refused to find a bridle for them. Smith, one of the soldiers, under orders of his superiors, killed the native in cold blood on the spot. When the war ended, a special court brought murder charges against Smith but he was subsequently acquitted. The court said, "I think it is a safe rule to lay down that if a soldier believes he is doing his duty in obeying commands of his superior, and if the orders are not so manifestly illegal that he must or ought to have known they were unlawful, the private soldier would be protected by the orders of his superior officer."

THE GERMAN VIEW

In the *Llandovery Castle* case (1922) two submarine officers, Ludwig Dithmar and John Boldt, alleged that they were following "superior orders" to sink a hospital ship, "Llandovery Castle",[16] a ship commissioned by the British government, to transport sick or wounded Canadian soldiers back to their country. The German Supreme Court turned a deaf ear to the defendant's defense of superior orders and declared—

> Military subordinates are under no obligation to question the order of their superior officers, and they can count upon its legality. But no such confidence can be held to exist if such an order is universally known to everybody, including also the accused, to be without any doubt whatever against the law. . .They should, therefore, have refused to obey. As they did not do so, they must be punished.[17]

A NEW SUPERIOR ORDERS RULE

To resolve the dilemma of the superior orders rule, some have suggested a new rule that would obviate the predicament of a soldier, whose judgment is understandably impaired, when finding himself fighting in the heat of battle. This new rule seeks to put a check upon excessive brutality and at the same time take account of the soldier's irregular position "between the devil and the deep blue sea." The following rule has been recommended for approval by an international criminal court as most nearly meeting these legal quandaries (presuming, of course, that it is supplemented by a sound sentencing policy): The act of a soldier in following the military command of his superior is not justifiable if, when he committed it, he either actually knew or, under the situation, had reasonable grounds for knowing, that the act ordered is illegal either under the laws and customs of warfare or under the criminal law of his country; and when the two systems conflict, the former shall be controlling.

The final condition is included because the most lawless of nations could justify their soldiers acts with impunity, for the most blatant violations of the law of nations, by merely rationalizing their acts, if committed against the enemy, to be at all times, lawful under their own law. This was the exact scenario the prosecutors at Nuremberg faced in bringing charges against the twenty-four Nazi leaders. As a rule, the law to be applied in order to establish the illegality of the order that resulted in atrocities would have to be the law of the soldier's country. He could not be expected to know the law of the enemy nation that prosecutes him. However, the laws and customs of war, as well as the commonplace principles of criminal law, are normally known and germane in Germany, Japan, and other Axis countries. By the way, a non-German court can lawfully disregard some of the Nazi legislation—such as that which denies legal status to Jews and other "non-Aryans"—because it is so contrary to the elementary principles of justice and fair play. (What Lon Fuller frequently refers to as "fidelity to law"). While a sovereign nation is at liberty to implement any legislation it sees fit, the point being the collective of civilized nations are not bound to recognize the tyrannical, unpredictable, and immoral Nazi laws.

This new superior orders rule cited above can circumvent harsh consequences if the sentencing procedure, post conviction, provides for allowances for the rank of the accused, and if his sentence is lessened for special circumstances, such as any of the following: he was not completely a free agent; there was no way for him to know with certainty, that he was violating the laws and customs of international conflict; the illegal order was obeyed under wartime conditions, at a episode of great danger, during warfare, or the like; or the command required instant compliance in carrying out an act that could not be deferred.

If these considerations were practical, many common soldiers would get off with insignificant or trivial punishment, while officers who had more familiarity of the law and greater liberty of action would be punished more harshly. The defense of "superior orders" and "ancillary clemency" should not, however, be relevant to the various private Nazi militias, such as the Gestapo, the Elite Guards, and Stormtroopers. Notwithstanding the fact that they had been integrated into part of the German army by law or decree, they evidently do not merit the typical protection accorded to ordinary soldiers because of their comparative elite training and status. Also, these specialized troops originated as private volunteer corps, and in any case their fellow comrades had full knowledge, and willingly accepted orders to commit their crimes, which are obviously "illegal orders" when they enlisted, which is what enticed these men to want to join these prestigious groups in the first place.[18]

To continue with Wyzanski's analysis of the Nuremberg Trials on the issue of the superior orders defense, he skillfully analyzes the diversity of historical legal opinion (even amongst the Allied nations judging at Nuremberg) furthermore, he seems to understand the imperative of the Nazi defendant's frequent reliance of this line of argument when he further writes:

> The defense of superior orders is, upon the authorities, an open question. Without going into details . . . , it may be said that superior orders have never been recognized as a complete defense by German, Russian, or French law, and that they have not been so recognized by civilian courts in the United States or the British Commonwealth of Nations, but they tend to be taken as a complete excuse by Anglo-American military manuals. In this state of the authorities, if the International Military Tribunal in connection with a charge of a war crime refuses to recognize superior orders as a defense, it will not be making a retroactive determination or applying an *ex post facto* law. It will be merely settling an

open question of law as every court frequently does.[19]

For example, under the Anglo-American common law system, trials are conducted under the guidelines of general rules of evidence.[20] The prosecutor and defense are responsible for constructing the best case for themselves based strictly on the evidence of the case at bar through discovery, seeking out all relevant facts, and identifying important legal issues and authorities of legal significance.

The judge, is by-in-large, relegated to the role of a referee; ensuring that each side follows the rules of evidence and proper procedure.[21] In the Continental legal system, this strict division of labor between the judge, prosecutor, and defense is not followed.[22] Instead, all parties work together to discover the truth, with the judge operating in a more inquisitorial role, even cross-examining witnesses himself.[23] The Nazi defense counsel at Nuremberg constantly protested what they perceived as the Tribunal's over-reliance on the Anglo-American legal system.[24]

Many jurists hold that the Continental legal system of the Occident is infinitely better adapted at determining the truth than the Anglo-American common law legal system. (I am increasingly moving toward this view particularly in the role of the judge that actively participates in the discovery of the truth).

Before I proceed further, one may wonder why I have seemingly departed from my examination of the "superior orders" rule, into this analysis of the differences between Anglo-American versus the Continental legal systems. The reason I do so and relate it for the former rule detailed above, is because at Nuremberg, the Nazis' defense counsel relied so heavily on *German* law to counter the charge of "conspiracy" or "common plan" as not being a recognized crime under the German legal system. Furthermore, the Nazi defense tactic of linking Austin's superior sovereign doctrine to that of superior orders as ipso facto related to the issue that they were following German law was belied by the fact that German law prohibited superior orders as an absolute defense to wartime atrocities. German law also prohibited the absolute defense to a person who "went beyond the order as given" or intended "that the superior's order referred to an act aimed at civil or military felony or misdemeanor."[25] Incredulously, Defendant Jodl claimed that he did not recall any charges under section forty-seven "in his thirty years of service,"[26]

German law actually had been used successfully prior to the Nuremberg Trials, to secure convictions of soldiers who committed atrocities during wartime. As cited earlier in the famous *Llandovery Castle* case—a 1922 German case originating from the First World War where two German submarine officers, Lieutenants Dithmar and Boldt were alleged to have shot at British lifeboats during World War I in violation of the accepted laws of war. The defendants tried to use German law to use the defense of "superior orders." A German Supreme Court not only found the defendant's Dithmar and Boldt guilty, but rejected out of hand the officers superior orders defense holding in part—

> Military subordinates are under no obligation to question the order of their superior officers, and they can count upon its legality. But no such confidence can be held to exist if such an order is universally known to everybody, including also the accused, to be without any doubt whatever against the law. ... They should, therefore, have refused to obey. As they did not do so, they must be punished.[27]

Incredulously, Wyzanski goes further and speculates whether the Tribunal has the legal legitimacy to even charge these twenty-four Nazi defendants with criminal acts. He appears affronted not only by the very existence of the Nuremberg Trials Tribunal, but outraged that the Tribunal, under color of law, could judge anyone, let alone the Nazi defendants who were protected citizens of a sovereign nation as Germany which he deems had the sole jurisdiction to hear and judge the Nazi defendants under German law.

Wyzanski further conjectures whether *any* Nazi soldier could be personally culpable for criminal acts committed by anyone else. In this, there is a form of "felony-murder rule" implied here. If the answer is yes, Wyzanski holds that it is fundamentally unjust because the law will blame the innocent for the acts of the guilty merely by association or conjecture. He further tries to make the distinction between the acts of the Nazi defendants on foreign soil, and those committed on German soil; as if one could have a safe haven, a refuge from the law, if one does the act in one's own country. To me this is a difference without a distinction, and does little to add clarity to the legal argument of the Tribunal's authority to judge crimes by German Nazi's wherever they occurred—Germany, France, Poland, Libya, or Russia. It should be remembered that during the war, Hitler sent eight German spies into America to cause mayhem via the planting of explosives at certain sensitive locations, and that when their plot was discovered, FDR demanded, and after going through the Supreme Court, received the authority to try and summarily execute seven of the eight German saboteurs. Writer, Joseph Persico, narrated those turbulent events in the case of *Ex parte Quirin* (1942)—

> On July 2 the President announced that the eight accused would stand trial before a military commission composed of seven generals, and they would be charged with violating the eighty-first and eighty-second Articles of War dealing with espionage, sabotage, and conspiracy. Court-appointed lawyers for the defendants made a game effort to move the trial to a civilian court, taking the constitutional issue all the way to the Supreme Court, but the justices backed the legality of a military tribunal. [Attorney General Francis]
>
> Biddle himself was to prosecute, an unusual move, having a civilian serve as prosecutor in a military proceeding. But FDR was taking no chances. The Army's Judge Advocate General was rusty and had not tried a case for over twenty years. FDR wanted his own man before the bar.
>
> On June 8 the prisoners, held in the District of Columbia jail, were shaved by prison barbers, lest they put the razor to their own wrists or throats, and hustled

> into two armored vans guarded by gun-toting military police. Nine Washington motorcycle patrolmen roared alongside, escorting the vans to the Department of Justice. Enterprising vendors soon were doing a thriving business selling ice cream and hot dogs to the crowds that gathered outside the department's iron gate every day to gawk at the enemy. The trial was held in Assembly Hall # 1 on the fifth floor of the Justice Department, the windows shrouded by black curtains. As the trial opened, Hoover, sitting next to Biddle, fed pages of evidence to the attorney general. During a recess, one of the defendants asked the presiding general for a cigarette. The general responded stuffily that Army regulations made no provision for such a request. A disgusted Hoover took out a pack of cigarettes and handed it to the German.
>
> In twenty-six days it was over. All eight were sentenced to death. The generals sent their verdict to the President. Roosevelt, acting, in effect, as the court of last resort, confirmed six of the death sentences, but commuted Burger's sentence to life and Dasch's to thirty years for their willingness to betray their comrades. August 8 was set for the executions, which would take place in the electric chair on the third floor of the District of Columbia jail. Eight weeks had elapsed from the night the first saboteurs had landed on Long Island.[28]

Contrast the eight weeks it took for FDR to fulfill the sixth amendment constitutional mandate of the defendant's "right to a speedy trial" with current war crime defendant's in American custody. The long, draw out mockery of justice liberal democrats, activist judges, and the liberal media are putting President George Bush through regarding Islamic fascist, Muslim fanatics that were fighting against American troops on foreign land and who are now prisoners of war is the natural result of ignoring the afore mentioned and other precedent in military tribunals. With these enemy combatants, we have much more evidence against them than President Roosevelt had against those eight Nazi saboteurs he had to deal with. The erosion of the rule of law from 1941 until today is astonishing, outrageous, and dangerous, as our government is needlessly hampered in its constitutional mandate to protect American citizens, "against all enemies, foreign and domestic."

It shouldn't matter *where* the Nazi war crimes took place, and to consider setting these vilest of vile men at liberty because of jurisdictional speculations would be the height of perversion of the law. In the end, Wyzanski believes that the tribunal lacked legitimate legal authority under *any* law to prosecute the defendants for murdering their own citizens. He completely rejects the legal theory that authority can be granted under natural law.[29]

NULLUM CRIMEN

Another criticism Wyzanski has toward the Tribunal is its violation of a standard rule of law which he believes is fundamental to justice and legality under any legal system. Namely, the ancient legal principle–*nullum crimen et nulla poena sine lege*, "[there can be] no crime and no penalty without [an already existing] law."[30] Allied prosecutor from Britain, Hartley Shawcross' remarks regarding this ancient legal maxim, *nullum crimen* are instructive:

> There is all the difference between saying to a man, "You will now be punished for what was not a crime at all at the time you committed it," and in saying to him, "You will now pay the penalty for conduct which was contrary to law and a crime when you executed it, although, owing to the imperfection of the international machinery, there was at that time no court competent to pronounce judgment against you." It is that latter course which we adopt, and if that be retroactivity, we proclaim it to be most fully consistent with that *higher justice* which, in the practice of civilized states, has set a definite limit to the retroactive operation of laws.[31]

Shawcross remarked, "The only innovation which this Charter has introduced is to provide machinery, long overdue, to carry out the existing law, and there is no substance in the complaint that the Charter is a piece of post factum legislation. . ."[32] Furthermore, Shawcross maintained that "the existence of law has never been dependent on the existence of a correlated sanction external to the law itself." [33] This is a very prescient distinction and that belies the sophistry at the heart of the Nazi defense attorney's argument on nullum crimen. Shawcross' legal analysis, infused with natural law philosophy (or what he referred to as "higher justice") was the type of common sense view of the law that paid homage both to our Anglo-American common law legal system which grew out of the Judeo-Christian tradition, while skillfully applying old law to new and complex questions about international law, jurisdiction, retroactive law, and war crimes in modern times.

On the other hand, Wyzanski continued his critique questioning the legitimacy of the Nuremberg trial as being contrary to the U.S. Constitution by criminalizing the Nazis' actions after the acts were committed. In his opinion, the Charter created new or *ex post facto* law, thus violating an expressed provision of Article I of the United States Constitution "No Bill of Attainder or ex post facto Law shall be passed."[34]

One of the most coherent and sublime expositions of the principle of legality, the prohibition of *ex post facto* law, and legal positivism regarding commentary on the Nuremberg Trials, is by Harvard University Professor of Philosophy Lon Fuller. In his famous article, *The Morality of Law*, Fuller presents his thesis that Nazi law lacked the vital element of all law—*fidelity to law*, a deficiency which precluded it from being considered actual law that one was bound to obey.[35] Jerome Hall in his book, *General Principles of Criminal Law*, stated that,

> The existence of law is one thing; its merit or demerit is another. Whether it be or not is one enquiry; whether it be or be not conformable to an assumed standard, is a different enquiry. A law, which actually exists, is a law, though we happen to dislike it, or though it vary from the text, by which we regulate our approbation or disapprobation." [36]

Wyzanski jurisprudence clearly argues the latter point, because in his opinion, the Charter that gave life to the UN Tribunal, breached the U.S. Constitution by including ex post facto elements; and that the Charter forfeited its very legitimacy as "law", by being unconstitutional. Although his analysis, at least rhetoric-wise, is plausible, in their analyses of the Nuremberg Trials it is ironic, that both Wyzanski and Robert Jackson repeatedly (and unavoidably) paid lip service to natural law, but then seemingly catch themselves, and curtly dismiss natural law, thereby refusing to acknowledge this moral-based philosophy of law as relevant to determining the legal parameters of the Nuremberg Trials. For example, Wyzanski says,

> [T]here exists, to cover the most atrocious conduct, a broad principle of universal international criminal law which is according to the law of most penal codes and public sentiment in most places, and for violations of which an offender may be tried by any new court, . . . [these principles] would not satisfy most lawyers.[37]

Here, Wyzanski concedes that "a universal, international criminal law" exists to punish the most heinous criminal conduct, but these legal principles are inadequate to most lawyers in a court of law." On this point I would question Judge Wyzanski about exactly *what* universal international criminal law is he talking about? The answer of course is "natural law." Wyzanski apparently doesn't have the intellectual honesty to even mention natural law by name even though it was the controlling legal philosophy of the Pilgrims and Puritans at the founding of America, it was the foundation for the Framer's of the Constitution, and it was the reason who fought the British Empire in a bloody revolution for over a decade in order to not to separate legality from morality, for the Framers well understood that this was the folly the French fell into with it's concurrent 'secular revolution' that overthrew the monarchy of King Louis XVI only to replace one totalitarian form of government with an even more evil incarnation (Robespierre and the Age of Terror).

Wyzanski's second point of why these (natural law) principles "would not satisfy most lawyers" is not explained, but one can assume that by the mid-1940s (the time of his writing), that most academic lawyers, professors, judges, intellectuals, as well as those who held views on legal philosophy, almost unanimously rejected a synthesis between law and morality as an unworkable, anachronistic philosophy of law from a bygone era.

The majority of academics and law professionals of the time virtually unilaterally embraced some form of analytical jurisprudence, otherwise known as positive law. That positive law was expressly design by its proponents and practitioners to follow social Darwinian thinking of the late nineteenth century, which, by 1945 with the establishment of the Nuremberg Tribunal, had so ingrained into every aspect of American society—law, culture, politics, economics, and even medicine by the 1940s, is an incredible admission and only underscores the arrogance of humanity to think they can dispense with the Judeo-

Christian aspects of the rule of law with such a cavalier attitude without regard to the detriment effects it imposes on our Constitution, American society, culture, law and politics. This arrogance is an ignominious perfidy with few parallels in the history of law. It suggests that Wyzanski ultimately believes that it is "lawyers, and lawyers alone" (not God) who determine what the law is. America's constitutional Framers would describe this form of domestic or international public policy, and its underlying legal philosophy, "legality without morality"—TYRANNY, which, had the citizenry not have been so utterly brainwashed and enticed by various political, scientific and academic mythologies (radical liberalism being the underlying religious/political foundation of them all under a social Darwinian paradigm), would have no doubt sparked a third American revolution by now. Albeit it appears the general public in contemporary times, like the people sixty years before during the Nuremberg Trials, seem satisfied with an activist judiciary that looks askance at the original intent of the Framers of the Constitution, a law academy that views natural law as an anachronism of past time, and so there is no call for reform of all our legal institutions while the America public, ignorant and apathetic of the moral foundations of Anglo-American law, walks in lock step with the Zeitgeist of the times—secularism and liberalism.

Wyzanski's concluding point questions the very necessity of even conducting trials such as those held at Nuremberg.[38] It seemed hypocritical to Wyzanski because in his view, the Tribunal was motivated by the Allies' desire to bring judgment to the Nazi defendants at all costs; that the Tribunal was merely a sham legal proceeding, and a Russia-style "show trial" and a mechanism of social propaganda–victor's justice. Here he states: "To some the count may appear as nothing more than the ancient rule that the vanquished are at the mercy of the victor."[39]

He goes further than accusing the Allies of victor's justice, accusing the Tribunal of being guilty of the same type of legal injustice for which they were condemning the Nazis. This moral equivalence argument subscribed to here is a ridiculous admissions by Wyzanski because to equate the Nuremberg Tribunal with at least making an attempt (flawed though it may be) at fair trial with the despicable, despotic, and evil atrocities of the lawless Nazi regime who willfully and wantonly murdered six millions Jews in addition to millions more in over a dozen European countries is a perverse logic with no substantive evidence, and is therefore indeed beyond the pale.

For Wyzanski, the principles of *nullum crimen* and *ex post facto* were absolute and any legal system that violates these precepts, the Tribunal notwithstanding, makes a mockery of justice and thus is considered by him to be an illegal entity. At the time the Nazis started World War II, "aggressive warfare" was not expressly prohibited by many international treaties in the sense of holding individuals liable for the crimes of others before an international tribunal outside of the laws of the aggressor nation.

In this respect, positive law, as the foundational and analytical jurisprudence of the Nuremberg Trials, is in reality a legal fiction since prior to World War II, there is no historical evidence of any Western nation holding legally liable, another nation during time of war for so-called, "illegal acts of aggression" although twenty-five years before, the same Allies tried to get Germany to bring several of its leaders before an international tribunal, but Germany only relinquished a handful of low level soldiers and the entire effort was eventually discarded. Based upon this history, Wyzanski holds that the genocidal acts of the Nazis against the Jews, as part of the "aggressive war" during World War II, was technically not a violation of law and that, "there is no convention or treaty which places obligations explicitly upon an *individual* not to aid in waging an aggressive war."[40]

In conclusion, Wyzanski considered, for those who were not chargeable with ordinary crimes but only with political crimes such as planning an aggressive war, that it would it have been better to proceed by an executive determination–that is, a proscription directed at certain named individuals. The form of the determination need not have been absolute on its face. It might have been a summary order reciting the offense and allowing the named persons to show cause why they should not be punished, thus giving the Nazi defendants a chance to show any mistake of identification or gross mistake of fact by the Tribunal prosecution.[41]

CHAPTER 5

REFUTATION OF JUDGE CHARLES WYZANSKI

> This doctrine [superior orders], alarming and unfounded, is repugnant to reason, and to the positive law of the land. No military or civil officer can command an inferior to violate the laws of his country; nor will such command excuse, much less justify the act. Can it be for a moment pretended, that the general of an army, or the commander of a ship of war, can order one of his men to commit murder or felony? Certainly not.
>
> ~ United States v. John Jones (1813)[1]

Although initially in my analysis of the Wyzanski-Jackson argument on the Nuremberg Trials, I thought that the legal philosophy of Wyzanski to be the more radical and liberal of the two, and therefore the one against whom I would most ardently direct my apologetic against, however, upon closer inspection, I found Wyzanski (at least in his rhetoric) to be the more prudent, reasonable, and conservative than Jackson not only in his jurisprudence and legal philosophy, his respective analysis of the Nuremberg Trials, but also in the legal conclusions drawn thereof. For example, in the opening paragraphs of his article, Wyzanski expressly and dramatically calls for "vengeance"—not only against the twenty-four Nazi defendants, but upon "several thousand Germans, including many defendants at Nuremberg, . . . either by death or by imprisonment [to] be permanently removed from civilized society."[2]

In contrast, Justice Jackson's *Opening Address* at the beginning of the Nuremberg Trials, at a point where critics like professor Alan Dershowitz and others have said that was one of his best moments, from my perspective, it is nothing a stringing together of bland platitudes which lacked the gravitas of law and moral authority.[3] However, my elation toward the validity of Wyzanski's critique of the Nuremberg trials was short-lived as he proceeded to wring his hands as he obsesses over what *theory* should be applied to judge the defendants? He states, "[i]f prevention, deterrence, retribution, nay even vengeance are ever adequate motives for punitive action, then punitive action is justified against a substantial number of Germans. But the question critical here is this—Upon what theory may that criminal action properly be taken?" [4]

Wyzanski further questions the legality of the existence of the Nuremberg Trials based on his strict Austinian interpretation of the superior sovereign doctrine to such an extent as to expresses doubt as to whether the defendants could be tried at the tribunal on the charges that encompassed crimes against German citizens on German soil.[5] His rationale is that since Germany is a sovereign nation, it can be judged only by Germans and only under German law. Wyzanski's logic here regarding German "sovereignty" inexorably leads to one of the frequent aberrations of positive law that provides a difficult and unavoidable problem for many theorists and philosophers who adhere to legal positivism's separability thesis or that school of analytical jurisprudence that mandates a strict separation between of legality and morality.

Accordingly, many positive law theorists and practitioners have discarded Austin's so-called "command doctrine" (law as a command of the sovereign that must be obeyed at threat of punishment), judging it to be ineffective, incompetent, unworkable, and, most significantly, in the Nuremberg and Tokyo cases, leading too a very miniscule number of indictments and an even smaller number of actual convictions, which I contend not only served as a gigantic mockery of the verity of the rule of law on an international stage, but in succeeding decades, embolden would be despots and tyrannical rulers all over the world to act with virtually impunity with the assurance that their acts, no matter how evil, anarchical, and genocidal in nature, would not be judge by the international community.

If jurisdictional issues of law can be viewed so narrowly and can be so easily detached from common sense, the common law rooted in moral/religious ethics out of the Judeo-Christian tradition, and the rule of law, the inevitable outcome of the Austinian command doctrine would essentially amount to providing secure jurisdictional havens for every international law criminal in the world. This result would be indeed an intractable situation, particularly from the establishment of the UN in 1945 up to modern times as the Western powers sought to battle communism, totalitarianism, and now a new menace—Islamic fascism.

Paradoxically, both Wyzanski and Jackson throughout their arguments, acknowledged the principles of natural law to counter the Nazis' defense that they were acting pursuant to superior orders based on the laws of Germany, or the "act of state" defense. However, in Article Seven of the Treaty of London (which had only been ratified by the Allied Powers four months before the Nuremberg Trials in November, 1945), expressly rejected the Nazi defense of "act of state," holding that "the official position of defendants, whether as Heads of State or responsible officials in Government departments, shall not be considered as freeing them from responsibility or mitigating punishment."[6]

Noted jurist, Hans Kelsen, who in 1945 became a legal advisor to the United Nations War Commission, in a famous paper written two years before the Nuremberg Trials in 1943 defined acts of state as "acts performed by individuals in their capacity as organs of the State and therefore acts imputed to the State"). An interesting historical fact is that Kelsen's paper was sardonically cited by Associate Defense Counsel, Hermann Jahrreiss, as substantive authority *for* the idea that "in questions of breach of the peace, the liability of the individuals to punishment does not exist according to general international law at present valid." [7]

Kelsen seriously disagreed with Jahrreiss' act of state defense. Anticipating the prosecution of Axis war criminals, Kelsen maintained that the characterization of rules, so as to affirm specific criminal liability retroactively, would be supported on a *moral* foundation.[8] I agree with Kelsen's prescient analysis of the requisite moral-based jurisprudence the Nuremberg Tribunal *ought* to have been conducted on, but few other voices were heard at that time, of the necessity of judging immoral acts on moral grounds to be therefore axiomatic. Kelsen, sadly, was a lone voice of reason crying out in the wilderness while the mainstream law academy, judges, and politicians continued down the Sisyphus path of putting their faith in the sophistry of positive law and the separation of law and morality. This blind faith in positive law we shall see later will have devastating consequences to the Jewish victims of the Holocaust.

At first surprisingly, then ironically, eventually, inevitably, Wyzanski time and time again found himself reverting to natural law arguments to counter the cruelty and irrationality of superior orders, command doctrine and other Nazi defenses, arguing that, "under well-known principles of German law, going back to the Middle Ages and differing from current Anglo-American theories, the superior order could be disregarded by a court applying German law, on the ground that it was so repugnant to 'natural law' as to be void." [9] This passage was indeed a rare admission by Wyzanski in that he actually wrote the unspeakable shibboleth, "natural law." As Kelsen urged the Allies must do two years before in citing the necessity of judging the Nazi war criminals on *moral*-grounds, Wyzanski was right to cite the natural law foundation not only in the history of German law but by association the entire Western Europe legal traditions that trace back to the Middle Ages. Even though Wyzanski's analysis relied principally on "positive law doctrine", his apologetic against the Nuremberg Trials frequent belied his reluctant reliance on natural law theory to make his arguments Nazi defenses based on analytical jurisprudence and positive law.[10] I criticize both of them for intellectual dishonesty because in the end of his argument like Jackson, Wyzanski deems natural law irrelevant in determining what the law actually *is*.

Contrary to the Nuremberg Charter which designated the international rules of war, until 1944, both the British, in their war rule book, *British Manual of the Laws and Usages of War on Land*, and the Americans in their war rule book, American Basic Field Manual, *United States Rules of Land Warfare*, expressly granted immunity from prosecution to any military soldier or officer for any criminal act committed during the commission of his military duties. These rules are contained in two primary sources, including—The British Ministry of Defense and the Manual of Military Law.[11] While both legal manuals allowed the defense, U.S. Military law also provided that the "[i]ndividuals of the armed forces will not be punished for these offenses [i.e., for violations of the laws of war] in case they are committed under the orders or sanction of their government or commanders."[12]

In 1944, both the British and the U.S. manuals abandoned the defense, the latter providing that "[i]ndividuals and organizations who violate the accepted laws and customs of war . . . pursuant to order of a superior or government sanction may be taken into consideration in determining culpability, either by way of defense or in mitigation of punishment. The person giving such orders may also be punished." [13] It is therefore evident, at least from the standpoint of American and British military law up until the advent of the United Nations Charter that established the Nuremberg Tribunal, that at least John Austin's superior order doctrine and command doctrine, far from being a legal anomaly, was if not an absolute defense to a charge of war crimes, was up until early 1945 both in Britain and American military law at least a mitigation to any charge where the defense of superior orders was raised.

Judge Wyzanski basically viewed the Nuremberg Trials as high politics masquerading as law. He questioned the very legal basis for the categories of criminality and standards of individual liability endorsed by the Charter. Wyzanski was not convinced that the Charter itself is valid "law"; if so, he asks, "by virtue of what authority?"[14] Wyzanski's views regarding the Nuremberg

Trials illustrate the danger of having a legal philosophy based solely on positive law, devoid of a moral context, hostile to religious traditions in the history and development of the law and presupposes a secular, naturalistic, and utilitarian approach to legal reasoning; an analytical jurisprudence scrupulously separate and distinct from any moral or religious-based ethical code. This is a very dangerous idea that can be easily exploited by a tyrannical leader like a Hitler.

For example, Wyzanski asserts that he knows of no international [law] convention "which in explicit words forbids a state or its inhabitants to murder its own citizens, in time either of war or of peace . . ."[15] This is an incredible admission. If there are no international laws that forbids a state from wantonly killing its citizens (which is patently untrue), then for Wyzanski, and others adhering to a positive law philosophy, ipso facto there must be an expressed law in order for such genocide to be illegal. This is because positive law must be "posited," positioned, or instituted by man and as Austin maintained—"law enforced by power or a threat of punishment." This analytical jurisprudence that looks with arrogant reproach at moral based legal systems with it's paradigm—Darwin's 'survival of the fittest' and Machiavelli's 'the ends justifies the means' or the anonymous aphorism, might makes right.

Any system of laws or legal structure that enacts these secular precepts is a legal structure that will eventually collapse upon sophistry of its own intrinsic contradictions. With sixty years of hindsight since the Nuremberg Trials, the anarchist and nihilist propensities of any nation governed by positive law jurisprudence, should serve as a sobering warning not only to America, but to the world legal community of all civilized nations—that a separation of legality from morality is a prescription for disaster of biblical proportions to any people who seek to *not* be governed by "moral precepts" in the rule of law.

Wyzanski's primary argument in his critique of the Nuremberg Trials centers on two well-known legal principles—*ex post facto* and *nullum crimen,*[16] And while he gives a reasoned exegesis on what these legal doctrines are, in relation to the Nuremberg Trials, Wyzanski neglects to give the reader the substantive history of these legal doctrines on which his argument so heavily relies in his assessment. I surmise that he omits delineation on the history of these ancient legal doctrines because he realized that both legal philosophies originated out of the natural law traditions dating back thousands of years, and that natural law philosophy was the basis of all early American law pre- and post-Constitution. Therefore, from the start of his argument, Wyzanski is on shaky ground by trying to bolster a positive law argument based on thoroughly natural law principles that he, in reality, neither acknowledges and respects, nor fully understands the critical role natural law has played in the history of Anglo-American jurisprudence.[17]

Conversely, Wyzanski does seems to realize that his arguments against the legitimacy of the Nuremberg Trials is on morally indefensible grounds, therefore he must constantly attempt to distance himself from the actions of the Nazis by frequent and perfunctory statements.[18] Wyzanski appears uncomfortable (on moral grounds) with his argument from the start against the validity of the Nuremberg Trials, which is evident by his constantly attempting to distance himself from the *acts* of the Nazi defendants (spirit of the law) as opposed to the actual, proper, legitimate application of the law and legal authority to judge the Nazi leaders (letter of the law). Although, in my opinion, he is wholly unconvincing at separating his legal philosophy of the classical positive law, secular humanism out of the Bentham-Austinian tradition that encouraged and gave legal sanction to Nazi atrocities, from the moral grounding of natural law—the legal foundation of Anglo-American law traditions, nevertheless, he is in a paradox and is therefore reliant upon and utilizes natural law principles to give credence to his arguments against the very Nuremberg Trials of whose existence he, by politics, ideology, culture and jurisprudence, despises.[19]

An example of Wyzanski's unintentional (I presume) tribute to natural law can be found in the following excerpt:

> Thus in Articles forty-six and forty-seven of The Hague Convention of 1907, the United States and many other countries accepted the rules that in an occupied territory of a hostile state family honour and rights, the lives of persons, and private property, *as well as religious conviction and practice, must be respected.*[20]

These emotionless words from the original Hague Convention of 1907 delineates arguments that are contradictory to his original opinion against the legal legitimacy of the Nuremberg Trials—a secular, humanistic view of legal philosophy rooted in positive law; an analytical jurisprudence which adhered to a strict wall of separation between law and morals. Under an analytical jurisprudence paradigm, the conception of positive law could countenance no reference in law respecting, in the words of The Hague Convention of 1907—"religious conviction and practice."[21] These conceptions of law are totally foreign to positive law and the philosophy of legal positivism which throughout his articles on the Nuremberg Trials Wyzanski espouses.

Wyzanski's understanding of *ex post facto* law, although natural law in origin and practice for centuries, is, through historical revisionism which reminds me of Orwell's lines in *1984*—("If the Party could thrust its hand into the past and say this or that even, *it never happened*—that, surely, was more terrifying than mere torture and death")[22] derived from a purely utilitarian perspective (policy to portends to do the most good for the most people), and leads to the logical conclusion that one could argue that the Nazis were being judged by a set of laws (i.e., UN Charter and the UN Tribunal) that did not exist at the time the crimes were committed.

However, by using natural law principles, the Nazi defendants have no such claim to refuge in nullum crimen (no crime without an existing law) or ex post facto law (no after the fact law) for their genocide against the Jews and others for murder has always been a crime in all civilized societies going back to ancient times. There is no "new law" here. The acts of genocide against the Jews by the Nazis would be considered murder by virtually any people or nation on earth—savage, barbarian, or civilized, regardless of whether the law is codified in international law (at the time the acts were committed) or not. This, in my opinion, is the sublime beauty of natural law—that such jurisdictional speculations which academics spend years and years arguing back and forth, over and over in seemingly endless repetition codified in voluminous academic journals that few people actually read or care about, fail to comprehend that such legal arguments under a natural law paradigm are wholly irrelevant in judging the Nuremberg Trials Nazi defendants.

As I stated in chapter two, natural law and to a lesser degree, even positive law,[23] contains a built-in exclusionary rule. Under a natural law paradigm where human institutions fail to undergird the universal moral order instituted by God, those laws lose their legitimacy as law, and are not to be obeyed. (*N.B.: that is construction can only work when the term "God" is the same deity referred to by the Framers of the Constitution, namely the God out of the Judeo-Christian tradition of intellectual thought. Since it was the God of Judeo-Christian tradition upon which all the suppositions of "natural law" were founded, Allah, Buddha, Vishnu, or other "gods" out of the Eastern religious tradition will not work under this analysis).

More importantly, a free, engaged, responsible, moral people are not under the obligation to obey the tyranny of a leviathan government that compels them to obey and respect inherently illegitimate and morally outrageous laws such as slavery, abortion, or same-sex marriage. To the contrary, history has proven that any nation under the unjust rule of a dictator or an intrinsically unjust, oppressive, or immoral system of laws has an unmitigated moral obligation, as human beings made in the image of God, to revolt, to seek to overturn these unjust laws even by force if other more diplomatic channels prove futile. This was the paradigm America's Founding Fathers took in the late eighteenth century to overthrow the tyranny of England and King George III. Thomas Jefferson penned those immortal sentiments in the Declaration of Independence—

> When in the Course of human events, it becomes necessary for one people to dissolve the Political Bands which have connected them with another, and to assume among the Powers of the Earth, the separate and equal Station to which the Laws of Nature and of Nature's God entitle them, a decent Respect to the Opinions of Mankind *requires that they should declare the causes which impel them to the separation.*[24]

(Of course by "separation" Jefferson meant from their present tyranny under England and King George III). If the United Nations Tribunal had relied on natural law principles in conducting the Nuremberg Trials, enshrined in all of America's founding documents including the Declaration of Independence, the Constitution, and the Bill of Rights, they would have effectively created a legal mechanism that would have summarily condemned Nazism as a fraudulent government, a sham state–antithetical to all known universal moral principles of humanity, which, ipso facto, would have condemned those laws that grew out of such an illegal, perverted state as contrary to all sound international laws. Tragically, since the Nuremberg Trials openly denigrated or ignored the theistic suppositions of natural law, they were conducted solely on secular, humanistic, empirical, relativistic, egalitarian, utilitarian, and positive law precepts like Austin's "act of state," "superior sovereign," and "command" doctrines.[25]

Analytical jurisprudence, like positive law and legal positivism, demands an almost fanatical allegiance to the doctrine of separation between law and morals. The academy understands the necessity of their religious devotion to this, and though they pay lip service to lofty ideals of "academic diversity" and "academic freedom", they walk lockstep to the beat of the Zeitgeist of our age—secular humanism.

These secular philosophies have no underlying moral authority parallel to that which is found in natural law. In analytical jurisprudence, like positive law and legal positivism, where questions of morality are measured against a utilitarian paradigm of what is best for the most people, worst for the least people, or what legal outcomes will allow the best utility for societal ends at that time, can only postulate such things in history, since it has no intrinsic moral underpinnings.

Novelist, George Orwell in his famous treatise on the apotheosis of the socialist state, *1984*, in his own unique, inimitable style put the above utilitarian philosophy in circumscribed, stark terms—

> Day by day and almost minute by minute the past was brought up to date. In this way every prediction made by the Party could be shown by documentary evidence to have been correct; nor was any item of news, or any expression of opinion, which conflicted with the needs of the moment, ever allowed to remain on record. All history was a palimpsest, scraped clean and reinscribed exactly as often as was necessary.[26]

Paradoxically, the root of Nazi totalitarianism was germinated by the Nuremberg Trials and has flowered in contemporary times in America and throughout Western Europe. For example, both America and Germany have thriving neo-Nazi movements that continue to spread terrorism, racial hatred, xenophobia, violence, and crime on a massive scale causing great societal upheaval.[27]

The Nazi ghosts have not all be exorcised from the marketplace of ideas in Germany, and there is still much respect and honor given to the socialist politics of Hitler. This state of affairs was brought to light a few years ago when several high-ranking German military officers were forced to resign for turning a blind eye to blatant neo-Nazi activity in their very ranks, as reported in a series of newspaper articles. The reporter chronicled the fact that two senior officers were reprimanded for allowing a convicted neo-Nazi to address soldiers at an elite military academy.[28]

Further evidence of a growing Neo-Nazi movement in Europe was noted in 1999. Joerg Haider, an Austrian politician, openly boasted of the great educational systems the Nazis had and how much he values his friendships with former SS Stormtroopers.[29] During the primary election, Haider commanded over twenty-five percent of the Austrian vote and has so affected the political climate to increasing nationalist ends, as to cause the ruling parties to "de facto adopt" many of his radical views in order to keep him from winning the popular vote during the general election and bringing further national embarrassment to the Austrian nation. Haider's comments have been so incendiary and anti-Semitic that they have sparked protests around the world, and caused some countries to break diplomatic ties with Austria. Among these comments, he has "praise[d] Nazi Germany's orderly employment policies" and he has characterized veterans of the Waffen SS, a branch of the feared Nazi organization, as "decent men of character."[30]

Bibilical Precedent of Natural Law

Wyzanski's argument that the Nuremberg Trials violated the principle *nullum crimen et nulla poena sine lege* (no crime without an existing law), is likewise without legal foundation when viewed through the lens of natural law which is derived from what Corwin called, "Higher Law" (See his legal/historical analysis of this subject in his excellent article in—Edward S. Corwin, *The "Higher Law" Background of American Constitutional Law*, which in turn goes back to 2000 years to the New Testament writings, which have their origins in the Torah or the Old Testament—the Bible.[31]

For example, the great Prophet/King Solomon, three millennia ago, wisely stated that, "there is nothing new under the sun."[32] This aphorism, applied to the principle of *nullum crimen*, would dictate that even before Moses codified the law of God into the Ten Commandments (what the Jews call "the Torah," God had already established these 'natural' laws in the moral universe enacted at the time of creation with the repeated biblical refrain—"And God said, let there be . . ."[33]

All creation is based on these immutable laws of nature upon which the foundation of science is based—gravity, the first and second laws of thermodynamics, Einstein's Theory of Space Time, the oceans and the seas abating at the shoreline, the fossil record, the structure of the smallest atom, DNA, etc. Based on such absolute laws, God was for instance, justified in judging Cain for killing his brother Abel [34] in cold blood 1500 years *before* the Ten Commandments were *verbally* given to the Jewish people by Moses at Mount Sinai and written on two stone tablets.[35] How could God judge Cain for killing his brother Able before the law of Moses was even written down and given to the people? (Sounds familiar to Wyzanski's retroactive law arguments?) Answer—the law of God was already known to Cain and Abel (presumably from the teachings of their parents (Adam and Eve) and all of ancient humanity by their very existence.

Cain knowingly and willingly violated God's universal, objective, moral order. Cain's conscience was fully engaged when questioned by God: "Where is thy brother Abel? His blood crieth out to me from the ground." Cain, without the least bit of contrition defiantly responded to God—"Am I my brother's keeper?" Man's adherence to God's "moral law" of the universe has stood throughout all civilizations since ancient times, and many historical examples are evident in both Eastern and Western religious and cultural traditions. If the Nazi defendants were judged innocent on positive law grounds, (which mandates a strong separation of legality and morality), because, according to Wyzanski (and others of this view), *at the time* the Nazi defendant's committed their acts of genocide against the Jews, they violated no known international law, then, following this logic to it's irrational conclusion, it would follow that all of humanity is guilty. To any rational person who is intellectually honest with themselves, can it be conceivable for a government such as Hitler's Third Reich, to create on a colossal scale, such unrestrained mayhem, destruction, and genocide and not be guilty of breaking the law? [36]

Stated another way, if the Nazi defendants are innocent because the world's brightest jurists could find no pre-existing law to judge them by, then society would be obligated to empty the prisons and never bring anyone else before the bar of justice again, and the concept of guilt/innocence would not exist in any meaningful sense and nihilism should become the political philosophy of the world.[37] Such a thought is ludicrous at best, however, the logical consequences of Wyzanski's argument, would in essence, discard over twenty-five centuries of Western civilization's adherence to the rule of law, natural law, and biblical theism whose antecedents date even to earlier civilizations of antiquity—the Hebrew, Greek, and Roman legal systems.

That American and European legal systems presently find it convenient to separate law from morality is both dangerous for American and European culture and its legal institutions. Historically speaking, it would be wise for America and the West to heed the fact that since ancient times, one common aspect of previous great world civilizations or world powers, are that they have all foolishly thought they could break God's eternal, universal moral laws with impunity or separate legality from morality without committing national suicide.[38]

CHAPTER 6

JUSTICE ROBERT JACKSON'S VIEW ON THE NUREMBERG TRIALS

[P]erhaps the Nuremberg tribunal asked for too little when it implicitly expiated the guilt of thousands of hands-on murderers by focusing culpability on a small number of leaders who could never have carried out their wholesale slaughter without the enthusiastic assistance of an army, both military and civilian, of wholesale butchers.[1]

~ Alan M. Dershowitz, America on Trial

Robert Jackson, (on leave as Associate Justice of the Supreme Court of the U.S.), as Chief Prosecutor for the U.S. at the Nuremberg Trials, in his *Opening Address for the United States in the Nuremberg Trials,* delivered in November, 1945, in addition to outlining his case, and the legal basis on how he believed the twenty-four Nazi were guilty of enumerated war crimes, appeared to be as focused on countering objections leveled by the Wyzanski articles on the Nuremberg Trials, published in the influential and popular magazine, *Atlantic Monthly* in the summer of 1945, several months before the actual Nuremberg Trials were to commence. Jackson argued that instituting an "aggressive war" clearly violated international law and that World War II was criminally entered into with full knowledge by the German people of the ghastly atrocities such a war would unleash, therefore, *ex post facto* and *nullum crimen* principles were not contravened by the Tribunal.[2]

However, Jackson appears contradictory when on the one hand, he says, "a Nationalist despotism . . . *took* from the German people, all of those dignities and freedoms that we had natural and inalienable rights in every human being,"[3] and on the other, "[i]f the German populace had *willingly* accepted the Nazi program, no Stormtroopers would have been needed . . . for concentration camps or the Gestapo . . . ."[4] (N.B.: Jackson's reliance on natural law rhetoric of "natural and inalienable rights" lifted from Jefferson's Declaration of Independence). I believe Jackson (at least at an intrinsic level), knew with certainty, that one could not bring charges on purely legal grounds, to such men that were so obviously guilty of moral crimes against humanity. The question then becomes this: which charge is correct? Did the Nazi government brutally deprive the German nation of liberty, or did the overwhelming majority of German citizens of the 1930s willingly cede their freedom and liberty for a greater German nationalism?

Conversely, Jackson also states, "[the Nazis] excited the German ambition to be a master race. . . *led* their people on a mad gamble for domination."[5] The implication Jackson seems to want to make here is that the German people were merely innocent bystanders during Hitler and his Third Reich's maniacal rise to power. However, I must agree with the view of recent (not revisionist) history; particularly of two noted historians—Daniel Goldhagen and Paul Johnson, who postulated that the Germans were indeed not only willing participants, but in numerous cases enthusiastic allies with Hitler and the Nazi genocide against the Jews.

For instance, Daniel Goldhagen in his prescient and controversial 1996 book, *Hitler's Willing Executions: Ordinary Germans and the Holocaust* wrote the following—

> I maintain that any explanation that fails to acknowledge the actors' capacity to know and to judge, namely to understand and to have views about the significance and the morality of their actions, that fails to hold the actors' beliefs and values as central, that fails to emphasize the autonomous motivating force of Nazi ideology, particularly its central component of antisemitism . . . Any explanation that ignores either the particular nature of the perpetrators' actions -

> the systematic, large-scale killing and brutalizing of people - or the identity of the victims is inadequate for a host of reasons. All explanations that adopt these positions, as do the conventional explanations, suffer a mirrored, double failure of recognition of the human aspect of the Holocaust: the humanity of the perpetrators, namely their capacity to judge and to choose to act inhumanely, and the humanity of the victims, that what the perpetrators did, they did to these people with their specific identities, and not to animals or things.
>
> . . . [T]he perpetrators, "ordinary Germans," were animated by antisemitism by a particular *type* of antisemitism that led them to conclude that the Jews *ought to die.* The perpetrators' beliefs, their particular brand of antisemitism, though obviously not the sole source, was, I maintain, a most significant and indispensable source of the perpetrators' actions and must be at the center of any explanation of them. Simply put, the perpetrators, having consulted their own convictions and morality and having judged the mass annihilation of Jews to be right, did not *want* to say "no."[6]

One of the more noteworthy absences regarding the Holocaust is the complete lack of attention regarding the perpetrators. A ten year debate centered on the initiation of the Holocaust, but of all this, only one member sought the question of why, once the killing began, did those receiving the orders to kill, do so. There appears the assumption the participants had no qualms about their orders, and similar lacking among the historians and social scientists, as well. The signal detail demonstrating the total lack of attention to this is the fact that there isn't even a specific number of people identified as "perpetrators" within the whole of Holocaust research. This is a significant issue in that the sheer numbers of victims delivers an almost unbelievable picture, were it not well recorded on film and paper.

It is a topic of substantial importance if we are to take the end result to be of any import. Were it but ten thousand who were called upon and performed the whole of it, we could lay it down to a horrifying aberration, and perhaps not be so consumed by the question. On the other hand, if the number were a half a million or a million or more, we would have to see it in an entirely different light. Such a thing would have to bear heavy weight when judging a society in this regard. Just the dearth of knowledge on this subject has far ranging implications, such as were they acting in civil office as police, or with military rank and orders as soldiers, and by what measure do we judge these possibilities?

The absence of curiosity on this issue has by no means kept some from making assertions about the role of ordinary German citizens in the Holocaust and their reasoning, but it has kept the question in the corner, unbidden, and uninvited. What is commonly put forth is more a matter of generalities applied to vague groups such as "guards" and "administrators," without delving into the personal side of the actual perpetrators—their vocations outside of the mainstream military machinery. Some of the generalities are laid on "The German People" in general, but the consistent thread through it all is that anonymity is always left for the viewer.

With many differing proffered explanations available, the primary ones can be brought down to some five, and an analysis of these can add some color to the black and white, stark picture. One of the explanations rests on "external compulsion", the perpetrators were compelled by threat, and by that token, "had no choice." With them in such hierarchies as the police, the military police and the parallel institutions, the strict chain of command, the expectation of immediate compliance with orders, and the certainty of the repercussions of simply turning the perpetrator into another victim is taken for granted.

The second explanation postulates the perpetrators as having been blind followers—an army of Manchurian Candidates if you will, simply following orders. Hitler's charisma has been called upon in this regard, along with the assumption of a general tendency of people to obey accustomed authority. Again, it is put that a German reverence for authority, and a noted tendency to follow orders without question, without moral considerations as a simple matter of conditioning, is submitted as reasoning.

A third explanation offered suggests the perpetrators were under extraordinary psychological and social pressure by the closeness of one's fellow soldiers of police officers, as may fit, and the common expectation of conformity to avoid being the lone hold-out. The mob effect, and the certain knowledge of its inevitable end, when aroused, can certainly fit here in this one. People adapt to those around them, and this being merely "the extreme."

As a fourth alternative, considering the perpetrators as petty bureaucrats and the natural "technocrats," whose lives revolve around standards and order, attracting those who prefer order and discipline above and beyond concern over human frailties, or simply too callous to consider such things. Such people exist everywhere, and are naturally attracted to such positions as meet their psychological needs. The institutions themselves can serve to dehumanize "cogs in machines" and lead people to lose sight of the fact of what they are doing, even to the point of ignoring death, or worse, coming to enjoy it.

Looking at the fifth apology, one almost must recoil from its meaning, suggesting that the perpetrators were of such enormous numbers, spread out with each performing such a small part of the whole, as to be impossible to conceive of what each act contributed, added up to in the whole. For this to carry any water, one must assume the absolute lack of connection to any part of it, that would not be absolutely and specifically one's own, and without contact between perpetrators. This would require an active, deliberate work to remain ignorant, and not casual, or a majority, but for reasonable effect, practically virtually comprehensive on the part of tens of millions of ordinary German citizens who were nevertheless willing Nazi sympathizers.

All of these explanations can be reduced to simpler, more useful terms, to actually account for the end result. Regarding the first, the only answer is postulating the perpetrator simply could not say "no." With the second and the third, one must maintain that the German people were just not capable—legally, morally, psychologically, of saying "no." With the fourth explanation, the contention is self-interest was sufficient to compel compliance. Of them all, perhaps the most galling is the suggestion that the individual acts were each, too small to apprise one as effecting a remedy to Germany's "Jewish problem"; an actual situation, while at the same time, far enough apart as to prevent any from having the knowledge of the totality of it all and therefore no reason to "say no."

While each one of these scenarios of why ordinary German citizens willingly participated in the genocide of millions of European Jews may sound plausible on its own, and isolated, and contain a germ of truth, can any come up to the level of reasonable? Consider the many common features, and the dubious nature of these commonalities. All are fraught with assumption and each of these assumptions requires one to believe in a level of parity across all the ranks and files. With these assumptions, it is suggested that we must demonstrate how people can be brought to commit grave acts to which they have strong antipathies for. There is no room in these explanations for the deliberate and intentional depredations done by people enjoying their work. We cannot deny that such are part of every group, there is no historical precedent for such a suggestion.

Treating these issues as if they were character traits of the German people does them no justice either. No doubt different people have different predispositions, but one cannot hang a natural predatory nature on a people just because one finds predators among them. In all of these explanations, one must consider the acts without considering the actors as people with moral and ethical sense, personal will, or common values, this reduces them beneath people in general, and that certainly won't hold water.

All of these explanations of behavior fail in two major areas: they do not explicate the extraordinary and horrific nature of the deed its self, the Holocaust, the mass killing of multiple millions of people, and they proceed forward, assuming there is little difference in ordering the mass killing, from perhaps a messy job cleaning up after burst sewer pipe, and people can be expected to follow such orders, just as they would any others.

Of all the things left out in all these rationalizations and excusing, the simple fact that the Holocaust was specifically aimed at the Jewish People, first, last and always, must be noted, always. From the other victims, one can draw an understanding of the mindset which set this in motion, the deliberate extermination of those seen as poor products, the sick, the criminal, the socially unacceptable homosexual, in fact, simply the laundry list of Eugenics, and in this selection, the statement is made two-fold: some citizens are not worthy of life, and some of these are recognizable by their religious and cultural heritage.

One must concede that this explanation leaves the fact that the vast majority of the victims were Jews, as "irrelevant." This then, was the crux of the matter, and it is this that truly defines the relationship between the victims of the Holocaust, and those ordinary German citizens who willingly perpetrated this tragic horror of biblical proportions upon their own friends, their neighbors and their fellow citizens.

Likewise, British Historian Paul Johnson, writes with a firm, unapologetic clarity on this issue the willing complicity and collective guilt of the German people regarding starting World War II and the Holocaust against the Jews. This devilish collusion between Hitler and ordinary German people crossed all social, economic, and religions ranks. Paul Johnson writes—

> From Hitler's silence downwards, the entire operation of genocide was permeated by unspoken, unspeakable guilt . . . . Hence security around the death-camps was elaborate. The wife of a German officer, who at a confused railway junction got onto a death-train by mistake, was ordered to the ovens nonetheless so that she could not relate what she had seen . . . . There were 900,000 people in the SS alone. Countless Germans heard and saw the endless trains rattling through the night, and knew their significance. . .[7]

In American history there are equally chilling examples of public complicity in the face of genocide. For example, Southern Whites fought and died five (for each slave) to one in their maniacal efforts to keep slavery the law of the land during the Civil War (1861-1865), but like the Nazis and average German citizens of the 1930s, good, well-educated, respected southern people of all social classes gleefully embraced and profited from the savage bondage of Black Americans. Moreover, the German people willingly followed Hitler and his Third Reich and zealously absorbed its nihilist propaganda of "purging" from the earth the inferior races of the world and seeking to establish on their charred corpses a strong, pure, White thousand-year Reich.

At the time the Tribunal convened in November 1945, there were several international treaties and agreements that expressly criminalized under the ubiquitous moniker, "aggressive warfare." Each of these treaties sought to set the parameters of the laws of war and bring these laws up to date with the strictures of modern warfare. These international treaties were ratified by many nations (including Germany) dating back to the early twentieth century. Moreover, Jackson contends the nations of the world have a right under international law to create new laws, to ratify new treaties and agreements that can become a foundation for the development and continual growth of international law.[8]

To this end, Jackson refused to allow the defendants to hide behind the Nazi defendant's frequent defense that international law would continue to "lag so far behind the moral sense of mankind." Therefore, the assertion by Wyzanski and the German defense attorneys that the Charter is not law because it's central precepts are *nullum crimen* and *ex post facto* law are according to the jurisprudence and legal philosophy of Justice Jackson, in my opinion is both sophistic and illogical.

To crystallize this distinction between Wyzanski's liberal view and Jackson's pragmatic view of the Nuremberg Trials, Jackson asks the rhetorical question that has strong overtones of natural law—"Does it surprise these men that murder is a crime?"[9] Jackson concludes that since genocide and torture are indeed crimes, it should not come as a surprise to any civilized person or nation that the venal deeds of these Nazi defendants should be severely punished. Furthermore, Jackson holds that it is rank hypocrisy for the Nazi party, whose very existence is owed to the complete annihilation of the rule of law, in furtherance of their genocidal madness of Hitler's Aryan supremacy, to then take refuge behind this same universal moral law to shield themselves from the bar of justice.[10]

Ironically, this deconstruction of the rule of law is exactly what occurred at Nuremberg and would tragically be repeated in subsequent war crime trials, even until this day of which I chronicle in detail in the Epilogue of this book.

CHAPTER 7

REFUTATION OF JUSTICE ROBERT JACKSON

Trying the culprits was plainly preferable to simply killing them. But trying so few of them sent out a powerful message that the "new legal order" would be lenient with those who were "just following orders."

Justice Jackson, who prosecuted the case for the United States, went so far as to suggest, early on, that it would be preferable to shoot Nazi criminals out of hand than to discredit our judicial process by conducting farcical trials.[1]

~ Alan M. Dershowitz

In response to Wyzanski's argument against the legality of the Nuremberg Trials, Jackson's opening statement to the Tribunal, although well written and delivered with sincerity, was essentially tentative, weak, mechanical, and generally lacking in moral authority imperative to legitimize an international criminal trial of this scope, and of whose precedent all future international war crimes trials would, under the doctrine of *stare decisis*, be obligated to follow. One primary criticism I have against the Nuremberg Trials, which I have repeatedly reiterated throughout this book, is that they were pathetically shortsighted and limited in scope. Stalin, (no doubt for bloodlust reasons), at the London Conference, argued for summary executions not only of Nazi leaders, but of soldiers, civilians, businessmen and all who were culpable. Jackson admitted as much during his opening remarks at the Nuremberg Trials when he stated, "[t]he case as presented by the United States will be concerned with the *brains* and *authority* back of all the crimes . . . We want to reach the *planners* and *designers*, the *inciters* and *leaders*. . . ."[2] Jackson further stated,

> Resort to a war of aggression is not merely illegal, but is criminal"; furthermore that the Nazi leader's complicity in the "planning and preparation" of these war crimes was clearly evident and that "inhumane acts charged in the Indictment, and committed after the beginning of the war, [that] did not constitute War Crimes. . . were all committed in execution of, or in connection with, the aggressive war, and therefore constituted Crimes against Humanity.[3]

To Jackson's laudatory statements above I would contend, why were the Nuremberg Trials concerned only with the *planners* and *designers*, the *inciters* and *leaders*?–the *brains*, if you will, and not the *brawn* of the perpetrators of Nazi genocide? For Jackson, the UN Tribunal and the Allied Powers who instituted the Nuremberg Trials, in the name of expediency, to so limit their jurisdiction to a handful of top Nazi officers as if they alone were response for the death of tens of millions of people, is beyond the pale. Here, I believe that Professor Dershowitz's portrayal that "trying so few of them sent out a powerful message that the "new legal order" would be lenient with those who were "just following orders."

The twenty-four Nazi defendants were not, "merely the German soldiers following orders of superior officers," they *were* the superior officers giving the orders for unbridled genocide against humanity. The pathetically limited scope of the Nuremberg Trials, (primarily on pragmatic grounds and political expediency), was truly one of the most ignoble episodes of the entire genocidal war against civilization, and in my opinion, an affront to the six million Jews who perished in Hitler's ovens, making this spectacle of a trial as the subtitle of my book intones—"the last tragedy of the Holocaust."

That Jackson offers no reasonable, sustainable explanation of the ridiculously constricted scope of limiting judgment only on the Nazi leaders, in my opinion, only increases the needless shame and outrage visited upon the Jews six decades later, when the Allies were literally given our enemies heads on a platter. Instead of executing swift justice to dissuade the all those who would deign to follow the Nazi's path, the Allied Powers instead, foolishly, arrogantly, and under color of law, abdicated our God-given responsibility to act with this authority and vindicate justice. I believe it not far-fetched to trace the rise of terrorism and radial political ideologies to this year 1945, for the Allied Powers showed the world that genocidal murder would be only symbolically punished, based on rank.

Furthermore, one could reasonably question whether the Tribunal in Nuremberg was even interested in bringing to justice. (That is an open question that I will address later). Furthermore, Robert Jackson was appointed to the Supreme Court by one of the most openly liberal and socialist politicians of the twentieth century—Franklin Delano Roosevelt. We must also remember that Robert Jackson was also hand-picked by FDR's successor, President Truman, a Big-government liberal, to be the chief prosecutor of the United States at the Nuremberg Trials, and finally it should be noted that President Franklin Delano Roosevelt appointed him to the Supreme Court in 1941 as part of his Machiavellian efforts to "pack" the Court with liberal activist judges to aid him in passage of his Leviathan government New Deal policies which was infamously referred to as "A stitch in time saves nine."

The Allied Powers were weary after suffering under the worst war in world history. They weren't interested in dispensing comprehensive justice to all the surviving Nazi officers, soldiers, businessmen, laymen—virtually the entire nations of Germany and Austria—a truly gargantuan task for nation or group of nations to undertake. Someone had to answer for Hitler's madness. I think that during the discussions by the Allied Powers at one of the subsequent conferences, (London, Potsdam, Crimea) that for pragmatic reasons, it was decided that only a symbolic number of Nazi leaders would be brought to trial, with the rest of the Nazis and Nazi aiders and abettors being "de facto" exonerated. Therefore the consensus was formulated by the Allied Powers—Let those men closest to him [Hitler] pay that price and pay it quickly so that America and the Allied Powers could get to the task at hand—rebuilding Europe from the ashes. The strategy sounded nice, neat, and clean, but was it?

Jackson further concedes the legal fiction of positive law as being "artificial" when he states that all wars from World War I, back to time immemorial, were not considered crimes (the twenty-six year period from 1919-1945, notwithstanding). Jackson further writes: "There was a time, in fact I think the time of the [F]irst World War, when it could not have been said that war inciting or war-making was a crime in law, however reprehensible in morals." [4] By these tepid remarks, Jackson belittles his position of strength, (one can hardly imagine having defendant's more guilty than Hitler and his principal henchmen), and plays right into the hands of the Nazi defense attorney's reliance on their one and only trump card—positive (secular) law—Law stripped of its moral content. What Hart calls "the gunman situation writ large." This reticence to argue natural law *a priori* (to the stronger), combined with an absence of any cogent analysis outlining a comprehensive overview of legal history, political philosophy, or history of warfare, throughout his opening remarks to the Tribunal, I contend, has to do more with his staunchly liberal and socialist politics than his jurisprudence. Was he not, after all, a liberal activist Justice appointed by Franklin Delano Roosevelt, himself?

Since the Age of Reason (1600-1750) (Enlightenment Period (1750-1830) of history, but especially since the Progressive Era (1900-1915), liberals have been adverse to characterizing vile acts of humanity as "evil" for this engenders in the liberal mind steeped in a secular humanist worldview—allusions to God, human nature, man's fall, the Bible, which the enlightened man now considers dead letter concepts. To illustrate this point, Jackson repeatedly demonstrates his aversion to the concept of *vengeance,* which is clearly a Biblical concept rooted in the common law and natural law traditions of Western jurisprudence. However, in his Opening Address, Jackson almost smugly iterates—"stay[ing] the hand of vengeance . . . is one of the most significant tributes that Power ever has paid to reason."[5] What does he mean by that? I find this statement to be a curious concept to come from the mouth of a prosecutor. Prosecutors are supposed to prosecute, not be a judge. Trying to balance vengeance (power) with reason is the domain of the judge. Here, Jackson is wearing a judge's hat when he should be wielding the sword of Achilles, as a prosecutor.

One of the fundamental objectives of a court of law is discover the truth, and once it is found, mete out justice, tempered with mercy (where warranted). It was not Jackson's nor any prosecutor's job to wax, however eloquently, on the noble cause of the Allied Powers, nor on the power they wish to wield to secure justice to the Nazi defendant's, nor because he wishes to "stay the hand of vengeance." His job, specifically, is to bring the evidence to court, and use it to achieve the objectives of a court of law. Why, in a court of law, arrayed against some of the most evil, despicable and unrepentant defendants in the history of criminal and international law, would a prosecutor, of all people, want to "stay the hand of vengeance?" This logic is indeed beyond the pale and in the Nuremberg Trials and the precedent setting cases that grew out of them, did pitifully little to forward the cause of justice.

To avoid the moniker of seeming like a conservative ideologue, I must state here that ironically liberals did not invent judicial activism but perfected it. Legislating from the bench began in earnest during the Progressive era with the infamous *Lochner v. New York* case of 1905 as the ongoing war between President Theodore Roosevelt's attacks against corporate trusts (i.e., monopolies) were shamefully given the color of law by a then conservative majority on the Court by reading into the Constitution their own *laissez-faire* ideals on economics and the primacy of corporate concerns over individual interests.[6] The Court in *Lochner* held that "there were no substantive arguments for precluding the right of freedom of contract by regulating the hours of labor."[7]

This so-called "substantive due process" jurisprudence was created by this conservative Supreme Court out of whole cloth without any legitimate or historical foundation in Constitutional law. This so-called "right" that the Court suddenly found in the 1905 *Lochner* case, was an unconstitutional usurpation of power by the judiciary branch over legitimate state law, that sought, for legitimate public health and public safety reasons, and rooted in Progressive politics, to limit the number of hours one could work per day.

Remember that this case was at the zenith of the industrial revolution (1850-1930) where good paying jobs were concentrated in large industrial cities, work was long and hard, and workers were cheap with few if any rights, and controlled with an iron hand by the captains of industry, the so-called "Robber Barons" who had little compassion for the lowly factory worker. If a worker couldn't keep up the pace or complained in any manner, they were summarily fired on the spot. The societal fallout from this great economic boon was oppressive, sweatshop conditions. The *Lochner* opinion is an ignominious example of conservative judicial legislation from the bench whereby justices used the power of their high office, under the color of law, (the Constitution), to tell states that they couldn't regulate the number of hours a baker could work.

The *Lochner* opinion was clearly in violation of the constitutional separation of powers doctrine where the Framers formulated a tripartite government—Executive, Legislative, Judicial—each branch with separate and distinct powers and no branch having authority to violate the domain of the other two. Despite the overstepping and unconstitutional nature of the *Lochner*, there appears to be little in this opinion that is unthinking or mechanical. *Lochner* was a well-written opinion with its own type of elegance, yes, even logic however, *Lochner* and it's progeny, remains to this day a *political* judicial opinion rather than *constitutional* one—the essence of judicial activism.[8]

Returning back to Jackson's Opening Statement at Nuremberg, he even seem to brag about the Allies' restraint when he stated, "stay[ing] the hand of vengeance . . . is one of the most significant tributes that Power ever has paid to reason."[9] As poetic and laudable as these sentiments appear to be in his opening address, Jackson seems to show no remorse regarding the hundreds of thousands of Nazis and Nazi sympathizers who escaped judgment, and no respect for the millions of innocent people they murdered. Unlike the blood of innocent Jews still unvindicated, still unjudged, still unrepentant, many Nazis leaders, soldiers, and their 'willing accomplices' (the complicit German public and the business community), with the blood of Jews and other innocents on their hands, are enjoying the fruits of freedom—some with great wealth accumulated through their "neutral" aiders and abettors, the Swiss and Swedish bankers via their closed banking system, even until this day. On this point one writer commented—

> Despite Hitler's boasts about autarky, the German economy was dependent throughout World War II on foreign imports: 23 of the 34 most important raw materials for conducting the war had to be imported. For this trade Germany required internationally recognized currency or gold-much of it "laundered" gold seized from European Jewry or from the government reserves of countries conquered by the Nazis.
>
> The Swedish National Bank also profited from the Nazi's stolen gold. From 1939 to March 1944 Sweden bought 34,564 kilograms of gold from the

> Reichsbank. In return, Sweden supplied Germany with a multitude of materials, including thirty-five million tons of iron ore. Gold was also exchanged for Swedish currency, which could be traded internationally. At America's insistence, following the end of the war Sweden handed back approximately 13,000 kilograms of gold to the national banks of Belgium and Holland, whose assets had been seized by the Nazis.[10]

The appalling, historical treachery of the country of Sweden, profiting from the plight of the Jews by their unholy alliance as Hitler's money launderer, further belies their hollow boasts of 'neutrality' during World War II, and is one of the darkest chapters of one country benefiting from bloodmoney of the Jewish people which Sweden continues to fabulously benefit from to this day, while denying any role regarding funding the Nazi State. At the same time, Robert Jackson gives credence to lessons learned from World War I, stating, "[e]ither the victors must judge the vanquished or we must leave the defeated to judge themselves. After the First World War, we learned the futility of the latter course."[11] With this stated, I have to ask, did America and the Allied Powers learn anything? If so, again I pose the question—why are there probably hundreds of thousands Nazis still alive today, living in peace, unrepentant, and unpunished, while millions of Jews must suffer the inconsolable pain and memories of having fifty percent of their friends, family, and countrymen murdered in Hitler's ghastly gas chambers of death, tortured by Mengele's ghoulish medical experiments, or unceremoniously shot in the head like a dog and dumped into mass graves by Nazi henchmen?

Indeed the Allied Powers learned nothing regarding just punishment from the debacle of the 1919 Versailles Treaty that literally, like the Nuremberg Trials afterwards, gave a tacit appeasement to German totalitarianism which only emboldened Hitler's maniacal drive for world domination, making the philosopher, George Santayana's words all the more prescient—'Those who do no learn from history are doomed to repeat it.' The appalling legacy of the Nuremberg Trials and the case law precedent that has come down from it, has demonstrated to the world that the international legal community that established the Nuremberg and Tokyo Tribunals under the analytical jurisprudence positive which mandates a separation of law and morality, have likewise, learned nothing.

Like Hitler, Wyzanski and Jackson's philosophical worldview is a legal system based firmly in the analytical jurisprudence of positive law and legal positivism—a legal system that is secular, humanistic and looks askance at any moral sentiments as guiding what the law *is*. While I mean no hyperbole here, I do wish show in a paradoxical sense how narrow an intellectual gap there is, (absent a moral base rooted in the Judeo-Christian tradition) to pervert law and to use it to justify any monstrous end one can imagine, once one makes the philosophical leap of removing all moral and ethical concepts from legal consideration.

Jackson's belief in the separation of law and morality is clearly evident in his Opening Address to the Tribunal when he boldly exclaimed, "[w]e charge guilt on planned and intended conduct that involves *moral* as well as *legal* wrong."[12]

Although throughout his remarks he makes token concessions to natural law like his veiled distinctions to charge guilt on *moral* wrong as well as *legal* wrong, however to Jackson's actions made the distinction between moral and legal little more than a rhetorical flourish—a distinction without a difference. Morality, to Jackson's ideal jurisprudence, has no intrinsic meaning to him that in any way influences his philosophy of law or his legal worldview. Jackson continues to pay homage to natural law philosophy without giving credit to the verity of this legal philosophy when he states, "[t]he Charter of this Tribunal evidences a faith that the law is not only to govern the conduct of little men, but that even rulers are, as Lord Chief Justice Coke put it to King James, 'under God and the Law.'"[13] Citing Justice Coke is a concession to the verity of natural law jurisprudence, for Justice Coke was one of the towering natural law jurists of his time and was not loath to challenge even the sovereignty of King James I himself–the potentate whose biblical translation of 1611 is still the most revered and popular English language version of the Bible, however this concession is never implemented in the final findings of the court.

Even though Wyzanski and Jackson, in their analysis of the Nuremberg Trials, frequently echo natural law ideas, they do so only in a perfunctory, sentimental way and thus I consider their approach cynical, impotent, and self-serving. Their positive law analysis appears designed only for the utilitarian purpose of bolstering their humanist arguments rooted in analytical jurisprudence, which have no moral foundation. I have seen little evidence that Justice Jackson thought for a moment, of natural law as viable, competent, legal philosophy; that it was the foundation of the common law and the rule of law or that natural law is in anyway relevant for a modern-day jurist in reaching a legal conclusion in the Nuremberg Trials or in any given case. If my supposition is true here, it is indeed lamentable, for the logical conclusions one is forced to reach, absent a moral foundation in any substantive legal system, reached its tragic apotheosis at Nuremberg and in the numerous international trials since Nuremberg, (the *Hamdan v. Rumsfeld* decision being the most recent case on this issue) only leads to disastrous results.

Specifically, in the *Hamdan* case, the U.S. military captured an American citizen, Yaser Esam Hamdan, fighting against American troops as an enemy combatant in Afghanistan. Following the precedent of Nuremberg, the *Hamdan* decision, for the first time in American jurisprudence, saw the Court violate the constitutional separation of powers doctrine, to decide what the rules of war would be regarding the defendant Hamdan. Prior to this case, the rules of war in American jurisprudence, and even under international law, was the exclusive province of the Executive and Legislative branches of government. The "*Hamdan* decision", a shameful example of judicial legislation from the bench, changes who sets "the rules of war" for the foreseeable future.

Returning back to Justice Jackson and his philosophical view of the Nuremberg

Trials, in his primary attack against the Nazi defendants, he noted in his Opening Address, the moral authority and primacy of the international law treaties that the Germans had signed, and under whose authority they knowingly submitted. Jackson commented: "Even the most warlike of peoples have recognized in the name of humanity, some limitations on the savagery of warfare. Rules to that end have been embodied in international conventions to which Germany became a party."[14]

However, international treaties, as important as they can be in maintaining civility among the nations of the world (at least in theory), in reality becomes merely symbolic posturing by politicians, and are usually broken before the ink dries on the document signed. Treaties are nice for diplomats, envoys, and ambassadors, but they are not worth the paper they are written on, absent mutual allegiance between the nations, to the rule of law based on moral precepts. Absent this, international law and international treaties signed between nations are all in vain. For example, who will forget the pathetic impotency of England's Prime Minister, Neville Chamberlain, naïvely waiving a "peace agreement" he had just signed with Hitler in the Munich Pact of 1938 and, as he arrived at the airport in England pompously proclaiming—"We have peace in our time."[15] Do we? . . . Did we then?

Hitler promised Britain and France, after his invasion of Czechoslovakia, (which he needed to expand Germany's borders for living space–*lebensraum*), that he would not invade Europe. England and France, in an ignominious act of appeasement, treachery, and cowardice, agreed to cede Czechoslovakia to Hitler, in their zealous (but ultimately vain) attempts to appease Him. These vain promises were made even as the tanks rolled toward Poland's borders—less than a year after the Munich Pact was ratified—thus leading to World War II on September 1, 1939.[16]

It is imperative to understand that treaties between secular nations are not sacrosanct, comprehensive, or immutable, their continued existence is based on their continued utility, and a failure to understand this demonstrates an ignorance of the intractable perversity of human nature—'The ends justifies the means'; 'Survival of the fittest.' Nuremberg psychiatrist, Dr. G. M. Gilbert, in his memoirs, *Nuremberg Diary*, commented on this obstinate human nature that seeks to rationalize its own twisted worldview, a conversation between Nazi defendants, Ribbentrop and Hess. Gilbert remarks—

> Ribbentrop was arguing with Hess but getting nowhere, since Hess has no recollection of the world events recounted in the Indictment. Ribbentrop then remarked to me "Why all this fuss about breaking treaties? Did you ever read about the history of the British Empire? Why, it's full of broken treaties, oppression of minorities, mass murder, aggressive wars, and everything."[17]

Moral equivalence, comparing Nazi atrocities as no different in scope than those of the historical British Empire, is reprehensible primarily because Ribbentrop actually appears to believe his own perverted rhetoric. The fairly recent history of two World Wars and as the world stands on the precipice of World War III, should give pause to all but the most partisan, of the futility of international treaties as a bulwark against the globalist expansionism of the nations.[18]

Jackson does not seem to understand the meaning, nor the true origins, of international law when he states, "[b]ut International Law is more than a scholarly collection of abstract and immutable principles. It is an outgrowth of treaties and agreements between nations and of accepted customs."[19] This definition is essentially incomplete because international law, prior to the Nuremberg Trials, was based on natural law, the rule of law, and the common law—legal systems all overtly rooted in a unity of legality and morality and following the intellectual tradition of Judeo-Christian theism. Prior to the advent of positive law in the early 1900s and it's apotheosis in international law, the Nuremberg Trials, the philosophical presuppositions of international law were not thought of in humanistic, abstract, secular terms, but in language of irrevocable, concrete, universal principles rooted in theism irrefutably linked to the Judeo-Christian tradition, the Bible, natural law, and moral order.

A case in point, in the Treaty of Versailles (1919) after World War I, the Allies left Germany's military virtually intact and turned a blind eye when Hitler became the only European power to rebuild his military forces, while America, Britain, France, and other world leaders of the West foolishly allowed their forces to languish (again). Thus, when Hitler's blitzkrieg rolled across Poland, the armies of the West were impotent to mount any viable counterattack until America entered the war two years later after Imperial Japan bombed Pearl Harbor in December, 1941.

Jackson spends considerable time condemning the Nazis for starting an "aggressive war." What is aggressive war? It is admittedly a term of art. Can aggressive war be distinguished from "non-aggressive" war? Is it even possible for one nation to mount a non-aggressive war against its another nation as to not be in violation of international law? I think not. This type of tough-sounding but ultimately meaningless rhetoric is indicative of a globalist philosophy born in the minds of the secularist, socialist bureaucrats who drafted the Charter. It is perverse UN-speak that makes otherwise very intelligent people like Secretary of War, Henry Stimson, say such inanities as—"War is an illegal thing," and not sound completely irrational. This extreme utopian liberal worldview held by the drafters of the UN Charter, the UN Tribunal, and the legal machinery of the Nuremberg Trials, indicates that they possessed a fatally flawed understanding of both human nature and military history that endures until this day? I will cover this topic in greater detail in the book's Epilogue in chapter 9.

Returning to the UN Tribunal and Jackson's repeated contention against the Nazi's for waging a "war of aggression" or "aggressive war"; how can war not be aggressive? War by definition involves not only aggression, blood, mayhem, killing, even the deaths of innocent civilians. Has there ever in the history of mankind been a "nonaggressive war"? Even the so-called "Cold War" between the United States and the Soviet Union (1945-1990) was aggressive in that these two superpowers used other countries as proxies in a series of wars with each other spanning the world.

Nations have warred since the beginning of human history and they have done so without UN bureaucrats micromanaging the war, and serving as referees and without any canon of rules of warfare except that of "victors' justice"—for good or ill, the winner of the war makes the rules. For jurists like Jackson, Wyzanski, liberal politicians in America, and United Nations bureaucrats, to naïvely hold to a utopian worldview that mankind's sinful nature can be reformed by man is fatuous, untenable, and as history has repeatedly shown, and poignantly exemplified in the Holocaust, ultimately genocidal.

What then should have been the legal philosophy the Allies should have used in the Nuremberg trials? Only by following the universal, theistic principles of natural law, with its emphasis on man's sins tempered with the iron rod of God's law, can the intractable gulf between man to man, man to God, and man to law be ultimately reconciled. Jackson's Opening Address at the Nuremberg Trials represents the birth and establishment of the diabolical philosophy of secular humanism which is the central tenant of positive law (legality separate and distinct from morality) and the death of the theistic suppositions of natural law and its antecedent philosophies—the English common law and the rule of law—ideas deeply entrenched in the Judeo-Christian school of intellectual thought.

One of my strongest contentions is that Jackson and the liberals and socialists in the United Nations had the humanistic idea that all of mankind's problems can be solved by man alone without resort to what liberal jurists such as, Wyzanski, Oliver Wendell Holmes, Benjamin Cardozo, Roscoe Pound, Karl Llewellyn, William Brennan, Thurgood Marshall, Richard A. Posner, Alan Dershowitz, Laurence Tribe, Ronald Dworkin, and the socialist bureaucrats of the UN consider anachronistic myths and naïve metaphysics of natural law; totally unnecessary and irrelevant in humanity's march toward utopia and salvation through their new gods—liberalism, humanism, secularism.

Remember the words of President Franklin Delano Roosevelt's own Secretary of State, and later, Secretary of War, Henry Lewis Stimson, who, regarding World War II, boldly proclaimed—"War. . . is an illegal thing," or the Briand-Kellogg Pact of 1928 that renounced war as an instrument of national policy.[20] At the outset, what type of policy could war be other than a national policy? Even America's Civil War had great national policy implications—England and Spain were allied within the confederate forces of the South; the French were allied with the Union forces of the North. Second, to try to make war illegal unilaterally, by international decree, or even in theory is about as effective as creating a law making it illegal for a raging bull to break glass in a china shop. Not only is this law unsustainable and futile, but the wasted time, wasted efforts, and misused resources squandered at trying to achieve the desired results only multiply the inevitable disaster—this indeed is why I call the pathetically symbolic Nuremberg Trials and their unreasonably limited scope at vindicated the atrocities against the Jewish people, truly the last tragedy of the Holocaust.

In studying the verbatim transcript of the Nuremberg Trials, it is easy to lose perspective that humanity, at that singular moment in the past, was trying to do something truly unique in history—impose some measure of justice on the Nazi criminals who were not only obviously guilty of multiple crimes against humanity, genocide, and war crimes, but were in fact, intrinsically wicked, some were pure evil, and together, the acts were utterly depraved; vile acts committed by unredeemable men. Reading the transcript of the Nuremberg Trials tends to lessen the impact of the totality of their actions, and reduces the force with which these manaical acts were committed gives us an even better understanding of how the use of "positive law" as a foundation for the Nuremberg Trials has reduced the effect of the totality of the genocide by removing the "moral impact" that is natural and critical to understand—the evil of human nature.

The fallacy and tragedy of Nuremberg was trying to establish under the strictures of liberal democracy, legal machinery to judge pure evil and give this incarnation of evil (Nazism) all of the due process rights and privileges expected by any defendant in a court governed by the "rule of law" as it exists in "natural law," as if this could be done without addressing the "evil" which can only be considered within the scope of "moral."

The Allied Powers, under the mechanism of the Nuremberg Tribunal, foolishly treated blatant war crimes that should have been judged by an international *military* tribunal, as tantamount to a local police concern to be tried by a local court of law; despite the fact the Nuremberg Trial Justices represented each of the four Allied Powers. This is establishment of the Nuremberg Trial precedent for treating international war crimes as a local police matter, is indeed, beyond the pale. While no reasonable person could doubt the sincerity of the creators of the UN, the Tribunal and the Nuremberg Trials, let me be frank—the road to hell is paved with good intentions.

Although it may be impossible for the secular, liberal mind to understand the necessity, in a civilized society, governed by the rule of law, to have law and morality integrated. Secular progressives are intransigent because of their reflexive aversion to anything related to the morality of law, the Judeo-Christian influence in the Anglo-American legal tradition, or any religious authority as relevant to what judges will do in a court of law. Yet it must be stated in plain language, that some people, because the acts they commit reach that rare level of evil and wickedness as to be beyond the reach of our courts or worthy of "due process"; it is here that secular "law" is always a total failure because it does not address the cause of the crime.

What then should have been done to the Nazi defendants? As FDR's lone Jewish voice of reason, Secretary of the Treasury, Henry Morganthau wanted; as well as Stalin, and certain of the Allied leaders like Churchill would have desired—Every Nazi officer and soldier that committed war crimes or other acts of atrocities such as what was done to the Jews at the concentration camps and other disparate episodes of wanton butchery during World War II, should have been summarily hanged and made a spectacle of for the world to see. Historians and academics must chronicle that at this pivotal time in history that humanity did not withdraw from its duty to derogate the war crimes, crimes against humanity, crimes against peace, and conspiracy to commit war crimes.

Remember what the Italians did when Mussolini's despotic regime was finally vanquished by the Allied Powers in April 1945? The Italian mob rushed into the dictator's palace, justly pummeling to death Il Duce (and his mistress) and hanging them both high upside down outside his palace for posterity to record. The Italians eschwed the sophistic pretense of a 'trial' to bring their hated tyrannical leader to justice for he wasn't worthy to receive the due process inherent in the rule of law. Note that summary justice for especially venal crimes is not without precedent in human history and the Bible. Note the two demonstrative examples below—

- Joshua and the Israelites commanded by God to destroy the ancient city of Jericho: And they [Israel] utterly destroyed *all* that was in the city, *both man and woman*, young and old, and sheep, and ass, with the edge of the sword—*Joshua* 6:22.[21]

- [Prophet] Samuel also said unto [King] Saul, the Lord sent me to anoint thee to be king over his people, over Israel: now therefore hearken thou unto the voice of the words of the Lord. Thus saith the Lord of hosts, I remember that which Amalek did to Israel, how he laid wait for him in the way, when he came up from Egypt. Now go and smite Amalek, and utterly destroy *all* that they have, and spare them not; *but slay both man and woman, infant and suckling, ox and sheep, camel and ass.*—I Samuel 15:1-3.[22]

My point here citing biblical precedent of summary execution is to illustrate that different circumstances requires different measures of justice. There can be no single law or even rules of war to address the infinite number of contingencies of man's inhumanity to man.

The conclusion of WW II was not the time to show mercy after the Nazi's wantonly and unreservedly murdered so many millions of people and plunged the world into a world war for the second time in 20 years, but like the biblical precedents cited above, certain acts of man are so vile and wicked that they do not merit the customary niceties of a trial. Remember the sentiments of Justice Jackson iterated at the onset of the Nuremberg Trials as quoted by Harvard Law Professor Alan Dershowitz—

> Justice Jackson, who prosecuted the case for the United States, went so far as to suggest, early on, that it would be preferable to shoot Nazi criminals out of hand than to discredit our judicial process by conducting farcical trials.[23]

The irony here is that Jackson probably had these radical ideas prior to President Truman's appointing of him as Chief Prosecutor for the U.S. at Nuremberg Trials. It was for prosecutor Jackson to make a mockery of America's judicial process and become a central figure in "conducting farcical trials" against the 24 Nazi defendants, he no doubt felt compelled to put on a pretense that he was in some measure chronicling Hitler's genocidal war and vindicating the Jews.

History has judged that the Allied Powers, by establishing the Nuremberg Trials, undoubtedly did not vindicate justice for the millions of Jews that perished in Hitler's death camps, but perverted justice for the Jews by setting up farcical, symbolic show trials, condemning only a handful of Nazi leaders. The Nuremberg Trials indeed created a mockery of justice by giving undeserved access to a court of law to pass judgment on the Nazi guilt, for causing the death of tens of millions of people, and virtually destroying much of Europe in its wake.

Nuremberg did not merely give the twenty-four Nazi defendants due process, but a world stage for these reprehensible criminals (especially Goering) to have a world stage to spew their perverse Nazi ideas of the necessity racial genocide to assure racial purity; to strut about and bloviate about the glorious Reich and how the Nazis were just defending the "fatherland" or "following orders." This vile, arrogant, outrageous, obsequious display from the outset, held the Nuremberg Tribunal hostage to Goering's long-winded rantings and remonstrations of his innocence and the verity of Hitler and his Reich. This brings to mind the old proverb—If Hitler (and by extension, his Third Reich) isn't guilty of *something*, then who among us could be innocent of *anything*?

During Jackson's cross examination of Goering, the climax of the Nuremberg Trials to most observers, Justice Robert Jackson, the American chief prosecutor and leading actor of Nuremberg, was exposed as a clumsy cross-examiner who lost practically every verbal battle with the wily and erudite Goering. In reading the Nuremberg Trial transcripts, Jackson were clearly unsuspecting, his courtroom demeanor shoddy, while Goering was prepared for every inquiry embellished with a particular Germanic recollection.

One well known example of Jackson's ineptness and Goering's competence was at a point in the trial when Jackson produced a document with the desired effect of demonstrating that in 1935 Goering was planning "the liberation of the Rhineland."[24] Unfortunately, this was not an accurate translation of the document which in fact related "cleaning of the Rhine"–removing physical obstacles in the Rhine River, such as sunken boats, that might hinder navigation.[25] This embarrassing event at trial devastated Jackson's confidence, and after it, Jackson became irritated, melancholy, and brooding, often exploding in open court, and then retreating alone to his residence at night.

Fortunately, Goering didn't get the last laugh. Jackson redeemed himself wonderfully by his opening and closing statements to the court, which were magnificent examples of culling together volumes of disparate documentary evidence. Jackson's especially powerful and expressive closing argument to the tribunal is a masterpiece in cadence, pacing, tone, and jurisprudence. One excerpt from the Nuremberg transcript recounted the following:

> We have presented to this Tribunal an affirmative case based on incriminating documents which are sufficient, if unexplained, to require a finding of guilt on Count One against each defendant. In the final analysis, the only question is whether the defendant's own testimony is that be credited as against the documents and other evidence of their guilt. What, then, is their testimony worth? The fact is that the Nazi habit of economizing in the use of truth pulls the foundations out from under their own defenses. Lying has always been a highly approved Nazi technique . . . .
>
> Even Schacht showed that he, too, had adopted the Nazi attitude that truth is any story which succeeds. Confronted on cross-examination with a long record of broken vows and false words, he declared in justification and I quote from the record: "I think you can score many more successes when you want to lead someone if you don't tell them the truth than if you tell them the truth."
>
> This was the philosophy of the National Socialists. When for years they have deceived the world, and masked falsehood with plausibilities, can anyone be surprised that they continue their habits of a lifetime in this dock? Credibility is one of the main issues of this Trial. Only those who have failed to learn the bitter lessons of the last decade can doubt that men who have always played on the unsuspecting credulity of generous opponents would not hesitate to do the same, now.
>
> It is against such a background that these defendants now ask this Tribunal to say that they are not guilty of planning, executing, or conspiring to commit this long list of crimes and wrongs. They stand before the record of this Trial as bloodstained Gloucester stood by the body of his slain king. He begged of the widow, as they beg of you: "Say I slew them not." And the Queen replied, "Then say they were not slain. But dead they are . . ." If you were to say of these men that they are not guilty, it would be as true to say threat there has been no war, there are no slain, there has been no crime.[26]

Without being redundant, Jackson's repeated historical allusions to the monarchy, where most law scholars would agree that the Anglo-American legal system was thoroughly grounded in natural law—a presumption of an integration between legality and morality. To this end Jackson and Wyzanski repeatedly, in their analysis of the Nuremberg Trials, were predisposed to cite natural law theory to make a substantive case against the Nazi defendants, yet refused to be intellectually honest enough to establish natural law as the jurisprudence the Nuremberg Trials. This constant use of "natural law" to achieve their substantive case is demonstrative of the fact that the trials should have been based upon the principle of natural law, and is demonstrative of the fact that natural law jurisprudence would have done far better to frame the issues of good and evil, right and wrong, following orders and war crimes, which admittedly, in the hands to the Nazi defense attorneys, such law/moral dichotomies were tragically obscured, ignored, or denigrated, only because of the precedent of positive law.

CHAPTER 8

CONCLUSION

The central idea of Machiavelli is that the state power is not bound by the moral law. The law is not above the state, but below it.

~ Lord Acton

Then said Samuel, Bring ye hither to me Agag the king of the Amalekites. And Agag came unto him delicately. And Agag said, Surely the bitterness of death is past.

And Samuel said, As thy sword hath made women childless, so shall thy mother be childless among women. And Samuel hewed Agag in pieces before the Lord in Gilgal. [1]

~ I Samuel 15: 32-33

Summary execution was the just punishment meted out by the Old Testament Prophet-Priest Samuel giving immediate and unmerciful justice to the notoriously wicked Amelekite king, Agag, whose nation not only prevented the nation of Israel from going through their land en route to the promised land of Canaan during the time Moses took the Children of Israel through the wilderness, but savagely and unprovoked, attacked Israel as they moved adjacent to their land. This sounds counterintuitive to our morally perverse, PC society of modern times—{*in a cynical voice*} *My word, a prophet killing a king 'before the Lord' and no reprimand be given. I never heard of such a thing!*

Samuel then chastised King Saul for his liberal view of warfare by showing a pagan king mercy when he and his people utterly hated the Jews. Fast forward 2,500 years to 1945. Where was swift, comprehensive justice for the Jewish people, who suffered on a Biblical scale at the hands of the Nazis? Sixty years later history has shown the world that the suffering of the Jewish people has not been vindicated; not by the thirteen Nuremberg Trials; not by the subsequent Tokyo Trials that sought to impose justice for the war atrocities committed by the Imperial Japanese empire, but only mimicked the injustices of Nuremberg; as have the subsequent international war crimes trials that have followed the Nuremberg Trials. To the Jewish people Nuremberg was a dream deferred.

In the end, who was right about the Nuremberg trials of 1945-1949? Were the trials a shameful example of "victor's justice," [2] as Judge Wyzanski and Nazi defendant, Hermann Goering derisively referred to them as, or was Justice Robert Jackson's characterization of the Nuremberg Trials as the establishment of a better legal order that would construct enforceable legal rules in opposition to aggressive war, crimes against peace, and crimes against humanity, the correct characterization? [3] I hold that neither side was correct. We have just passed the sixtieth anniversary of the end of World War II, and the end of the ghastly Holocaust against the Jews, however, the fact that there were only a mere token number Nazi war criminals—officers, soldiers, the aiders and abettors of the German public, that have yet to be brought to justice, seems, on this occasion, to have only added salt to the wounds to Jewish suffering. Admittedly, to do so then as well as trying to bring ultimate justice for the Jews and others who suffered at the hands of Hitler's madness sixty five years ago is nigh an impossible task. Time passes, and at some point, the Jews can only put it ultimate vindication of the crimes visited against them, in the hands of their God—"the God of Abraham, the God of Isaac, and the God of Jacob."

It is undoubtedly too complicated at this point in time, to determine with any degree of certainty, the effectiveness of the Nuremberg tribunal (and the successive trials of Nazi judges, doctors, businessmen, and abettors) on the condition and advancement of international law that found only 177 Germans and Austrians guilty of war crimes. Though this number may to many like Wyzanski, Jackson, and most academic and law scholars of the academy who hold views on such issues, seem to be enough to establish the idea of vindication, yet I would stand alone against the whole world in stating unequivocally that Nuremberg did *not* grant the Jews vindication, but on the contrary was the last outrage done to them by a cruel, wicked world that had other things on its mind after the war. Things other than vindicating the rights of such a small, despised minority group as the Jewish people, who have given the world so much, only to receive in recompense, so much evil.

A major argument about the efficacy of the Nuremberg trials was whether the captured chief Nazi leaders—those who did not kill themselves or get away—should have been placed on trial rather than immediately executed. These two camps were the focus of much controversy. Secretary of the Treasury Henry Morgenthau (an inconspicuous Jew and the lone voice of reason in the Roosevelt administration regarding the necessity to stop Hitler), like English Prime Minister Winston Churchill, regarded the seriousness of the Holocaust long before the conclusion of the war. Morgenthau had planned that a record of major war criminals be drawn up, with the hopes that if they were identified and arrested they would be summarily executed.[4] President Roosevelt was, at the outset, open to such radical justice, but in due time, ultimately both he and President Harry Truman, were convinced by Secretary of War Henry Stimson that summary execution was inconsistent with the American jurisprudence of due process and the rule of law. Herein is the crux of the matter; one of the fatal flaws, if you will, of Nuremberg. Whose advise would FDR follow—Morgenthau or Stimson? FDR, by following the politically expedient advice of Stimson I surmise was a critical reason why the Nuremberg Trials were so pathetically limited in scope and largely symbolic in comparison to the gargantuan atrocities Hitler and his Third Reich unleashed upon the Jewish people and upon most of the world during World War II.

At the creation of the United Nations, at the San Francisco Conference, in April 1945, it was decided therefore, to assemble an international tribunal to rule in judgment over the most notorious Nazi leaders. However, this plan had numerous legal problems. Under the rule of law, justice must not only be viewed as being executed, justice must also be executed with in surety and swiftness. A show trial, with conventional verdicts and predictable sentences, would be scarcely an improvement over no trial at all. In reality, Justice Jackson, who prosecuted the case for the United States, early on at Nuremberg even favored summary execution of all the Nazi criminals out of hand, rather than to bring disrepute to the judicial process by conducting superficial show trials.[5]

The paradox of the Nuremberg tribunal, therefore, was to try to conduct actual justice in the milieu of a trial by the victors against the defeated. In aiming particularly at those leaders of the vanquished, who had been most influential in the savage genocide and mass murder of civilians in the history of the world, the very fact of a trial was indicative of the paradox before the world; trying men who had only used "trials" for mockery purposes. With the corpses of the millions Hitler butchered were still unburied when the Nuremberg Trials began on November 20, 1945, the possibility of findings of facts and prosecuting on the basis of evidence, rather than outrage was scarcely possible in the climate of that day.

Furthermore, the full scope of the ghastly ignominy of Nazi crimes was still being discovered by many for the first time, during the days of the trial itself. The operative question here is this–with all of the emotional angst that World War II engendered, could the trials at Nuremberg be considered fair and just punishment of the Nazi leaders?—A trial of a mere twenty-four men? Daunting legal and philosophical obstacles notwithstanding, the retroactive nature of what was then, recently announced laws, and the jurisdictional challenges imposed by this form of UN Tribunal—there was an elemental problem of justice, as presented. Modern legal scholars wondered if judges designated by the triumphant Allied Powers—and politically responsible to those governments—could be likely to listen with an unbiased mind, to the prosecution evidence presented by the Allies, and to the defense claims proffered against this evidence, by the Nazi defense team. This is indeed the paradox of Nuremberg.

Sixty years after the Nuremberg Trials, the premise for its existence: the bringing of Nazi leaders, planners, organizers to justice, to the conclusion that the judges were competent jurists that provided the Nazi defendant's equal justice under the law cannot possibly be upheld based on the facts of the actual outcome for the defendants. If anyone has illusions of the "fairness" of the Nuremberg Trials, isn't it true that these same judges, in the first Nuremberg Trial, acquitted three of the twenty-two defendants, and sentenced another seven to short prison terms, rather than sending them to the gallows? However, just as with Cicero's defense of Cornelius Balbo in fifty-six B.C., the exception proves (or disproves the rule). Stated another way, if there were no rule, no exception would be needed.

The Allied Powers looked to the end results of the Nuremberg Trials to judge the credibility, yea, the necessity of even having trials, however, the facts at the end of the days, belie the idea of justice imposed. It is impossible to establish in hindsight, exactly who Justice Robert Jackson referred to in his Opening Address at Nuremberg, as the "brains . . . leaders and planners." Was he referring to men such as Goering, Ribbentrop, Hess, and Rosenberg? If he was, then an argument could be made that the fix was in. That these men never had a reasonable chance of vindication from the allegations against them, nor the chance of freedom, or of attaining some other sentence less than death suggests the purpose of the trial was to impose an already decided penalty. At the same time, were the minor sentences and acquittals for majority of the other Nazi defendants merely a sham to make it seem that equal justice under the law was indeed meted out to these people?

It was the voluminous and damning documentary evidence (which the Germans were infamously known for) describing in the most minute detail, their own meticulous records of their evil schemes, acts of aggression, and of genocide, that as the Nuremberg trials progressed, ironically became the death knell to the Nazi defendants. Manuscript after manuscript, text after text, letter after letter, movie reel, after movie reel, showed to all but the most partisan or insane, that Hitler and his Third Reich orchestrated a grand, complex evil scheme to kill two entities—Europe and the Jews. Alan Dershowitz, a professor of law at Harvard Law School, states the following regarding this point:

> Document after document proved beyond any reasonable doubt that the Nazis had conducted two wars: One was their aggressive war against Europe (and eventually America) for military, political, geographic, and economic domination. The other was their genocidal war to destroy "inferior" races, primarily the Jews and Gypsy populations within the control of the Third Reich were systematically murdered while the rest of the world—including those nations sitting in judgment—turned a blind eye.[6]

For sixty years, conventional wisdom has held that the Nuremberg tribunal and the subsequent trials that followed it, dispensed justice to a small percentage of those guilty of the worst savagery ever inflicted on humanity. Was justice achieved for humanity? I don't think justice was in any manner served to the Jewish people. I believe that the Jewish people got a raw deal at Nuremberg. Why do I believe this? Because the overwhelming majority of the Nazi murderers, torturers, and yes, even leaders, were eventually "de-nazified" and permitted to live ordinary, and often fruitful lives, in peace ofttimes upon the very ground where the Jewish blood cried out in vain for vengeance but, alas there was none to hear their pleas. The international community, headed by the fledgling UN, simply and callously agreed to stage a dozen symbolic trials which we collectively call, "The Nuremberg Trials" while millions of Germans—citizens, soldiers, businessmen, and respectable citizens (aiders and abettors), went unjudged, unpunished, and in an increasing number of public cases, unrepentant.

In the midst of those Nazis convicted and sentenced to death, was one who arguably never murdered or ordered the murder of anyone. This case was possibly the most paradoxical one because without his venomous pen and outrageous rhetoric, there might have been no genocide—at least to the degree suffered by the Jews, if for no other reason than ineffective communications. I am referring to Julius Streicher, the infamous editor of *Der Stürmer*, the notorious anti-Semitic propaganda newspaper that became the Bible of Hitler's genocide machine against the Jews. Streicher was a vitriolic extremist who added insult to injury at the Nuremberg Trials by insisting on being represented by an anti-Semitic lawyer, because in his view the Nuremberg tribunal was a "Jewish" court.[7] He further ranted that Jackson was a Jew whose real name was "Jacobson" and that Roosevelt ("Rosenfeld") and Eisenhower were also Jewish. I am no psychologist, but this appears to be a classic example of 'projection'—being obsessed over the possibility that the people he treated so shamefully would do the same to him, so he ascribed or "projected" onto the tribunal, the evil deeds he himself instigated on the Jewish victims.

In *Der Stürmer,* editorials and speeches added significantly to a racist atmosphere that fanned the flames Germany's irrational hatred of the Jews leading to institutional discrimination, destruction of Jewish business and Synagogues, and ultimately to conspicuous genocidal acts against all European Jewry by Hitler's Nazis. But Streicher's weapon was the letter (the poison pen if you will), not the sword, though his incendiary words would compelled Germans to the sword, and inevitably helped to send the Jews to the gas chambers. Streicher's prosecution offered the characteristic—if excessive—challenge to the restrictions of free speech. Ironically, however there was no free speech for those who did not hold to Streicher's extremely fanatical anti-Semitic views. In Streicher's world of Hitler's Germany there was no marketplace of ideas only the dominion of vile propaganda, hatred, racism, nihilism, and death.

Although Streicher's contemptible rants in his own defense were second only to Goering wicked remonstrations, at the conclusion of the trial, the Nuremberg Judges gave Streicher the death sentence "without much difficulty."[8] However, during the deliberations regarding Streicher's guilt, not all the Judges were in agreement. For example, American judge Francis Biddle at first contended that it would be "preposterous" to judge Streicher a conspirator merely because he was a "little Jew-baiter", however Biddle was eventually convinced to regard Streicher as a "accessory" to murder.[9] The metaphor of the cheerleader was used to refer to Streicher's role in Hitler's grand Nazi scheme, who "by his continual goading of the crowd to frenzied excitement . . . is a key personality in his teams' success."[10]

I find a better analogy akin to ubiquitous propaganda movie of the early twentieth century, *Birth of a Nation* (1915), where the protagonist, a fair White woman of virginal purity, was viciously assaulted by wild, Black savages who happened upon her as they burned and pillaged the town. This movie so enraged Whites across America that it caused them to riot all over America—North to South, East and West, murdering hundreds of Black men by hanging. To satisfy their bloodlust enflamed by this scurrilous movie whose greatest sin, was that it was purposely conceived to engender and inflame White passions against the innocent (and defenseless) Black minority population at a time in history where, because Jim Crow (de facto) and legal (de jure) racism was at full power, were virtually defenseless in the face of the uncontrollable bloodlust of White mobs. This degenerate movie would be a more fitful comparison to what Streicher did to the Jews albeit on a substantially smaller scale.

The analogy of the Tribunal's reasoning mandating a separation of law and morals is further unsound, particularly when compared to the Anglo-American legal tradition, which differentiates between *speech*—even racist propaganda—and *actions*. Like the famous statement from a Justice of the Supreme Court who stated in an opinion regarding the limits of free speech—"You cannot yell fire in a crowded theatre" because of public safety issues. You can't say, "I'm going to kill you!" because it expresses an intent to commit a crime.

This is a case in point, demonstrating that some speech (libelous, infamous, violent, or obscene) can under certain circumstances, proscribe conditions in the law to be prohibited, therefore the ubiquitous idea of absolute freedom of speech isn't so free after all. Conceivably the court was basing its decision on the classic, though controversial, limitation of free speech that is tantamount to violent actions (the so-called "clear and present danger" test). However, it is seems apparent that the Nuremberg judges "failed to debate [the] fundamental question of whether Streicher's words could be linked directly with others' deeds." [11]

Historically, critics of the Nuremberg Trials have incessantly been vexed by the fact that Streicher was sentenced to death not "strictly on the law, but on the physical and moral revulsion he evoked."[12] Other critics have cited the historical fact that literally hundreds of thousands of Nazi murderers (soldiers and citizens alike) went unpunished to this day because they did not "look" or "act" like the savages they were, perpetrating the genocide during Hitler's wars. In a comparable case in modern times, in 2003 the international court at The Hague, with jurisdiction over the Rwandan genocide, likewise found media inciters guilty. In the Epilogue I go into greater detail regarding this case and other international trials post-Nuremberg.

A pivotal question of this chapter; and even of this book is this: can the civilized world say with assurance, that sixty years after the Nuremberg Trials, did those trials do more good to society and the rule of law, than harm? In the opinion of this author, that the Nuremberg Trials were ultimately, pathetic show trials concocted by the Allies purely out of expediency and with the intent to dispense symbolic justice so that they could get on with the work of rebuilding Europe which had been so utterly devastated by the war. Furthermore, by convicting and executing an insignificant and symbolic number of the most brazen Nazi 'planners and leaders,' the Nuremberg court allowed the international community to quickly return to some semblance of normalcy after the comprehensive genocide of World War II. This rationalization, some have said, was imperative to preserve the world's psyche.

The next question logically follows—Was it just for the world return to business as usual while literally hundreds of thousands or even millions of complicit Nazi solders, officers, and German civilians live their lives in peace? I say, No! And even more sinister, but as Hitler, Mussolini, Stalin, Mao and later Ho Chi Mihn, Pol Pot, Edi Amin, Saddam Hussein, Osama bin Laden and other would-be dictators present and future carefully watched America, Europe, and the international community do nothing as Imperial Japan annexed Manchuria in 1931, Franco wantonly murdered the Basque separatists in Northern Spain, Mussolini invaded Ethiopia in 1936, and Hitler annexed the Czechoslovakia in 1938 setting the stage for World War II—the war to end all wars. And what was the aftermath of the Nuremberg trials? The German economy was rapidly rebuilt, forty-five years later unification between East and West Germany became a certainty— and irrational, ubiquitous Jewish hatred is once again, rampant throughout Europe and the Middle East, with World War III, the new and better "war to end all wars" well begun, in earnest.

Dershowitz's remarks were prescient in stating that Morgenthau asked too much (perhaps for geopolitical or pragmatic reasons?) and the Nuremberg tribunal asked too little in judging such a minuscule number of Nazi murderers, and even acquitting a noticeable percentage of those brought up on initial charges.

On this point Dershowitz further expounds:

> Perhaps Henry Morgenthau was asking for too much when he demanded that German industry and military capacity be destroyed "forever." And that Germany must be "reduced to a nation of farmers." [13] But perhaps the Nuremberg tribunal asked for too little when it implicitly expiated the guilt of thousands of hands-on murderers by focusing culpability on a small number of leaders who could never have carried out their wholesale slaughter without the enthusiastic assistance of an army, both military and civilian, of wholesale butchers.[14]

Dershowitz's analysis of the Nuremberg trials above states in clear, stark terms the essential dilemma Nuremberg created by limiting the jurisdiction of their judgment to a token few men. I believe that Nuremberg set the predicate not for an efficient, consensus manner to deal en masse with war criminals, but gave a tacit approval that war crimes would from hence forth be dealt with not comprehensively, but symbolically. Professor Dershowitz added a further caveat, suggesting that the other creation of Nuremberg was "the possible beginning of a 'new legal order' of accountability." Was it?

Nuremberg was indeed a high water mark in international criminal trials, especially when you compare those symbolic trials of a minuscule number of guilty Nazis, to the utterly farcical international war crimes trials of today such as the Korean, Vietnam, and Cambodia Trials (which never happened), Rwanda, where only a few token low level soldiers saw any prison time and Serbia, where the Serbian leader, Slobodan Milosevic was shamefully scapegoated by the United States (under President Clinton) and the international community, and died under mysterious circumstances, just before he was to deliver his testimony at The Hague on 11 March 2006.

Dershowitz also looses me when he states that "[t]rying the culprits were plainly preferable to simply killing them."[15] Given that trying so few of them sent out a powerful message that the "new legal order" would be lenient with those who were "just following orders", why wouldn't killing the vicious murders of over half the Jewish population in Europe not be more "preferable" than letting them go free as the Allies virtually did? Certainly the whitewash scenario regarding the vindication of the Jewish people at Nuremberg that people in polite circles have come to esteem isn't more preferable to the millions of Jewish families whose generations were wiped off the face of the earth simply because of their nationality.

Paradoxically speaking, how can Professor Dershowitz, being a Jew, be as seemingly callous of the historical plight of his own people not favor summary execution of all Nazi high command? This reasoning is beyond the pale. I surmise that in our present day existence—in all of our post-modern excess, irrelevance, existentialism, liberalism and ease, our secular progressive culture is rather smug and unbelieving when faced with pure evil as displayed by the Nazis during WW II. I do not share that optimistic view.

TO JUDGE OR NOT TO JUDGE? THAT IS THE QUESTION

Further, it has become politically incorrect to 'judge' and thus Nazi war crimes of sixty years ago don't rise to the level for the average American or Westerner to resort to such drastic means to judge the perpetrators no matter what evil they have committed against humanity in the past. Conventional thinking contends that secular society has evolved beyond all notions of anachronistic terms as "good" and "evil". This leads to the question: and what of this "new legal order" Dershowitz alluded to? This liberal utopian dream that Dershowitz so glowingly and longingly expresses, when at the time of this writing, his people are waging a two front war for their very survival, being attacked by the Palestinian Muslim fanatics in Gaza in the south and from the north by Hezbollah, backed by the puppet government of Lebanon, and their puppetmasters—Syria and Iran.

This new legal order or "new world order" as President George Bush Sr. referred to it, is for the Jew, for America, and for the few remaining allies we have left in the civilized world, has brought an active and increasing axis of evil that seeks nothing less than a Muslim Caliphate established throughout the Western world and is willing to accomplish this by the blood of the infidels (Jews and Christians), by force of arms, by lies, subterfuge, and by any means necessary against what Muslim fanatics view as the cowardly, decadent, and immoral West.

In the final analysis, what has Judge Wyzanski, Justice Jackson, and the Framers of United Nation and the Nuremberg Tribunal's faith in secular humanism, positive law, progressivism, and utopian liberalism given the world these past six decades? The shameful legacy of the Nuremberg Trial philosophy with its international policy of appeasement and token show trials, has in modern times, (and with a degree of irony), created more brutal dictators who fear no retribution for their crimes; produced more war, more chaos, more genocide than even the much maligned Middle Ages (400-1400).

Let me write with perfect clarity here. The pacification-laden, consensus policies that led to the establishment of the United Nations, the secular legal philosophy of the Nuremberg and Tokyo Tribunals, and the impotence of the largely symbolic Nuremberg Trials, has to a degree spawned the war between South Korea and North Korea, the escalating Israeli-Palestinian conflict, the American-Iraq Wars (Operation Desert Shield/Storm),[16] and America's present war with Iraq (Operation Iraqi Freedom), the anarchy and savagery of Haiti, the Rwandan genocide, and general anarchy throughout virtually all sub-Saharan Africa, and the perpetual Bosnian-Croatian-Serbian-Albanian quagmire in the Balkans and its subsequent War Crimes Tribunal of the former Yugoslavia. And what of the major international organs of the United Nation—The World Trade Organization (WTO), the World Court in The Hague, the International Monetary Fund, and the World Army that was given sanction to exist by member states in 1999, what of them?

And finally, consider the most diabolical and dangerous threat to America's sovereignty, its moral authority that undergirds its rule of law:[17] the ongoing assault by the United Nations member States, particularly our historic Allies—the Soviet Union, France, Germany, Canada, China—reflexively voting against the sovereignty of the United States through the United Nations at every opportunity. This intransigence against American interests that promote freedom and democracy throughout the world, has recently been made the more acute with the current international crises of communist North Korea blatantly flouting the will of the international community by testing nuclear weapons. These are but a few of the many "aggressive war" situations that Justice Jackson promised the world the United Nations would historically prevent, in his Opening Address at the Nuremberg Trials. History has shown quite the contrary; that the United Nations, with its secular, positive law mandate and aversion to any law/moral constructs, has, for the past sixty years since its establishment, been virtually impotent at stemming the tide of international totalitarianism and now international terrorism.

Legal realism is a philosophy of law that originated in American legal history in the early 1930s. It has most effectively codified and integrated the original tenants of Jeremy Bentham and John Austin in modern times, probably more than any other branch of positive law. Along with this, one of legal realisms most illogical and entrenched views, held by Oliver Wendell Holmes, Roscoe-Pound, Karl Llewellyn, Judge Richard A. Posner, professor Laurence Tribe, and other secularists and left-leaning jurists, is that general ideals do not decide hard cases and that rules should not (or cannot) control court decisions. On the other hand, law Professor Karl Llewellyn, although a noted legal realist, breaks ranks with this standard realist positions, for example, in the first edition of *The Bramble Bush*, Llewellyn assigned himself unreservedly to the legal ideas that "what these officials do about disputes is, to my mind, the law itself" and "rules . . . are important so far as they help you . . . *predict* what judges will do . . . . That is all their importance, *except as pretty playthings*."[18]

What does this mean? In Llewellyn's philosophy of law *the judge* is pre-eminent—singular and paramount within himself, and not subjected to any notions of higher law and that the "rules" (i.e., laws) are merely as playthings in his hands—a means to an end. In the second edition Llewellyn, no doubt feeling the vocal criticism from the academy (and perhaps the public) revised his ideas that those were "unhappy words when not more fully developed, and they are plainly at best a very partial statement of the whole truth . . . . [O]ne office of law is to control officials in some part, and to guide them even . . . where no thoroughgoing control is possible, or is desired . . . . [T]he words fail to take proper account . . . of the office of the institution of law as an instrument of conscious shaping . . ." [19] There are few examples in the history of law where the writer so clearly and unmistakably describes judicial activism ('conscious shaping') or infusing into the marketplace of ideas one's own personal policy preferences—more popularly known to today as 'legislating from the bench.' The Nuremberg Trials are the apotheosis of judicial activism, legislating from the bench, and 'conscious shaping' of the grandest scale.

As a final point in his Opening Address to the Nuremberg Trials, Prosecutor Robert Jackson also stated that history would judge their efforts at Nuremberg; and judge them it has. The UN's entrenched, arrogant secular worldview, and the ingrained philosophy of legal positivism on which it is based, has proven repeatedly despite the myriad of subsequent "war crimes" tribunals and the international treaties that they have spawned to be totally inadequate, incompetent, and impotent at preventing either "aggressive war," "crimes against humanity," "crimes against peace," "conspiracy to commit war," or any type of war for that matter. Mankind will continue to wage war at every opportunity that it is able—that is one of the most irredeemable and intractable aspects of human nature, a fact about human nature many secular progressives seemed utterly blind to recognize, nevertheless the perversity of human nature is a reality of life.

If civilization is to have any hope of avoiding self-annihilation, America, as the leader of the free world and in the words of philosopher Dr. William Bennett, is "the [world's] last best hope," thus must return to its original law/moral synthesis of a natural law, common law, rule of law where all legitimate legal concepts are thoroughly based in the Judeo-Christian tradition. Judges and lawyers alike must support a natural law approach to the Constitution and the to the rule of law that presupposes the unity of legality and morality; an accord between law and morals that won't lead to petty sectarian squabbles which only yields xenophobic nationalism and the present anarchy the world is in with wars raging incessantly across the globe.

Could public policy choices made by the Allied Powers sixty years ago during the aftermath of World War II somehow adversely affect international law and geopolitical harmony amongst the nations in modern times? And if so, could the solution be as simple and sublime as a return to a synthesis of legality and morality into all of our law, treaties, and constitutions? A synthesis between law and morality that the Framer's of the U.S. Constitution, the Bill of Rights, the Declaration of Independence considered so obvious as to refer to this synthesis with these sublime words—'We hold these Truths to be self evident.'

Indeed a return to the original natural law philosophy the constitutional Framers relied on when they wrote America's founding documents; words that had such lofty, moral and inspiring rhetoric that though America in the late eighteenth century had not adequately resolved it's original sin and the moral dilemma of slavery, yet the very seeds of freedom for the slave and eventually equality for all humanity, were enshrined in the very stanzas of those transcendent founding documents for a later, more enlightened generation to bring to fruition sadly after much bloodshed and an end to that noble experiment called democracy. Unless and until America returns to legitimate constitutional jurisprudence, and to a worldview rooted in the immutable principles of objective moral order, a Constitution based on the original natural law precepts of the Framers and the primacy of the rule of law, America's end will be the same as the end of all other great nations of antiquity—Egypt, Babylon, Assyria, Persia,

Greece, Portugal, Spain, Italy, France, Great Britain. What brought the demise of these great empires?—unprincipled public policy, democracy, socialism, societal breakdown and deconstruction, anarchy, nihilism, and death.[20]

CHAPTER 9

EPILOGUE

THE NUREMBERG TRIAL PHILOSOPHY IN MODERN TIMES

At the end of the Road Map—to be presided over by the Quartet: The UN, EU, Russia, and the U.S.—lies Auschwitz.[1]

~ Don Feder

How has the positive law philosophy utilized in the Nuremberg Trials sixty years ago evolved in modern times? By various estimates, in the six decades since Nuremberg, more than 100 million people have been killed in wars — millions of them as victims of genocide in countries from Cambodia to Rwanda to the former Yugoslavia. Nuremberg was supposed to put an end to those crimes. The great question begging an answer is: why is the world still deficient in the means to stop war crimes and crimes against humanity? Has what I will refer to here as the "Nuremberg Trial philosophy" given efficiency, coherence, and structure to international law or has the Nuremberg Trial philosophy plunged international law (and international relations) into the abyss of incoherence, irrelevance, and anarchy?

A more profound question is has what I consider the "Nuremberg Trial philosophy," its symbolic and tentative judgments, only emboldened would-be dictators of contemporary times? Can the judgment of this be somewhere in between these disparate polarities?—Between a Judeo-Christian worldview and secularism, between theism and humanism, between Jerusalem and Athens (or Mecca), between Good and Evil, between God and the devil, between life and death . . . between natural law and positive law? This is our choice, the choice of civilization from time immemorial.

Albert Carr in his classic, *Napoleon Speaks,* wrote eloquently of these paradoxical times; an epic that, although written over sixty-five years ago, could have been about these contemporary times. An age of what the nineteenth century Romantics called their passionate literary movement—*Sturm und Drang* (storm and stress):

> Much could be written on the importance of love as a factor in the greatest political successes—not sexual love, but what might be called social love. Men, as well as dogs, know instinctively when they are really loved, without regard to mere words; and it is then that they give love in return. Hitler adores Germans, not as individuals, but in the mass, as members of a race; and those Germans in who the racial consciousness is strong adore him in return. The great statesman offers his people programs, but their cerebral approval is of little value to him; he needs their intuitive recognition of his passionate feeling for them.[2]

The pages below are a brief synopsis of the effects on positive law jurisprudence on war crimes trials in modern times. Has the secularist movement infused in international called the Nuremberg Trials worked? Could it work sixty years later after some tweaking by the secular progressive elites? History has made the judgment and the precedent the Nuremberg Trials set for subsequent war crimes tribunals is clearly not commendable by any measure.

WAR CRIMES TRIALS IN MODERN TIMES

THE KOREAN WAR CRIMES TRIALS?

The Korean War (1950-1953) was fought primarily between the United States, Korea and later China, five years after the war to end all wars (World War II) was concluded.[3] Although the war was largely fought as a proxy war with the United States on one side and Russia and China on the other as surrogates to Korea, the war ended in 1953, and was considered by historians as a draw. This book is focused on the question of the necessity of war crimes tribunals, something which never occurred in Korea, but *should* there have been a war crimes tribunal?

Were there wartime atrocities committed during the Korean War? Thousands of American troops were captured by the Koreans, and the aftermath of the war showed that they were brutally tortured and many of them murdered by exposure, starvation, torture, and summary execution. Why didn't the international community, embodied in the United Nations, convene a war crimes tribunal like it did five years earlier at Nuremberg? Herein lies the deficiency and treacherous legacy of the UN and the "Nuremberg Trial" philosophy. First, we have the machinery and bureaucracy of the UN, and the five permanent members of the UN Security Council. This body must give unanimous approval before any "legal war" can be declared or any "war crimes tribunal" convened. All matters delineated by "committee" are at best difficult and intractable, but the latter, (a war crime tribunal) would prove to be not only difficult, but impossible in this ideological battle between democracy and freedom on the one hand and state controlled totalitarianism or communism on the other; a dualism that history called *The Korean War*.

The application of a "war crimes tribunal" would have exposed two of the five members of the security counsel, two unofficial nations—China and Russia, to have aided and abetted the "war of aggression" initiated by North Korea, to the international community, and demonstrated the correctness of the action taken by the United States, and were the cause of the calling for a truce, rather than a calling for an actual "win" over what was exactly the form of "aggressive war" the United Nations was supposed to prevent. The truth regarding the Korean War would open to world, elements truth deliberately hidden by the United Nations in its organs,—truths that would bring the light of international condemnation upon China and Russia and provide a "new paradigm." This scenario could not be tolerated at all, so the war crimes trials for the Korean War would be a tribunal that would never be established. All the evidence of Chinese and Russian duplicity and treachery remains swept under the rug even to this day!

The treachery of the Truman administration, by not insisting on convening a war crimes tribunal after the Korean War, to vindicate the vicious atrocities committed by the Koreans against U.S. prisoners of war, was indeed one of the darkest chapters of this poorly fought battle, and set the stage for an even greater catastrophe for America, in the next war against communism, Vietnam.

VIETNAM WAR CRIMES TRIALS?

Like it's predecessor the Korean War, the Vietnam War (1955-1972), was an ideological proxy war (between the U.S. and Russia) fought first between Vietnam's colonial occupier, France, and the communist propagators, but after the disastrous battle of Vinh Yen, France was driven out of the country in 1954, leading to the U.S. taking the helm, first only in an advisory capacity, but gradually finding America sucked into a full scale war with Russia and to a lesser degree, China, as the puppetmasters of Vietnam, against the lone standard bearer of a republican-democracy, the United States.[4]

Why were no war crimes tribunals convened after the end of the Vietnam War? Certainly there were numerous war crimes atrocities by the Vietnamese army against Vietnamese civilians, U.S. solders, and prisoners of war, Senator John McCain, R-AZ, being one of the most notable POWs of the Vietnam War. Like the Korean War, the necessity of establishing a war crimes tribunal after the Vietnam War was squashed by the UN, due to complicity and duplicity of Russia and China as proxies in that war against South Vietnam, and the US, and was facilitated by their ensconced position as two of the five permanent members of the UN Security Council.

CAMBODIA WAR CRIMES TRIALS?

Will Cambodia have Nuremberg-style war crimes trials? If so, will they be only token or symbolic trials like Nuremberg or will they go further to make a legitimate attempt at vindicating the genocidal acts of the Cambodian regime? December 1998 marked twentieth anniversary of the Vietnamese invasion of Cambodia, which ended the bloodthirsty four-year rein of terror of the Khmer Rouge. Soon the Phnom Penh government would be conducting war crimes trials for some of the former, infamous leaders. The horrific times of the "Killing Fields" by the Khmer Rouge had, for the previous twenty years, been an indelible stain on Cambodian history. Literally one out of every five Cambodian citizens (some 20 percent) had either died from exhaustion, starvation, torture, or cold-blooded murder by this genocidal regime.[5]

A Khmer Rouge Trial Task Force was established by the Cambodian government in 1997 and was designed to create a legal and judicial framework to bring the existing leaders to justice for war crimes and other crimes against humanity. However, progress with bringing these leaders to trial was frequently delayed, due primarily to the political machinations of Prime Minister, Hun Sen, a former leader of the Khmer Rouge, and influential member of the Cambodian government. Additionally, an impoverished and moribund Cambodian economy, along with a lack of financing for the trials, further prevented a full funding of the tribunal. This bureaucratic ineptitude despite the fact that numerous countries agreed to assist Cambodia pay for the tribunal, most notably, India and Japan. To date, as late as January 2006, the financial shortfall for the war crimes tribunal—US$56.3 million had not been fully overcome.

On the ground, the task force progressed in its work at creating a tribunal, when it took possession of two buildings on the grounds of the Royal Cambodian Armed Forces (RCAF) High Command headquarters, in the Kandal province, near the capital of Phnom Penh. The tribunal task force expects to use the remainder of 2006 for the preparation of the judges and additional tribunal staff, prior to mid 2007; the actual time the trial is expected to occur. Secretary General of the United Nations, Kofi Annan, in March 2006, appointed seven judges for a trial of the Khmer Rouge leaders. Justice Minister Ang Vong Vathana, announced in May 2006, that Cambodia's leading judicial court sanctioned 30 Cambodian and UN judges to be in charge of the war crimes tribunal for the few remaining leaders of the Khmer Rouge.

On July 17, 2006, the United Nations and the Cambodian government of Prime Minister Hun Sen are planning to charge the surviving Khmer Rouge culprits with various criminal acts including crimes against humanity, genocide, and other international war crimes through a newly-created war crimes tribunal. These trials, modeled after the famous Nuremberg Trials of sixty years before, are designed to judge the ageing past leaders, and are projected to commence by mid 2007. However, all of those most culpable will not face the international bar of justice. Pol Pot, the supreme leader of the Khmer Rouge, had long since died peacefully, of natural causes on July 16, 2006,[6] one of the most infamous and bloodthirsty Khmer Rouge leaders, Ta Mok, known as "The Butcher," paradoxically fell quietly into a coma. The age of the few of possible defendants like Ta Mok and the almost US$60 million cost to conduct the trials, however, has a number of critics questioning the necessity and validity of even having a war crime tribunal convened at this point.

In reality, the Cambodian war crimes tribunal is faced with two critical questions: First, will those defendants found guilty by the war crimes tribunal actually be brought to justice? Secondly, will it bring closure to the Cambodian people, who are still grappling with their ghastly experiment of self-suicide almost twenty years ago? In addressing these questions, it is wise to avoid the assumption that only convictions will achieve closure. History has show that a contrary outcome is more likely; that the collective memory of the Cambodian nation hints that it is improbable. If the war crimes trials are to assist restoring the mental and psychic health of the Cambodian people, they will need a further element—the narratives of the victims who suffered. I contend these narratives, due to a variety of reasons many of which are stated earlier, will not be allowed to be heard. The pain and suffering is still too raw, too real, too existential in a society that would rather get on with living in the present, than in any manner, reliving the nightmare of its recent past.

RECONCILING CAMBODIA'S PRESENT BY REMEMBERING IT'S PAST

The chronicles of collective memory in Cambodia exemplify two trends - the production of a politicized, revisionist history to eliminate the evil done, and the exploitation of that contrived, distorted history to suppress individual victims' recollections. The Vietnam invasion of Cambodia in 1978, forever changed Cambodian history, tragically for the worse. Almost immediately after its forming, the new Hanoi supported government of Cambodia, started to proliferate an "authorized account" of the Khmer Rouge years. To a great degree, this revisionist and contrived history, still controls Cambodian belief from those turbulent years of 1976-1979.

Journalist Margaret Scott describes this accepted view as "Pol Pot time." Pitting the minority against the majority—a recognizable tactic of the Cambodian past—this description maintains that Pol Pot and a gang of high-ranking staff deceived and exploited the Cambodian people, creating a second Holocaust. However, unlike the first Holocaust which although conducted initially as German against German, despite the shared nationality, Nazi's sought to show the Jewish as distinct and apart from the *pure* Aryan Germanic race. In the Cambodian "second Holocaust" such racial distinction, though contrived in the German example, did not exist in the Cambodian Holocaust because the Cambodian people, racially speaking, were largely monolithic. Therefore, "Pol Pot time" is about as fine a distinction as a moustache on the Mona Lisa.

Why set in motion, a history of Cambodia that disregards international pressure, covert hatred towards Vietnamese, the function of ideology, and the number of Khmer Rouge faction amid other things? Basically, the "Pol Pot clique" theory gave considered legitimacy to the revived communist regime. This theory demonized Pol Pot and his cohorts, who struck fear in the populace even in hiding, as though the perpetrators were other than "Cambodian."

The Pol Pot clique propagated a communist-backed, propagandizing interpretation of political actions and history that was comprehensive—affecting all aspects of society from the cradle to the grave. Significantly, the Pol Pot clique subtly and with a tinge of irony, maligned Khmer Rouge ideology, which, as time passed, had become vituperative against anything related to the Vietnamese, burying the fact that the "Pol Pot regime" was perpetrating genocide against its own people, and the issue of Vietnam was only one of short duration with the express purpose of ending the genocide. Virtual propaganda was considered legitimate news by liberal journalists, who supported the new government's idealized image as liberator, thus cultivating emergent international legitimacy.

That contrived, revisionist, propaganda-driven history provided legitimacy, though this is an old lesson. The salient issue here is that, in Cambodia, officials wrote and maintained the authorized history in the marketplace of ideas (i.e., the public). Here, in this, private memories would be summarily suppressed, fought against, and forgotten. To show their national contrition, the new government, the Pol Pot clique, created a national museum out of the S-21 prison camp in Phnom Penh; tried Pol Pot and his deputy Ieng Sary, for war crimes in absentia; exhumed mass graves; inaugurated memorials at several "killing fields"; and established a holiday called the "Day of Anger", when people were to simmer in bitterness at the suffering the Cambodian people had to endure, (ironically, with no revulsion at what the Cambodian people were led to do to one another). So entrenched and ingrained was the national denial of the atrocities of the Khmer Rouge that it wasn't until 2001 that schools taught anything on the subject of that infamous period. To this day, many schools in Cambodia still don't.

Regarding Cambodia's recent ignoble history, shouldn't the international community follow that famous aphorism?—"let the past stay in the past." Why go to the extreme extent of imprisoning history in a community sphere of exhibition and oratory? The Pol Pot clique did this to limit the power of individual memories. A large number of ex-Khmer Rouge officers continued on in government. Finding them culpable instead of Pol Pot - as memories would - could have destabilized the social order and probably the weakened the government itself. This tyranny of concealed memories continues to take an appalling psychological toll on the psyche of the Cambodian people as they try to exorcise the demonic influence of the Khmer Rouge. USAID calculates that approximately 40 percent of Cambodians suffer from PTSD, post-traumatic stress disorder. This statistic is particularly shocking in light of the fact that over half of the existing population was not yet born when the Khmer Rouge ruled.

THE CAMBODIAN WAR CRIMES TRIALS

Many nations of the international community look with optimism, hoping that the upcoming Cambodian "War Crimes Tribunal" will alleviate the psychological burdens left by the Khmer Rouge. This consideration is based on the supposition that the trials will function as what the French historian and memory theorist Pierre Nora terms a "lieu de mémoire," or site of memory. Sites of memory, Nora conjectures, are things, places, or events to which people connect a memory, eliminating that memory's closeness, and give support to it the memories passage toward resolution and a disconnected history.

Supposing that the trials will mechanically bring a spiritual or psychic "healing," however, is wishful thinking. The tribunal is remote; it provides no intrinsic mechanism for people to connect or share their memories, and has little connection with the realities of the time of the atrocities. In reality, distant from the paradigm of lieu de mémoire that facilitate the release memories, the tribunal may in fact sustain the official history and further suppress the freedom of the Cambodian people. Following the pathetically limited precedent of the Nuremberg Trials, by prosecuting a token number of leaders, the tribunal imply that just a small number of officials were guilty. Admittedly, prosecuting many more would be difficult if not unreasonable, given the hold revisionist history has on the event and issue, but charging these minuscule number of Khmer Rouge leaders is of little value, other than for propaganda purposes. Cynically speaking, the Pol Pot clique propaganda machine has enacted "Pol Pot time" yet again.

Furthermore, the tribunal will only solidify the contrived, revisionist official history favored by the Pol Pot clique which as stated above is a cynical legitimization project of rewriting out of history, blotting out of memory, the communist war crime atrocities committed in the killing fields. Assigning guilt to a symbolic, token few, undeservedly exonerates the countless former Khmer Rouge leaders, soldiers, and officials remaining in the Phnom Phen government—undoubtedly a worry in the mind of current Prime Minister Hun Sen, himself an old Khmer Rouge official. Likewise, collaboration with the UN allows the Pol Pot clique government to assume the color of law and international legitimacy.

I do not wish to convey the idea that establishment of the tribunal is bad or irrelevant. These murderous criminals participated in appalling acts of genocide against their own people and should be judged by a competent international court of law. However, if commenced unilaterally, the trials undoubtedly will be counterproductive. Barring some supplementary component, the Cambodian tribunal will not only legitimize a dubious, despotic regime, but they will further squeeze the life out of the private memories with politicized public history.

THE RWANDA WAR CRIMES TRIALS

The war in the central African country of Rwanda, and its subsequent genocide, was the ghastly massacre of an estimated 800,000 to 1,071,000 ethnic Tutsis and moderate Hutus in Rwanda, typically carried out by two extremist Hutu militia factions, the Interahamwe and the Impuzamugambi, throughout a 100 day period from April 6th through mid-July 1994.[7]

The Rwandan genocide is a conspicuous episode and historically momentous, notwithstanding the enormous number of innocent people, virtually all civilians, murdered with such speed and efficiency, but moreover because of how weakly the Untied Nations (above all, its Western members such as the United States and France) responded. In the face of intelligence provided prior to when the killing began, and international news media exposure reflecting the horrific degree of violence as the genocide quickly extended throughout the borders of Rwanda, most first-world countries, particularly France, Belgium, and the United States, stubbornly refused to intervene or even speak out against the premeditated massacres.

To address the increasingly volatile and destabilizing political situation in Rwanda, UNAMIR (United Nations Assistance Mission for Rwanda), was established by the United Nations in October 1993. Furthermore UNAMIR's mission was defined "to help implement the Arusha Peace Agreement signed by the Rwandan parties on August 4, 1993." Remarkably and regrettably its "mandate" ended in 1996.[8]

Leading up to, and during the genocide, the UN did not sanction UNAMIR to intervene and to use military power decisively to stop the killing and other atrocities in Rwanda. While it "adjusted" UNAMIR's "mandate and strength", on a number of occasions, in the face of the tragic events of the genocide and the changing situation in the country",[9] the makeup and the politics of the UN Security Council and a range of procedural restrictions and other limitations demanded in UNAMIR, prevented the U.N. from accomplishing anything worth noting, and allowed the genocide to continue to demonstrate the utter failure of the United Nations.

In the weeks leading up to the Rwandan genocide, the UN did not take action on the report of Hutu militias buildup of weapon's caches, and abandoned any tactics for a pre-emptive interdiction these disparate, lawless gangs. UN ineptitude notwithstanding the many pre-and present-tribal clash warnings that were made by the principal of the UN mission, Canadian Lieutenant-General Romeo Dallaire. Despite warnings from its own chief of the Rwandan tribal conflicts, the United Nations was adamant on preserving its infamous bureaucratic hierarchy—maintaining its rules of engagement and averting its peacekeepers in Rwanda from engaging in battles with the militias or firing their weapons, except in self-defense. The UN's failure to act proactively and in an opportune and effective manner to arrest the killing, became the center of bitter attacks toward the United Nations, and Western Nations in particular, notably, Britain, France, and the United States, along with individual policymakers, including Jacques-Roger Booh-Booh and U.S. President Bill Clinton, who later characterized the U.S. inaction as "the biggest regret of my administration."[9]

The genocide in Rwanda finally concluded when a Tutsi-controlled expatriate rebel movement referred to as the Rwandan Patriotic Front, led by Paul Kagame, defeated the Hutu government and seized military and political control of the country. Fearing revenge, hundreds of thousands of Hutu warlords, foot soldiers, and other refugees fled into eastern Zaire (now the Democratic Republic of the Congo). The wanton genocide and its attendant psychological trauma, the crime, famine, disease, and its memory, have repeatedly thwarted subsequent efforts by the UN and the international community to positively stabilize the country and the region. Deep running hatreds based on ethnicity and tribal origin, which were the spark that started the initial genocide in Rwandan, quickly spilled over into Congo, continuing after it ended in Rwanda, and fueling both the First and Second Congo Wars. Ethnic rivalry between Hutu and Tutsi tribal factions is also a major factor in the Burundi Civil War.

To bring justice to the Rwandan people who suffered greatly from the short but devastating genocidal tribal war between the Hutus and the Tutsis, the United Nations established The International Criminal Tribunal for Rwanda (ICTR) which is an international court established for the prosecution of the war crimes and crimes against humanity committed in Rwanda, during the genocide that took place there, in the 100 days following April 6, 1994. The court was established with the limited jurisdiction to prosecute crimes which happened during the year of 1994.

ICTR was establised on November 8, 1994 by Resolution 955 from the United Nations Security Council, in order to judge those people accused of perpetrating genocidal acts, war crimes, and other grave violations of the rules of war, and international law, perpetrated in the territory of Rwanda, or by Rwandan citizens in nearby states, between January 1 and December 31, 1994.

The tribunal was convened in Arusha Tanzania (UN Security Council Resolution 997) and had jurisdiction over genocide, crimes against humanity, and war crimes, which are defined as violations of Common Article Three and Additional Protocol II of the Geneva Conventions, which specifically address war crimes committed during internal conflicts.

To date, the Tribunal has completed twenty-one trials and convicted twenty-eight accused culprits of various war cimes charges. Currently, eleven other trials remain in progress. fourteen defendants are still in custody awaiting trial, but the prosecutor plans to transfer five for trials under Rwanda national jurisdiction. Eighteen other named defendants remain at large, several of which are suspected to be dead. In 1997, the first trial began against the defendant, Jean-Paul Akayesu. At that time, interim Prime Minister Jean Kambanda, pled guilty. Based on the ICTR's Completion Strategy, under the expressed authorization of Security Council Resolution 1503, all of the intitial cases are due to be by the end of 2008 with the entire trials to be finished by 2010. However, several commentations doubt the ICTR will be able to complete its work, given the number of defendants, the complexity of the evidence, and the difficulty of constructing a viable narrative, of what actually occurred.

JULIUS STREICHER REVISITED AND THE TRIAL AGAINST "HATE MEDIA"

Julius Streicher was that imfamous editor of Hitler's vile propaganda newspaper, *Der Stürmer,* during the Nazi's rise to power (1932-1945). Although Streicher never personally killed a single Jew, nevertheless his poison pen daily spewing racial hatred and speading vile lies against the Jews in Germany and throughout Europe, and had a direct cause and effect relationship by inciting genocide against the Jewish people. In this sense Shakespeare was right: "The *pen* is mighter than the *sword.*"

One unique aspect of the Rwandan War Crimes Trials was the charging regarding the critical role the so called "hate media" had in spreading vicious propaganda and exploiting tribal hatreds. The trial against the "hate media" began on October 23, 2000. In accordance with its UN mandate, this aspect of the Rwandan Trubunal was authorized for the prosecution of the government-controlled media, which fanned the flames of intra-tribal hatred and the genocide of 1994.

On August 19, 2003, three journalists were sentenced by the Rwandan Tribunal, in Arusha with the prosecutor requesting that life sentences be given for the owners of the Radio Television Libre des Mille Collines, Ferdinand Nahimana, and Jean Bosco Barayagwiza. All three defendants were charged with genocide, incitement to genocide, and crimes against humanity, before and during the period of the genocides of 1994. On 3 December 2003, the court found all three defendants guilty and sentenced Nahimana and Ngeze to life imprisonment and Barayagwiza to imprisonment for thirty-five years. The case is currently on appeal. In addition, Hassan Ngeze, the editor and director of the Kangur newspaper was also charged.

THE FORMER YUGOSLAVIA WAR CRIMES TRIALS

Where are we now in our sixty year effort to punish genocidal war criminals under the mechanism of international law? Scholars like Richard Wilson, who, in his 2005 article titled, "Judge History" wrote: "The Historical Record of the International Criminal Tribunal for the Former Yugoslavia," as well as numerous legal officials, have contended that it is counterproductive for courts endeavor to write authoritative historical accounts of extensive human rights violations."[10] The argument put forth to support this contention, is that since law and history have vastly different modes of amassing and interpreting history, any attempt to reconstruct a comprehensive history of a conflict, carries the probability that such a legal account will be acutely defective, and probably just plain uninteresting.

These condemnations have also appeared notably in deliberations of Holocaust trials in the domestic courts of Israel and France. So far, the Tadić and Krstić judgments handed down by the The International Tribunal for the Prosecution of Persons Responsible for Serious Violations of International Humanitarian Law Committed in the Territory of the Former Yugoslavia since 1991 (ICTY), are distinguished by the in depth contextualization of criminal acts and broad historical understanding.

Wilson, in his article, further suggests that the Tribunal's historical evidence represents a departure from preceding courtroom accounts of mass atrocities for two reasons. First, since it is an international tribunal, it has been less predisposed to rule based on vague narratives on national character. Second, the ICTY has utilized legal terminology such as genocide, which stress the cooperative nature of the perpetrators of crimes against humanity. and this obliges the court to position individual acts within enduring, logical policies.[11]

INTERNATIONAL CRIMINGAL TRIBUNAL FOR THE FORMER YUGOSLAVIA

The International Criminal Tribunal for the former Yugoslavia (ICTY), is an organ of the United Nations (UN), created to prosecute war crimes in the former Yugoslavia. The tribunal functions as an auxillary court, and is headquartered in the Netherlands, at The Hague.[12]

ICTY was enacteded by UN Resolution 827 of the UN Security Council, which was authorized on May 25, 1993. ICTY has jurisdiction to try people charged with various war crimes committed within the territory of the former Yugoslavia since 1991, for the specific violations of the 1949 Geneva Conventions, violations of the laws or customs of war, genocide, and crimes against humanity.

ICTY only has jurisdiction to try individuals. It does not have legal authroity to bring charges against organizations or governments. The maximum sentence ICTY can impose is a life imprisonment. Different countries have signed accords with the UN to authorize custodial sentences. The last indictment was handed down by ICTY on March 15, 2004. Its purpose is to complete all trials by the end of 2008, and all appeals by 2010. Like the Rwandan Genocide trials before them, the complexity of conducting an international trial of this magnitude, and the constraints of its jurisdiction will make it virtually impossible for them to complete the entire legal effort by the year 2010.

ACCOMPLISHMENTS OF THE COURT

In 2004, the ICTY published a list of five successes which it claimed it had accomplished:

> 1. "Spearheading the shift from impunity to accountability", pointing out that, until very recently, it was the only court judging crimes committed as part of the Yugoslav conflict, since prosecutors in the former Yugsolavia were, as a rule, reluctant to prosecute such crimes;
>
> 2. "Establishing the facts", highlighting the extensive evidence-gathering and lengthy findings of fact that Tribunal judgments produced;
>
> 3. "Bringing justice to thousands of victims and giving them a voice", pointing out the large number of witnesses that had been brought before the Tribunal;
>
> 4. "The accomplishments in international law", describing the fleshing out of several international criminal law concepts which had not been ruled on since the Nuremberg Trials;
>
> 5. "Strengthening the Rule of Law", referring to the Tribunal's role in promoting the use of international standards in war crimes prosecutions by former Yugoslav republics. . .[13]

Due to the involvement of the UN, and its use of the UN Security Council in the establishment of The International Criminal Tribunal for the Former Yugoslavia as opposed to the precedent of the General Assembly establishing tribunals, there has been a chorus of the criticisms addressed against the court. A number of these criticisms center around the initial establishment of ICTY by the UN Security Council as opposed to the UN General Assembly. Former president of Serbia Slobidan Milosevic, the principal defendant of the ICTY, repeatedly and vociferiously contended that the court has no lawful jurisdiction based on the allegation that the UN used the "Security Counsel" to establish the tribunal, because it did not have the full acceptance of the international community.

ICTY was created by the UN Charter, specifically under Chapter VII.

Significant excerpts of the charter reads "the Security Council can take measures to maintain or restore international peace and security", this specific section was used to justify the use of the "security counsel" to establish the tribunal. It is argued that the tribunal could be considered as a means to uphold and restore international peace and stability to area of the former Yugoslav republics. The idea to utilize Chapter VII, and the section giving the "security counsel" authority to "take measures to maintain or restore international peace and security", was originally made in a report from the Secretary-General to the Security Council.

Conspicuously, a disproportionately high number of defendants are Serbs (to the degree that a large portion of the Bosnian Serb and Serbian political and military planners have been prosecuted), with scant prosecutions of war crimes perpetrated against Serbs (numerous Croat defendants were also charged with war time attrocities against Bosnian Muslims). In addition to these irregularities, generally speaking, Serbian defendants are of higher rank as compared with those of other nations, and were accused of many more crimes and acts. Supporters of the Tribunal counter that Serb authority over the permanent command structure (and most of the weaponry), command of the Yugoslav People's Army (JNA) from the begining of the conflagragation, validates the proposition that the Serbs were complicit in the commission of crimes on a grander and more protracted scale. Moreover, the Serb command structure aided the identification of those with command authorization for war crimes. Nevertheless, these arguments fall short of justifying why numerous other allegations of war crimes perpetrated against Serbs were not prosecuted.

Regrettably, to date, the majority of the defendants are still at large, and have not been brought into custody, setting a poor precedent for the UN Security Council and the ICTY. In response to this problem, supporters point out that the Tribunal has no powers of arrest, and is entirely dependant on other agencies (particularly national governments, EUFOR and KFOR) to capture and extradite defendants. In addition to the above problems, the Tribunal's authority to hand down secret indictments fosters uncertainty among people who consider themselves as possible indictees, adding to the questionable authority, an unanswerable burden on the possibility of possible indictees, to proceed with their everyday lives, both in the short and long term.

The Tribunal has not prosecuted the citizens of any NATO countries regarding NATO's connection in the war in Kosovo. NATO spokesman Jamie Shea stated the following about the court:

> NATO countries are those that have provided the finance to set up the Tribunal, we are amongst the majority financiers, and of course to build a second chamber so that prosecutions can be speeded up so let me assure that we and the Tribunal are all one on this, we want to see war criminals brought to justice and I am certain that when Justice Arbour goes to Kosovo and looks at the facts she will be indicting people of Yugoslav nationality and I don't anticipate any others at this stage.[14]

Critics have argued that the Tribunal is counterproductive; that it actually increases national, racial, and sectarian tensions rather than fostering reconciliation, as is claimed by Tribunal supporters. Polls seem to indicate a primarily negative reaction to the Tribunal within from the Serb and Croat perspective. At this point, the majority of Croats and Serbs question the tribunal's integrity and doubt the viability of its legal procedures (despite the fact that the Serbs's and Croats's beliefs on the court are usually positive regarding the cases impacting both parties). On the other hand, Kosovo Albanians and Bosnian Muslims have frequently expressed their high regard for the court, and trust in its impartiality.

Critics, including officials of the United Nations, have been surprised by the exceedingly high cost of the Tribunal. The two-year budget for the Tribunal for 2004 and 2005 was $271,854,600 (USD). The cost is borne by all UN members, albeit not proportionately. There can be no doubt the U.S. is once again, bearing the brunt of the exorbitant cost of liberals, playing court games with taxpayer money, of the American people.

Critics have also expressed reservations regarding the actual time it is taking for the trials to come to a conclusion, with some taking as long a three years or more. Supporters of the Tribunal counter that numerous defendants are charged with multiple crimes against a plethora of victims, all of which must be proven beyond reasonable doubt, which leads to lengthly trials. The added dimension of having to simultaneously translate all the proceedings of the court, during the trials, also makes the trials slower than they would ordinarily be.

Within the milieu of political discourse, one can frequently encounter examples of the aphorism, "court's decisions should not successfully re-write history". Historians have chronicled the fact that trials like the Nuremberg trials, or the Tokyo trials proceedings, all failed to affect German and Japanese citizens, respectively, in the desired manner. They each resulted in national homogenization that helped form a uniform, self-defensive opinion, which treated these judicial processes as show trials or a weapon of revenge wielded by occupying forces. Only after more than two decades and the onset of economic prosperity did German general public come to agree with the most of the assumptions delineated in the Nuremberg trials indictments and findings. On the other hand, repeated Sino-Japanese and Korean-Japanese diplomatic discord regarding the truth of Japanese history textbooks, report that the Japanese citizenry have not, in general, agreed to the interpretation of the WWII history, conventional in the US, the EU, and the Asian countries surrounding Japan, most notably Korea and China.

Criticism along this line of inquiry has also been raised with regard to the ICTY. The conventional wisdom, particularly or the Serbs's and Croat's, expect the Court will be loath to hold or follow the judicial opinion of the Hague court that is contrary to the mainstream intellectual Brahman's (especially with regard to historiography, political, economic and sociological analyses; as well as, political journalism, geopolitical analyses and military history), and that, in their august wisdom, they will feign to hand down the final, definitive verdict on the troublesome periods of their national histories.

A synopsis of Croatian and Serbian history books and best-selling political journalism, in addition to opinion polls, reveal the inevitable tide of events has manifested: nationalism dictates national histories, especially if these historiographies are seen as being largely politically motivated. Because the majority of Serbs and Croats, a minority of Bosnians and Albanians, and a large proportion of the international community legal experts believe the ICTY lacks legitimacy as a court of law and is merely a political court and tool of Anglo-American geopolitical benefit—the likelihood that the ICTY's verdicts will be considered impartial, in a near future by the newly warring factions it has been established to punish, to the furthest extent of the law, is virtually nil.

Since March 16, 2006, the ICTY had indicted 161 defendants. Only six of these remained "at large." The cases against eighty-five of the indicted had been concluded: Forty-three were found guilty, eight acquitted, twenty-five had their indictments withdrawn, and six had died—three of these in custody, three while on parole. Four cases had been sent to national courts for trial. Fifteen of those convicted had completed their sentences and been released by March 2006.[15]

The defendants varied from ordinary soldiers to generals, and from police commanders, all the way to Prime Ministers. Slobodan Milosevic was the first sitting head of state indicted for war crimes.[16] Other "high level" defendants included Milan Babic, Croatian Serb prime minister of Republika Srpska Krajina; Ramush Haradinaj, Albanian prime minister of Kosovo; Radovan Karadzic, Montenegrin former President of Republika Srpska; and Ratko Mladic, Bosnian Serb army commander.

Those indicted and currently on trial and those who were denied a conditional release are held in custody at a prison facility in Scheveningen, located some four km from the courthouse. There are four floors of twelve cells each. The indicted are housed in private cells which have a toilet, shower, radio, satellite TV and other comforts. They are allowed to phone family and friends daily and can have conjugal visits (Serb general Nebojsa Pavkovic became a father at the age of fifty-nine as a result of one such visit). There is also a library, a gym and various rooms used for religious observances. The inmates are even permitted to cook for themselves. All the inmates socialize freely and are not segregated on the basis of nationality.

THE IRAQ CASES AND THE FARCICAL TRIALS OF SADDAM HUSSEIN

> Justice Jackson, who prosecuted the case for the United States, went so far as to suggest, early on, that it would be preferable to shoot Nazi criminals out of hand than to discredit our judicial process by conducting farcical trials.[17]
>
> ~ Professor Alan M. Dershowitz
> America on Trial

> During an interview with the Arab news agency al-Arabiya nfollowing the opening of the trial, Hussein's eldest daughter Raghad branded the court a "farce." [18]
>
> ~ Raghad Hussein

The first trial of Saddam Hussein, the former dictator and President of Iraq, was convened before the Iraqi Special Tribunal on October 19, 2005. In the Dujail case, Hussein, together with seven other defendants, was tried for allegations of genocide, war crimes, and crimes against humanity, with regard to events that took place after a failed assassination attempt on his life by the Shiites, in Dujail in 1982. In August 2006 a second and separate trial began bringing charges against Hussein along with six other co-defendants, for genocide during the Anfal military operation in Northern Iraq, against the Kurds.[19]

Saddam Hussein may also be tried for atrocities dating to the Iran-Iraq War (1979-88), and the invasion of Kuwait (1991) including war crimes, crimes against humanity, and genocide. At this point, such a trial would be for airing the charges and supporting the allegations since Hussein has already been executed based on his conviction in the first tribunal.

Hussein was given over to the interim Iraqi government to stand trial on June 30, 2004 and was held in custody by U.S. forces at Camp Cropper in Baghdad, along with eleven senior Ba'athist officials. Exacting consideration was given regarding the allegations of violent reprisals against the Kurds in the north during the Iran-Iraq War, and against the Shiites in the south in 1991 and 1999, as he sought to quell several insurrections at that time. Saddam contended that he had been illegally deposed, and he adamantly insisted that he remained the President of Iraq, to the end.

As the trial against the former dictator of Iraq proceeded, Saddam's defense continually argued for a postponement in the deliberations, insisting that some legal technicality had been breached by the prosecutor, including allegations the defense had not been given certain evidence, had not been given adequate time to make an assessment of any prosecution documents, however, these inquiries by the defense have received no response at the time, and are now moot, given the final finding of the court.

In the interim, international human rights groups, including Human Rights Watch, Amnesty International in addition to UN bodies such as the Working

Group on Arbitrary Detention and the High Commissioner for Human Rights, have argued that the Iraqi Special Tribunal and its legal process did not meet international standards for a fair trial. At the same time, the United Nations Secretary-General had likewise refused to sanction the proceedings, conveying unease over the question of evenhandedness in addition to the prospect of a death sentence, which was ultimately handed down in the case. The UN's present aversion for associating itself with trials that have a death penalty component is at odds with history. The UN's first international trial, the Nuremberg Trials, had twelve of the original twenty-two defendants executed by hanging.

AL-DUJAIL TRIAL

On October 19, 2005 four days after the October 15, 2005 referendum on the new constitution Iraqi, authorities put Saddam and seven other former Iraqi officials on trial. The tribunal expressly charged the defendants with the killing of 143 Shiites from Dujail, in retribution for the unsuccessful assassination attempt of 8 July 1982. Factions of Saddam demonstrated against the trial in Tikrit.[21] Saddam's co-defendants are:

- Barzan Ibrahim al-Tikriti, his half-brother and former chief of intelligence;
- Taha Yassin Ramadan, former Vice-President;
- Awad Hamed al-Bandar Al-S'adun, a former chief judge;
- Abdullah Kadhem Roweed Al-Musheikhi, Al-Dujail Baath party official;
- Mizher Abdullah Roweed AL-Musheikhi, (son Abdullah Kadhem), Al-Dujail Baath party official;
- Ali Daeem Ali, Dujail Baath party official;
- Mohammed Azawi Ali, Dujail Baath party official

As in his pre-trial appearance, Saddam, at the opening of his trial on October 19, appeared defiant and refused to subject himself to the tribunal's authority and proclaimed independence from the authority of the foreign occupation. Hussein remarked: "I do not respond to this so-called court, with all due respect to its people, and I retain my constitutional right as the president of Iraq." He added, "neither do I recognize the body that has designated and authorized by you, nor the aggression, because all that has been built on a false basis is false." When the judge asked for his name, Saddam said "I am the president of the Iraq," refused to state his name, but returned the question, asking Kurdish judge Rizgar Mohammed Amin, "Who are you? I want to know who you are." When Amin addressed Saddam as "the former president," Saddam objected emphatically, saying he was still the President of the Republic of Iraq, and had not been lawfully deposed.

After the charges were read to them, all eight defendants pleaded not guilty. The first session of his trial lasted about three hours. The court adjourned the case until November 28, 2005, because some of the witnesses were too frightened to attend, as well as to allow the defense more time to study the evidence.[22] During an interview with the Arab news agency al-Arabiya, following the opening of the trial, Hussein's eldest daughter Raghad branded the court a "farce" and boasted that her father behaved like a "lion" during the proceedings. "My father is brave, a lion, I am proud of him," she said. "He is a man who dedicated his life to serve his country, he was brave in his youth, so how can he be afraid now?" she added. Was Raghad correct in her assessment that the case of Saddam Hussein was a "farce"?[23] I for one, believe she was right.

Below is a brief summary of the main proceedings in the Trial of Saddam—a macabre parade of the harlequins:

- October 20, 2005—attorney Saadoun Sughaiyer al-Janabi, charged with the defense of Awad Hamed al-Bandar, was abducted from his office by gunmen, and found shot dead near his office a few hours later.
- On November 8, 2005, attorney Adel al-Zubeidi, who had been representing Vice President Taha Yassin Ramadan and Abdullah Kazim Ruwayyid, was killed by three gunmen in Baghdad. Barazan Ibrahim's lawyer Thamer Hamoud al-Khuzaie was also wounded in the attack.
- On November 28, 2005, Chief Judge Rizhar Mohammed Amid adjourned the trial until December 5 to allow time to find replacements for two defense lawyers who were slain and another who fled Iraq after he was wounded.
- On December 5, Saddam's legal defense team stormed out of the court after questioning its legitimacy and asking about return of defense papers seized by U.S. Army troops and security issues regarding the protection of the defense. Saddam, along with his co-defendants, railed against Chief Judge Amin and the tribunal.
- On December 6, after listening to hours of testimony against him, he lashed out at the judge. He said he was exhausted, did not intend on returning to the trial, and to "go to hell."
- On December 7, 2005, Saddam refused to enter court, complaining of the conditions in which he was being held and the conduct of the trial. Saddam's complaints included, among other things, that he had not been able to change his clothes for four days. [10] "A defiant Saddam pleads innocent, scuffles with guards in stormy hearing."

- On December 12, 2005, instead of cross-examining witnesses, Saddam used the time to accuse his American captors of torturing him, saying, "I have been beaten on every place of my body, and the signs are all over my body." "Saddam alleges that he was tortured by the Americans" at BBC News.
- On January 23, 2006, Rauf Rashid Abd al-Rahman was nominated interim chief judge of the tribunal. He replaces former chief judge Rizgar Amin, also a Kurd, who resigned after complaining of government interference. "Court names new judge" at BBC News] Hussein and his co-defendants objected to the change in judge, citing bias after he ordered defendant Barzan Ibrahim al-Tikriti out of the court, and announced they would boycott the trial under Rahman.
- On February 1st Saddam and the seven defendants failed to show up to court.
- On March 15, 2006, Saddam was called by the prosecution as a witness. On the stand, he began making political statements, insisting he was still President of Iraq. He got in an argument with the judge, who eventually closed the trial to the public in response ["Judge closes trial"].
- On June 19, 2006, Chief Prosecutor Jaafar al-Moussawi called for the death penalty for Saddam and four other defendants including Barzan al-Tikriti, Saddam's half-brother, Taha Yassin Ramadan, former Iraqi Vice President and Awad Hamed al-Bander, former chief judge of Saddam's Revolutionary Court. The suspects face execution by hanging if convicted and sentenced to death.
- On June 21, 2006, Saddam's chief defense lawyer, Khamis al-Obeidi, was assassinated in Baghdad. In protest of the lack of international protection for lawyers, Saddam began a hunger strike. On June 23, 2006, Reuters reported that Saddam ended his hunger strike, having missed only one meal.
- On June 27, 2006, two of Saddam Hussein's lawyers, Ramsey Clark, a former US Attorney-General, and Curtis Doebbler, held a press conference at the National Press Club in Washington, D.C., to call for immediate security for all the Iraqi defense lawyers and to complain in a lengthy and documented statement of the unfair trail being conducted by the American authorities, using Iraqis as a front. The two lawyers claimed that the United States had refused to provide adequate protection for the defense lawyers despite repeated requests that were made, and that the United States was intentionally ensuring an unfair trial.
- On September 20, 2006, the Iraqi government removed chief judge Abdullah al-Amiri. This is the second judge to be removed.

- On October 2006 the third judge, Rizgar Amin, publicly and effusively lavished praise on Saddam Hussein in open court.
- On November 5, 2006, after several false starts the first guilty verdicts were handed down against Saddam and his seven co-defendants in the Dujail case. Commentators close to the trial expect Saddam to hang before year's end even with the appeals process yet to begin.

CRTICISMS OF THE TRIAL OF SADDAM

Numerous critics arose at the beginning of the trial against Saddam Hussein, stating that for all of the atrocities he committed during his thirty-five plus year reign as the dictator of Iraq, along with the hundreds of thousands, perhaps millions of people he murdered, to have the prosecutors choose to begin tribunal proceedings with the Dujail case rather than the Anfal campaign where Saddam unleashed weapons of mass destruction (WMDs) in the form of chemical weapons to quell an insurrection in the Kurdish north, was inappropriate, to say the least.

Another problem in the trial against Saddam involved American complicity in funding the Saddam regime with weapons and money for years, as a buffer against their hated enemy, Iran, including aid during the Iran/Iraq War (1979-1988). The selection of cases to be prosecuted is considered by some to be caused by strong opposition from the United States, which supported Iraq diplomatically during the Iran-Iraq War. Extending the trials to these crimes might result in publishing material collected from Hussein's administration, confiscated by the United States occupying forces. Opening the archives might give clues or verify the US's involvement with arming of Iraq and intelligence in the 1980s. This could result in negative effects on the ruling administration in US domestic politics.

The United States is in a paradox regarding the trial of Saddam. On the one hand, the United States is pushing for a speedy trial against a vicious dictator that has thwarted America's foreign policy and fomented international terrorism in that area of the world for years. On the other hand, there is the desire to scrupulously censor what evidence is brought against Saddam, because of America's concerns that such information would be a great embarrassment of past American foreign policy blunders.

To ensure that all the court proceedings of the Trial of Saddam is controlled by America, the television link for the trial is supplied by a US company which regularly censors out the sound of what Saddam and the defendant say, and sometimes cuts the video line also. This is allegedly edited in compliance with commands issued by the presiding judge. As an example, if a defendant's microphone is turned off as a sanction for obnoxious behavior by the defendant in court, the defendant's speech is not transmitted. There are guests and observers in audience at all court proceedings apart from the little number that the presiding judge has affirmed closed. An additional grave dilemma for this court is the absence of a trustworthy transcript. This has hindered efforts by all parties to adequately maintain evidence, and supervise the proceedings.[24]

Numerous other criticisms of the trial of Saddam Hussein abound, including crass political opportunism by the Bush administration, alleging that the date in which the verdict will be released publicly to the world, November 5, 2006, was intentionally motivated by officials of the Iraqi government to manipulate the U.S. midterm elections scheduled just two days later. Other observers view the Saddam trials as an unmitigated farce, bereft of sound international law and consensus from the international community. There have been allegations that the trials are unhelpful, quick, and are generally poor quality.

Whether a just trial in occupied Iraq is even possible has also been questioned. In light of the rampant and numerous assassinations and assassination attempts on Saddam's defense team, judges, and family members of those associated with the trial, security of participants has been criticized. Several defendants have claimed that they have been tortured by the American forces that are holding them. Human rights witnesses and the defense attorneys, who are comprised of two previous ministers of justice, maintain the defendant's human rights have been abused to such an extent, that a fair trial is no longer likely.

Various international spectators have blamed the special Iraqi Court itself of being unlawful since it was established as one of the consequences of the United States-led invasions of Iraq, which they also regard as against international law. Iraqi governmental demands on the court and interfering with its independence, chiefly by selective enforcement of the de-Ba'athification condition (providing that no associate of the previous Ba'ath Party may work in the court) have been criticized. As subsequent cases in the Saddam Trials come about, much of the speculation surrounding the inequities of these trials are moot—Saddam was hanged on December 30, 2006, and his equally infamous cousin, Ali Hassan al-Majid, (a.k.a. "Chemical Ali"), was sentenced to be hanged on June 24, 2007 for his role as for masterminding the genocide against a Kurdish insurrection of Northern Iraq in March 1988, by gassing them with lethal chemicals, murdering over 5,000 Kurds.

One of the oft-repeated ironies of history is the cycle of nature and humanity—that social degeneration, revolution, and "dark ages" breed counterrevolution, enlightenment, and societal renaissance, frequently serving as the genesis of "great awakenings" and revivals.

September 11, 2001, a date that will live in infamy, a day where nineteen Muslim religious fanatics commandeered four planes and killed several thousand people, to date has not led to a trial, since the actual perpetrators all died in the plane crashes. However from the 9-11 terrorist acts, have come a litany of cases, that together, comprise a pivotal legal event of the twenty-first century—The Padilla case and its progeny.[25]

VARIOUS TERRORIST CASES POST-9/11

As this book goes to press, there have been plea bargains and accusations, but no notable trials of the 300 or so Muslim enemy combatants held at Guantanamo Bay. To Dershowitz, liberal Democrats (*sans* Sen. Lieberman, D-CT), and other critics who favor granting full constitutional rights enjoyed by U.S. citizens, to enemy combatants that seek to destroy America. They refer to the fact that post-9/11, there have been no "criminal trials" in America of terrorists, which to them, "may suggest a dangerous trend in our nation's approach to terrorism. I am not one of those apologists. To give people like the Guantanamo detainees; vicious blood-thirsty religious fanatics, literally caught in the act of plotting to kill Americans as part of a worldwide Muslim jihad against the "American and Jewish infidels," would be tantamount to lighting the fuse of the bomb that would not only destroy America, Israel, but every civilized, non-Muslim majority nation in the world. This would indeed be a most untenable situation; nevertheless the American courts have to address terrorist related issues. The treacherous and ignoble legacy of the Nuremberg Trials can be clearly seen in four major terrorist cases cited below which have caused great controversy in the United States Courts of Appeals and has divided the nation. The Supreme Court has given *certiorari* to review two of them and may choose to examine others as well.

THE PADILLA CASE

One of the most significant of these cases, and the one that will in all probability, have the most definitive effect, constitutionally speaking, is Jose Padilla, the so-called "dirty bomber." He is a suspected Al Qaeda terrorist who was arrested in Chicago, and originally held as "a material witness." Subsequently, President Bush selected Padilla, who is an American citizen, who was deemed to also be an "enemy combatant," and intended that he be detained in the custody of the military where he had been detained for the past several years, in the brig at a military prison in Charleston, N.C. with no access to his lawyer, his family, or his friends. He is undergoing "ongoing questioning regarding the Al Qaeda network and its terrorist activities in an effort to obtain intelligence"[26]

Padilla, an American citizen born in New York, was convicted of murder in 1983. In 1998 he moved to Egypt and in 2001 he traveled to Afghanistan, where he became involved with the radical Islamist terrorist group, Al Qaeda with the end plan "to build and detonate a 'dirty bomb' within the United States." The government does not charge that he became "a member of Al Qaeda" but it does allege that "he was closely associated with known members and leaders" of that Islamic terrorist organization.

The government is in a bind for they don't want to put Padilla on trial for conspiracy to detonate a dirty bomb, because the sources of its information continue to be confidential and sensitive to national security. Therefore it is satisfied to hold him, perhaps forever, as an enemy combatant. It cites as precedent for this power "the President's authority, settled by *Ex Parte Quirin* (1942) to detain enemy combatants in wartime—authority that is argued to encompass the detention of United States citizens on United States soil." The *Quirin* case concerned Nazi saboteurs—including at least one U.S. citizen—who, during World War II, landed by submarine on Long Island, with plans to bomb designated sites in New York. Instead, they were speedily caught, tried by a military tribunal, and hanged, with the sanction of the Supreme Court.[27]

The Court of Appeals for the Second Circuit (located in New York) restricted its ruling to "the case of an American citizen arrested in the United States, not on a foreign battlefield, or while actively engaged in armed conflict against the United States."[28] It differentiated this case from another one, that also regarding an American citizen, this one named Yaser Esam Hamdan, who was apprehended by American soldiers during battle in Afghanistan. It agreed with an opinion by a judge of the United States Court of Appeals for the Fourth Circuit (located in Virginia) that "to compare this battlefield capture [of Hamdan] to the domestic arrest [of Padilla] is to compare apples and oranges." The fourth Circuit had upheld Hamdan's confinement, emphasizing the fact that he was captured by American troops on a foreign battlefield.

The Second Circuit overturned Padilla's confinement, citing that "the President lacks inherent constitutional authority as Commander-in-Chief to detain American citizens on American soil outside a zone of combat." It differentiated the *Quirin* precedent on the argument that during World War II, Congress had sanctioned the president to keep in custody American citizens arrested here, for an indefinite period and without any appearance of a trial.

The court ordered Padilla's discharge within thirty days unless the government should relocate him to civilian authorities for a criminal trial, or confine him "as a material witness in connection with grand jury proceedings." The government has appealed the Padilla judgment to the Supreme Court, requesting an "expedited" hearing. The lawyer for Hamdan has requested review , contending that the Padilla verdict, ordering the detainee's release, "clearly conflicts" with the Hamdan opinion ordering his continued incarceration. On January 9, 2004, the Supreme Court issued a writ of certiorari in the *Hamdan* case.

Journalist, Linda Greenhouse, in a New York Times op-ed, stated that the *Hamdan* case had become, "the rallying cry for all those people concerned about how far the president can go." He defined the *Hamdan* case as "the case that goes to the very heart of the nationwide debate about whether the administration has gone too far."[29]

Obviously, it is unknown how the Supreme Court will rule on Hamdan, or whether the High Court will regard the *Padilla* and *Hamdan* cases as "apples and oranges" given the fact that Padilla was arrested here and Hamdan on an overseas battlefield, or whether it will consider them both as "fruits" given they both entail American citizens. What does seem probable is that the justices will reflect on the issues raised in both *Padilla* and *Hamdan* and will come to a decision whether a detainee's standing as an American citizen, in addition to the place of his original apprehension, determines how he is to be regarded by the American legal system.[30]

THE GUANTANAMO BAY CASES

The recent Supreme Court decision regarding the status of the hundreds of detainees, currently being held at a U.S. controlled prison at Guantanamo Bay, Cuba, has the potential to decide whether our courts can detain persons in custody, under military control, as an enemy combatants indefinitely, or must accord them all of the rights and privileges of "American citizens", under our criminal justice system. The Court, in a 5-3 decision (Chief Justice John Roberts rescued himself due to his participation in the same case at the appellate level), has determined to attend to the narrow question of whether "United States' courts lack jurisdiction to consider challenges to the legality of the detention of foreign nationals captured abroad in connection with hostilities and incarcerated at the Guantanamo Bay Naval Base, Cuba."[31]

The Court of Appeals for the District of Columbia circuit ruled that "Cuba—not the United States—has sovereignty over Guantanamo Bay," and therefore U.S. courts have no authority over foreign detainees being held there. The U.S. Supreme Court recently affirmed that lower court's ruling. The U.S. Court of Appeals for the Ninth Circuit in California came to a different conclusion, determining that the United States had showed absolute jurisdiction over Guantanamo for more than a century, has operated the Base as if it intended to keep hold of Guantanamo permanently, and has established the exclusive, unrestricted right, to exploit this land as it wished. Furthermore, the United States also detains persons who commit crimes at Guantanamo, to try in its criminal justice system. Liberal or Left-leaning legal scholars like Dershowitz, Tribe, Kennedy (Harvard), Akhil Reed Amar (Yale), Richard Posner, Cass Sunstein, Richard Epstein (U. of Chicago), M. Cherif Bassiouni (DePaul), Jonathan Turley (George Washington), and the Leftist Justices of the Supreme Court—Ruth Bader Ginsburg, David Souter, Stephen Breyer, Sandra Day O'Connor [retired], Anthony Kennedy and John Paul Stevens, hold that these legalistic formulations hide some of the most conflict-ridden and essential issues that effect our nation.

Is the Constitution a patriotic document that demands that all American officials, wherever they may be, and whomever they may take into custody for whatever legal reason, must follow with accord, the restrictions of the Bill of Rights? Do overseas combatants, taken into custody outside of our nation, have any rights? Are those rights less than, equal to or greater than those "inalienable" rights enjoyed by American citizens during normal circumstances? And, most imperative, will the present Supreme Court ascend to the event and fulfill its mandate of checking and balancing the Bush administration's otherwise unchecked and unbalanced methods of fighting terrorism?

If the triumvirate of President George W. Bush, Secretary of Defense

Rumsfeld and his Attorney General, John Ashcroft, could fully implement its foreign and domestic policy to combat terrorism, the court would simply take a *laisse faire* approach, allowing the executive and the military *carte blanche* to fight the war against terrorism by any means that they deem effectual, without concern to the protections extended by the Constitution American citizens. In their defense, the Bush administration mention the actions of preceding great presidents—particularly Lincoln and Roosevelt—as precedents for the necessity for tough and unrestrained executive action during war time.

While it is factually accurate that Abraham Lincoln (1861-1865) suspended the writ of *habeas corpus* during the Civil War allowing him to imprison hundreds of his political enemies including journalists, politicians, and Southern sympathizers and Franklin Delano Roosevelt (1933-1945), who during World War II ordered the confinement in internment camps of more than 100,000 Americans of Japanese origin, as well as the military trial and quick execution of the German saboteurs—and that equally these men acted with little obstruction from the Supreme Court. But historical revisionists and secular progressives insist unconvincingly, however, that it was not these illegal actions that made Lincoln and Roosevelt great presidents. Certainly, these departures from conformity with the rule of law, lessened the magnitude of their presidencies, in the opinion of many historians. These undemocratic actions were perhaps, not among their finest hours, but hindsight is never an accurate gauge. At the same time, there is there no proof that our nation's war aims would have been compromised had the Constitution been staunchly upheld.

Almost certainly there can be no singular substantive decree to the countless issues presently dividing our nation. The Supreme Court will more than likely rule that an American citizen has greater rights under the Constitution and in our legal system and courts, than some stranger, whose only relationship to America, is his aim to carry out a terrorist plot against our people and to attack America's national interests. However, it is doubtful that the Court will decide that the Constitution follows the flag—that is, that American soldiers would be constrained by all constitutional restraints, wherever they may be, and whomever they may be imprisoning or interrogating in the course of war. On the other hand, it is likely that it will rule that Guantanamo, which is leased from Cuba on a long-term basis and is home to a large U.S. military base, is essentially part of the United States, for legal purposes. Inevitably, the circumstances of these cases will compel the justices to make new law to deal with America's and the West's, no end in sight, war against Islamic terrorism.

Certainly, new law is desperately needed, because the since World War II the corpus of international law has become treacherously anachronistic as we face warfare in modern times.

THE SADDAM HUSSEIN CASE

The Iraqi dictator Saddam Hussein was hanged on December 30, 2006 for crimes against humanity, war crimes, and other crimes against the Iraqi people, particularly his brutal genocide to quell a Shiite uprising in the Dujail province of Iraq in 1982. On January 9, 2004, the Defense Department formally called Saddam Hussein a "prisoner of war." The POW category guarantees the imprisoned dictator certain rights under international law. It is rather sardonic that, under the Defense Department's approach, this genocidal murderer, who is directly to blame for many war crimes against his own people, as well as against foreign civilians, will be accorded many more rights than an enemy combatant of the Taliban, captured in the battle fields of Afghanistan. Not only is this an egregious example of the shameful legacy of the Nuremberg trials, where dictators, military tyrants and mass murders get a "trial" i.e., an international stage to rant and rave and pontificate to humanity, of their unfair treatment, this also underscores as fact, how perilously obsolete current international law has become in the age of terrorism, and the advent of World War III.

At the time of this writing it is not known if the Supreme Court will give a writ of certiorari to hear other terrorism cases and if so, how many and of which types. The Court's choice not to make this decision can sometimes be the most important decision the justices could make, because it demonstrates to the lower courts or to the executive branch, not only how the Court ruled on a given terrorist case, but more importantly, the probable direction the Court would go in other cases of this nature. The early direction of the courts is mixed—some of the lower courts have decided in favor of the government, others have been decided against the government's argument. Since the government has substantial influence to direct cases in the direction of these sympathetic courts, a ruling by the Supreme Court to not make a decision would be a definitive triumph for the Bush administration.

America's legal structure of checks and balances also includes the legislative branch, but the Senate and the House of Representatives have historically been tacit regarding executive exercise of power in the war against terrorism. It is axiomatic that the public wants a strong leader during times of national attacks to stand up against to National enemies, such as the terrorists who wish to do us harm—there will be no political price to pay for being too harsh in the war on terror. However, only unelected federal judges, and particularly the justices of the Supreme Court, can, in effect, check excesses in the use of the executive power, during a national crisis such as the war on terror. The war against terrorism will be a prolonged test as to whether this Supreme Court will fulfill its mandate to balance executive power, with the rule of law.

The terrorism cases now on the docket in our courts may shift our legal system in a different and more precarious course. The pivotal question here is this—will criminal trials in terrorism cases become an anachronism as military tribunals assume the primary role in such cases? The jury is still out on this question, but the Supreme Court hasn't signaled yet that it doesn't have jurisdiction to decide this question.

In the near future, it seems safe to conjecture that the Criminal Court system will have a substantive role in ruling on terrorist cases that are perpetrated by citizens, and are perpetrated on American soil. However, if the Supreme Court determines that "illegal enemy combatants" and "terrorists, operating on American soil" do not have our traditional constitutionally recognized rights, then this war, unlike past wars which ended on specific dates. has the ability to persist for the foreseeable future, carrying these issues into that unforeseeable future, with it. It is fitting, therefore, to end this chapter with the authoritative warning issued by an earlier Supreme Court in the aftermath of the Civil War:

> [Our Constitution] foresaw that troublous times would arise, when rulers and people would become restive under restraint and seek by sharp and decisive measures to accomplish ends deemed just and proper; and that the principles of constitutional liberty would be in peril, unless established by irrepealable law.
>
> This nation . . . has no right to expect that it will always have wise and humane rulers, sincerely attached to the principles of the Constitution. Wicked men, ambitious of power, with hatred of liberty and contempt of law, may fill the place once occupied by Washington and Lincoln, and if this right [to suspend provisions of the Constitution during the great exigencies of government] is conceded, and the calamities of war again befall us, the dangers to human liberty are frightful to contemplate.[32]

While the above words are lofty and eloquent in word and in deed, it is axiomatic that the rules, out of necessity, do change and must change to deal with a new enemy who shares no such compunction to abide by "principles of constitutional liberty" or "irrepealable law" except that law which is the eight century Sharia law, of Islam, that forces women to wear head-to-toe burkas and commands all men who call themselves Muslims by the words of the prophet Muhammad himself to "kill the infidel (i.e., unbeliever, Christians and Jews) where you find him."

In conclusion, when I speak of the "shameful legacy" of the Nuremberg trials, what precisely do I mean? It would be to easy to lump every UN scandal, bureaucratic inefficiency, "cut and run" UN peacekeeping mission, dictator appeasement policy or inept, symbolic international trial at the Hague, as being directly linked to the authoritative declaration of the original Nuremberg Trial utopian mandate—to judge Nazi leaders for their war crimes against humanity, however that rules out the impact that people serving in such posts have, individually. At the same time, I tried to make a convincing case in this book that the Nuremberg trials did indeed sow the seeds that bring about the death of the rule of law. How? By creating and expanding a international-governed criminal court for a special category of "war crimes", based on "positive law" which allowed the foundation of "Natural Law" to be excluded in such tribunals.

The precedent set by this international court, (now located at the Hague), has provided little justice over the past sixty years to tyrants, dictators, and genocidal maniacs like Pol Pot, Osama bin Laden, Slobodan Milosevic, Saddam Hussein, but has only burdened those bound by traditional morality, with extraneous demands lacking any merit, and preventing the swift justice or victor's justice of pre-Nuremberg trial cases where the obviously guilty tyrant and his henchmen, the enablers and those who profited from his crimes of infamy, were not accorded the respect and decency of a "trial" but were rightly summarily executed if they didn't, like Hitler, Goebbels, Goering or Himmler, have the courage to save humanity the cost of a bullet to the head or the rope of the hangman, and commit suicide.

On the contrary, it has allowed liberal legal scholars like Dershowitz, Laurence Tribe (Harvard), Jonathan Turley (George Washington), M. Cherif Bassiouni (DePaul), Akhil Reed Amar (Yale), Cass Sunstein, Richard A. Posner, Richard Epstein (U of Chicago), Erwin Chemerinsky, Lawrence Lessing, Richard Dworkin, Eugene Volokh and the majority of law professors and liberal legislators who hold ideas or write about international criminal Tribunals in law reviews, or the legal status of the prisoners at Guantanamo Bay, to pontificate on the idea of "equal rights" which are specifically linked to our moral and ethical Judeo-Christian culture, as applying to *anyone* who is found to be involved in this war in any way, including those specifically designated as "illegal combatants" by Geneva Convention, as well as such terrorists who we find in America, despite the fact that the Constitution merely "recognizes" "unalienable rights", and said Constitution only having authority over American Citizens. In trying to link the procedures of their detention to the FISA Court and see these enemy combatants as having the right to our criminal court system, by using the civil rights movement's rhetoric comparing Islamist radical's rights on equal terms with American citizen's constitutional rights is beyond the pale. Incidentally, not even the utopian bureaucrats that drafted the Geneva Conventions expected them to apply to: (1) illegal enemy combatants (i.e., people who dressed up like civilians to blend in fighting soldiers); (2) radical Islamic terrorists (or others if this ilk) who have no country. Ironically, a recent Supreme Court decision regarding the status of the Guantanamo detainees, has said the Geneva Convention protocols do apply to enemy combatants, and they must be accorded all of the rights and privileges ensconced in the Constitution of The United States of America. Even the Defense Department, perhaps reacting to pressure of the liberal media and thier pressure groups, has treated the Guantanamo detainees with such deference and respect that the facility is colloquially called by conservative radio commentator, Rush Limbaugh as, "Club Gitmo."

It is prudent to remember that historically, the Geneva Conventions was a treaty which outlined the rules of war and treatment of captured soldiers between *nations*, not individuals. In a sane society, where evil men threaten to destroy the peace of civilized nations that respect a democratic republic, the rule of law, and the Judeo-Christian tradition, the only rule of war can be to quickly rise up and utterly destroy those people who, by their very existence, are sworn to annihilate the very existence of civil societies. The best example of this is the Israeli Defense Force, as it is presently doing as it wages war against its sworn enemies, Hamas in the south (Gaza) and Hezbollah in the North (Lebanon). May America, before its too late, have the fortitude to withdraw from the treaty that gave us the Geneva Conventions, suspend habeas corpus as Lincoln courageously did, and utterly destroy our sworn enemies. We must not give them a

Nuremberg-style trial which only makes a mockery of the rule of law, justice, and our sacred Judeo-Christian traditions.

The treacherous, ignoble legacy of Nuremberg, so clear in hindsight, is that UN bureaucratic bungling and inefficiency plunged the world as it was into the perpetual abyss of genocide after genocide after genocide after genocide—in Cambodia, the former Yugoslavia, and Rwanda. The Nuremberg Trials have demonstrated to the world, that legal machinery alone will never put an end to man's inhumanity to man. Professor Dershowitz argues that the very purpose of the tribunals were to set up a court system to condemn at least some of these war crimes, genocide, and crimes against humanity and show a unity in the world community for some level of broadly accepted the rule of law.

The United States, perhaps because of the pathetic legacy of the shortsightedness and ineptitude of Nuremberg still ringing in its ears, has, to date, refused to officially support or participate the International Criminal Court based at The Hague, which has just recently come into existence. The "International Criminal Court" has the same mandate to prevent, deter, and punish the kinds of crimes against humanity, which the Nuremberg Tribunal had, and is based on the same form of "positive law" for its foundation. I have to disagree with the statement that: "only time will tell whether the Nuremberg trials were the beginning of a new regime of enforceable international criminal law or merely an important incident in history." [33] History has spoken as what some writers have already called, "World War III" rages at Israel's northern and southern borders, while the "international community" sits on the sideline and reflexively urges Israel to exercise "restraint" against a religiously fanatical entity that has, as part of it's religious duty, to "wipe Israel off the map" and "to push Israel into the sea." This is the ignoble legacy of Nuremberg—the apotheosis of liberal utopianism.

Following the precedent of the Nuremberg Trail philosophy long, ignoble legacy is the present the Iraq Trials. Saddam Hussein has been hanged, his cousin, "Chemical Ali" has recently been hanged, and however, they are but two men in a genocidal Baathist regime that lasted forty years. This was a regime that murdered hundreds of thousands of Iraqi Jews, Sunni and Shiite Muslims as well as tens of thousands of Iranians. For what purpose were these Iraq trials? So that he and his cousin, and a few other low level soldiers can face an international tribunal? As others come before the Iraqi tribunal which, despite multiple murders of defense attorneys and prosecutors, is still functioning, (no doubt by his Baathist cohorts and Sunni Arab sympathizers) the question remains, will the current precedent remain with Saddam's Goering-esque rants and raves having turned the entire Iraq Trials into a three-ring circus?[34] Dershowitz remains committed to the UN and its machinery to dispense justice—the International Court, and states that the essence of the Nuremberg Tribunal was, in the eyes of the international community, "that must do justice and be seen to do justice. It will be a daunting task." [35]

To Professor Dershowitz, I demur. This Gordian knot [the UN and its tribunals] cannot be untied for it was conceived and birthed in futility, vanity, inefficiency and irrelevance. How can one do justice when the Nuremberg Tribunal made two intractable and egregious errors as its foundation from the very beginning—(1) It judged only a minuscule number of Nazi murders, spitting in the face of every Jewish person who lost a loved one, a friend or an acquaintance in Hitler's ghastly crematoria; (2) The UN's Nuremberg Tribunal reliance *solely* on positive jurisprudence; a philosophy of law that insists on the complete separation and rigid segregation between law and morality, where former adherence in Anglo-American law insisted on moral justice out of the Judeo-Christian tradition, was officially viewed as anachronistic, unworkable, and sectarian. If history has taught us anything is that natural law, "the law of Nature and Nature's God" is evitable and that as a nation that venerates the rule of law comes into conflict with a savage, brutal people; an evil nation if you will, whose law is their own perverse creed—Power trumps Truth. On this issue, recently one of our astute readers of WorldNetDaily wrote the following prescient remarks:

> Western civilization ceased to exist in the 20th century and it's decline was evident long before the Nazi Holocaust in which Europe, as the pinnacle of Western civilization, was complicit. It may even be argued, as professor Paul Eidelberg does in *A Jewish Philosophy of History*, that "the demise of Western civilization began with Machiavelli, whose ethically neutral political science came to fruition in the democratic atheism of the European Enlightenment." [36]

Lord Acton once famously remarked: "The central idea of Machiavelli is that the state power is not bound by the moral law. The law is not above the state, but below it." For this reason, who was right—St. Thomas Aquinas or Machiavelli—the Constitution's Framers or modern-day liberal academics? . . . Jerusalem or Athens? Does, as JFK stated, the rights of man come from the generosity of the State, or from the mouth of God? I believe St. Aquinas was right. What supreme law can We the People put our faith and hope in when confronted with the pure evil and savagery of Hitler's Holocaust against the Jewish people? Or our would be Hitler's of modern times?—Osama bin Laden, president Mahmoud Ahmadinejad and the Iranian Mullahs, the Saudi Arabian Sheiks, Hezbollah, Hamas and the world-wide Muslim jihad against Jews, Christians and the West. The answer is found in the sublime words of Thomas Jefferson, one America's greatest presidents and the father of the Declaration of Independence—". . . the law of Nature and of Nature's God."

'The law of Nature' (= Natural Law) and 'Nature's God' (= the Bible) was the precious heritage bequeathed to all Americans by the Constitution's Framers. If we squander so great a gift by our forefathers, how shall we escape the collapse of Western civilization that will inexorably follow?

Appendix

* *The material for this section has been used with expressed permission of Wikipedia.org.*

The main trial

The International Military Tribunal was opened on October 18, 1945, in the Supreme Court Building in Berlin. The first session was presided over by the Soviet judge, Nikitchenko. The prosecution entered indictments against 24 major war criminals and six criminal organizations - the leadership of the Nazi party, the Schutzstaffel (SS) and Sicherheitsdienst (SD), the Gestapo, the Sturmabteilung (SA) and the High Command of the German armed forces (OKW).

The indictments were for: Participation in a common plan or conspiracy for the accomplishment of crime against peace Planning, initiating and waging wars of aggression and other crimes against peace War crimes Crimes against humanity

The 24 accused were:

"**I**" indicted "**G**" indicted and found guilty "º" Not Charged

Name	**Count**				**Sentence**	**Notes**
	1	**2**	**3**	**4**		
Martin Bormann	I	º	G	G	Death	Successor to Hess as Nazi Party Secretary. Sentenced to death in absentia, remains found in 1972.
Karl Dönitz	I	G	G	º	10 years	Leader of the *Kriegs-marine* from 1943, succeeded Raeder. Initiator of the U-boat campaign. Became President of Germany following Hitler's death. In evidence presented at the trial of Karl Dönitz on his orders to the U-boat

						fleet to breach the London Rules, Admiral Chester Nimitz stated that unrestricted submarine warfare was carried on in the Pacific Ocean by the United States from the first day that nation entered the war. Dönitz was found guilty of breaching the 1936 Second London Naval Treaty, but his sentence was not assessed on the ground of his breaches of the international law of submarine warfare.
Hans Frank	I	o	G	G	Death	Reich Law Leader 1933-1945 and Governor-General of the General Government in occupied Poland 1939-1945. Expressed repentance.
Wilhelm Frick	I	G	G	G	Death	Hitler's Minister of the Interior 1933-1943 and Reich Protector of Bohemia-Moravia 1943-1945. Authored the Nuremberg Race Laws.
Hans Fritzsche	I	I	I	o	Acquitted	Popular radio commentator, and head of the news division of the Nazi Propaganda Ministry. Tried in place of Joseph Goebbels.

Walther Funk	I	G	G	G	Life Imprisonment	Hitler's Minister of Economics. Succeeded Schacht as head of the Reichsbank. Released due to ill health on May 16, 1957.
Hermann Göring	G	G	G	G	Death	Reichsmarschall Commander of the Luftwaffe 1935-1945, Chief of the 4-Year Plan 1936-1945, and several departments of the SS. Committed suicide the night before his execution.
Rudolf Hess	G	G	I	I	Life Imprisonment	Hitler's deputy, flew to Scotland in 1941 in attempt to broker peace with Great Britain. After trial, committed to Spandau Prison; died in 1987.
Alfred Jodl	G	G	G	G	Death	Wehrmacht Generaloberst, Keitel's subordinate and Chief of the O.K.W.'s Operations Division 1938-1945. Subsequently exonerated by German court in 1953.
Ernst Kaltenbrunner	I	o	G	G	Death	Highest surviving SS-leader. Chief of RSHA 1943-1945, the central Nazi intelligence organ. Also, commanded many of the Einsatzgruppen and several concentration camps.

Wilhelm Keitel	G	G	G	G	Death	Head of Oberkommando der Wehrmacht (OKW) 1938-1945.
Gustav Krupp von Bohlen und Halbach	I	I	I	I	----	Major Nazi industrialist. C.E.O of Krupp A.G 1912-1945. Medically unfit for trial. The prosecutors attempted to substitute his son Alfried (who ran Krupp for his father during most of the war) in the indictment, but the judges rejected this as being too close to trial. Alfried was tried in a separate Nuremberg trial for his use of slave labor, thus escaping the worst notoriety and possibly death.
Robert Ley	I	I	I	I	----	Head of DAF, The German Labour Front. Suicide on October 25, 1945, before the trial began.
Baron Konstantin von Neurath	G	G	G	G	15 years	Minister of Foreign Affairs 1932-1938, succeeded by Ribbentrop. Later, Protector of Bohemia and Moravia 1939-1943. Resigned in 1943 due to dispute with Hitler. Released (ill health) November 6, 1954.
Franz von Papen	I	I	o	o	Acquitted	Chancellor of Germany in 1932 and Vice-Chancellor un-

						der Hitler in 1933-1934. Ambassador to Austria 1934-1938 and ambassador to Turkey 1939-1944. Although acquitted at Nuremberg, von Papen was reclassified as a war criminal in 1947 by a German de-Nazification court, and sentenced to eight years' hard labour. He was acquitted following appeal after serving two years.
Erich Raeder	G	G	G	o	Life Imprisonment	Commander In Chief of the *Kriegsmarine* from 1928 until his retirement in 1943, succeeded by Dönitz. Released (ill health) September 26, 1955.
Joachim von Ribbentrop	G	G	G	G	Death	Ambassador-Plenipotentiary 1935-1936. Ambassador to the United Kingdom 1936-1938. Nazi Minister of Foreign Affairs 1938-1945.
Alfred Rosenberg	G	G	G	G	Death	Racial theory ideologist. Later, Minister of the Eastern Occupied Territories 1941-1945.
Fritz Sauckel	I	I	G	G	Death	*Gauleiter* of Thuringia 1927-1945. Plenipotentiary of the Nazi slave labor program 1942-1945.
Dr. Hjalmar Schacht	I	I	o	o	Acquitted	Prominent banker and economist. Pre-war

						president of the *Reichsbank* 1923-1930 & 1933-1938 and Economics Minister 1934-1937. Admitted to violating the Treaty of Versailles.
Baldur von Schirach	I	°	°	G	20 years	Head of the *Hitlerjugend* from 1933 to 1940, *Gauleiter* of Vienna 1940-1943. Expressed repentance.
Arthur Seyss-Inquart	I	G	G	G	Death	Instrumental in the *Anschluss* and briefly Austrian Chancellor 1938. Deputy to Frank in Poland 1939-1940. Later, Reich Commissioner of the occupied Netherlands 1940-1945. Expressed repentance.
Albert Speer	I	I	G	G	20 Years	Hitler's favorite architect and personal friend, and Minister of Armaments from 1942. In this capacity, he was ultimately responsible for the use of slave labourers from the occupied territories in armaments production.
Julius Streicher	I	°	°	G	Death	*Gauleiter* of Franconia 1922-1945. Incited hatred and murder against the Jews through his weekly newspaper, *Der Stürmer*.

"I" indicted **"G"** indicted and found guilty **"o"** Not Charged

Throughout the trials, specifically between January and July 1946, the defendants and a number of witnesses were interviewed by American psychiatrist Leon Goldensohn. His notes detailing the demeanour and personality of the defendants survive. The death sentences were carried out October 16th 1946 by hanging using the standard drop method instead of long drop. The French judges suggested the use of a firing squad for the military condemned, as is standard for military courts-martial, but this was opposed by Biddle and the Soviet judges. These argued that the military officers had violated their military ethos and were not worthy of the firing squad, which was considered to be more dignified. The prisoners sentenced to incarceration were transferred to Spandau Prison in 1947.

The definition of what constitutes a war crime is described by the Nuremberg Principles, a document which was created as a result of the trial. The medical experiments conducted by German doctors and prosecuted in the so-called Doctors' Trial led to the creation of the Nuremberg Code to control future trials involving human subjects.

Of the organizations the following were found not to be criminal: Reichsregierung, Oberkommando and Generalstab der Wehrmacht.

ENDNOTES

ACKNOWLEDGMENTS

1. Dictated in Che's café (his home in Southfield, Michigan) on 9 June 2005.

2. Paul Johnson, "Quctes, " *Spectator*, January 2005, quote at: http://homepage. eircom. net/~odyssey/Politics/Quotes/Paul_Johnson.html.

PROLOGUE

1. Albert Carr, *Napoleon Speaks* (Viking Press, New York, 1941), p. 383.

2. Ellis Washington, *The Inseparability of Law and Morality: The Constitution, Natural Law and the Rule of Law* (Maryland: University Press of America, 2002), See, e.g., Chapter 4—*The Nuremberg Trials: The Birth of the Death of the Rule of Law.*

3. ELLIS WASHINGTON, "The Nuremberg Trials: The Death of the Rule of Law (In International Law)" 49 *Loyola Law Review* 101 (2003), pp. 76-95.

4. Hermann Jahrreiss, Professor of Law at Cologne and associate defense counsel for defendant Jodl, skillfully and with some success utilized the "act of state" defense and the doctrine of absolute sovereignty. Both legal philosophies came directly out of John Austin's *Providence.* Jahrreiss presented a lengthy apologetic on jurisprudence considerations of the trial. His discourses epitomize the most extensive attempt by defense counsel to specify a philosophical foundation for the defense's case. 17 IMT 458-94. For an interesting and engaging commentary by Jahrreiss reflecting on his Nuremberg Trial experience, see his testimony before the United States Military Tribunal at Nuremberg as an expert defense witness on German constitutional law. 3 IMT 252-84. *See also* 2 *Hermann Jahrreiss, Die Fortentwicklung des Volkerrechts, Jahrbuch fur Internationales und Auslandisches Offentliches Recht* 654-66 (1949), *reprinted in Hermann Jahrreiss, Mensch und Staat* 233-53 (Cologne ed., 1957).

5. *See generally* Jean Bodin, *Six Books of the Commonwealth* 25, 28 (M. J. Tooley trans., Oxford ed. 1955) (1576) (providing a comprehensive starting point for the study of legal history). The previous Western conception of law as subsequent and superior to man was now beginning to be replaced with law as a mere tool or servant of the state. *Id.* However, in Bodin's work, *The Prince,* though freed from the *law of man* and a law unto himself, medieval understandings of the law still constrained him to the *universal natural law* precepts as well as to certain common ecumenical precepts to which all mankind must adhere. Nonetheless, the break with the medieval world of "the Law of Nature and of Nature's God" as Jefferson codified two hundred years later as natural law philosophy in America's Declaration of Independence, was in the sixteenth century already being rent in two like the Temple veil of the Bible when Christ died on the cross. *Matthew* 27:51 (King James). *See generally,* The Declaration of Independence (U.S. 1776) (exposing a natural law philosophy).

6. The rough draft of the Declaration of Independence 28 June, 1776—

> As it probably read when Jefferson submitted it for corrections. In the original text there are some changes: these are indicated by [.....].

Most of these changes seem to be by Jefferson himself, but some of these are in a handwriting that resembles that of Adams.

A Declaration by the Representatives of United States of America, in General Congress Assembled

When, in the course of human events, it becomes necessary for a people to advance from that subordination in which they have hitherto remained, and to assume among the powers of the earth, the equal and independent station to which the laws of nature and of nature's god entitle them, a decent respect to the opinions of mankind requires that they should declare the causes which impel them to the change

We hold these truths to be [sacred and undeniable] selfevident, that all men are created equal and independent; that from that equal creation they derive in rights inherent and inalienables, among which are the preservation of life, and liberty and the pursuit of happiness; that to secure these ends, governments are instituted among men, deriving their just powers from the consent of the governed; that whenever any form of government shall become destructive of these ends, it is the right of the people to alter or to abolish it, and to institute new government, laying its foundation on such principles and organizing it's powers in such form, as to them shall seem most likely to effect their safety and happiness. prudence, indeed, will dictate that governments long established should not be changed for light and transient causes: and accordingly all experience hath shewn that mankind are more disposed to suffer while evils are sufferable, than to right themselves by abolishing the forms to which they are accustomed. but when a long train of abuses and usurpations, begun at a distinguished period, and pursuing invariably the same object evinces a design to [subject] reduce them to arbitrary power, it is their right, it is their duty, to throw off such government, and to provide new guards for their future security. --

Such has been the patient sufferance of these colonies; and such is now the necessity which constrains them to expunge their former systems of government. the history of his present majesty is a history of unremitting injuries and usurpations, among which no fact stands single or solitary to contradict the uniform tenor of the rest, all of which have in direct object the establishment of an absolute tyranny over these states. to prove this, let facts be submitted to a candid world, for the truth of which we pledge a faith yet unsullied by falsehood.

He has refused his assent to laws, the most wholesome and necessary for the public good:

He has forbidden his governors to pass laws of immediate and pressing importance, unless suspended in their operation till his assent should be obtained; and when so suspended, he has neglected utterly to attend to them.

He has refused to pass other laws for the accommodation of large districts of people unless those people would relinquish the right of representation [in the legislature], a right inestimable to them and formidable to tyrants only:

He has dissolved representative houses repeatedly, for opposing with manly firmness his invasions on the rights of the people.

[He has dissolved] he has refused for a long space of time, to cause others to be elected, whereby the legislative powers, incapable of annihilation, have returned to the people at large for their exercise, the state remaining in the meantime exposed to all the dangers of invasion from without, and convulsions within:

He has endeavored to prevent the population of these states; for that purpose obstructing the laws for naturalization of foreigners; refusing to pass others to encourage their migration hither, and raising the conditions of new appropriations of lands:

He has suffered the administration of justice totally to cease in some of these colonies, refusing his assent to laws for establishing judiciary powers:

He has made our judges dependent on his will alone, for the tenure of their offices, and the amount of their salaries.

He has erected a multitude of new offices by a self-assumed power, and sent hither swarms of officers to harrass our people, and eat out their substance.

He has kept among us, in times of peace, standing armies and ships of war:

He has affected to render the military, independent of and superior to civil power:

He has combined with others to subject us to a jurisdiction foreign to our constitutions, and unacknowledged by our laws; giving his assent to their pretended acts of legislation, for quartering large bodies of armed troops among us;

For protecting them, by mock trial, from punishment for any murders [which] they should commit on the inhabitants of these states; for cutting off our trade with all parts of the world;

For imposing taxes on us without our consent;

For depriving us of the benefits of trial by jury;

For transporting us beyond seas to be tried for pretended offenses;

For taking away our charters, and altering fundamentally the forms of our governments;

For suspending our own legislatures, and declaring themselves invested with power to legislate for us in all cases whatsoever;

He has abdicated government here, withdrawing his governors, and declaring us out of his alegiance and protection;

He has plundered our seas, ravaged our coasts, burnt our towns, and destroyed the lives of our people:

He is at this time transporting large armies of foreign mercenaries to compleat the works of death, desolation and tyranny, already begun with circumstances of cruelty and perfidy unworthy the head of a civilized nation:

He has endeavored to bring on the inhabitants of our frontiers the merciless Indian savages, whose known rule of warfare is an undistinguished destruction of all ages, sexes and conditions of existence:

He has incited treasonable insurrections of our fellow citizens with the allurements of forfeiture and confiscation of our property:

He has waged cruel war against human nature itself, violating it's most sacred rights of life and liberty in the persons of a distant people who never offended him, captivating and carrying them into slavery in another hemispere, or to incure miserable death in their transportation hither. this piratical warfare, the opprobium of infidel powers, is the warfare of the Christian king of Great Britain. [determined to keep open a market where MEN should be bought and sold,] he has prostituted his negative for suppressing every legislative attempt to prohibit or to restrain this execrable commerce [determining to keep open a market where MEN should be bought and sold]: and that this assemblage of horrors might want no fact of distinguished die, he is now exciting those very people to rise in arms among us, and to purchase that liberty of which he had deprived them, by murdering the people upon whom he also obtruded them: thus paying off former crimes committed against the liberties of one people, with crimes which he urges them to commit against the lives of another.

In every stage of these oppressions we have petitioned for redress in the most humble terms: our repeated petitions have been answered only by repeated injury. a prince, whose character is thus marked by every act which may define a tyrant, is unfit to be the ruler of a people who mean to be free. future ages will scarce believe that the hardiness of one man, adventured within the short compass of twelve years only, on so many acts of tyranny without a mask, over a people fostered and fixed in principles of liberty.

Nor have we been wanting in attention to our British brethren. we have warned them from time to time of attempts by their legislature to extend an unwarrantable jurisdiction over these our states. we have reminded them of the circumstances of our emigration and settlement here, no one of which could warrant so strange a pretension: that these were effected at the expence of our own blood and treasure, unassisted by the wealth or the strength of Great Britain: that in constituing indeed our several forms of government, we had adopted one common king, thereby laying a foundation for perpetual league and amity with them: but that submission to their parliament was no part of our constitution, nor ever in idea, if history may be credited: and we appealed to their native justice and magnanimity, as well as to the ties of our common kindred to disavow these usurpations, which were likely to interrupt our correspondence and connections. they too have been deaf to the voice of justice and of consanguinity, and when occasions have been given them, by the regular course of their laws, of removing from their councils the disturbers of our harmony, they have by their free election re-established them in power. at this very time too they are permitting their chief magistrate to send over not only soldiers of our common blood, but Scotch and foreign mercenaries to invade and deluge us in blood. these facts have given the last stab to agonizing affection, and manly spirit bids us to renounce forever these unfeeling brethren. We must endeavor to forget our former love for them, and hold them, as we hold the rest of mankind, enemies in war, in peace friends. we might have been a free and a great people together; but a communication of grandeur and of freedom it seems is below their dignity. be it so, since they will have it: the road to [glory and] happiness [and to glory] is open to us too; we will climb it apart from them [in a seperate state] and acquiesce in the necessity which denounces [pronounces][our [everlasting Adieu!] eternal separation!

> We, therefore, the representatives of the United States of America, in General Congress, assembled do , in the name, and by the authority of the good people of these states, reject and renounce the allegiance and subjection to the kinds of Great Britain and all others we may herafter claim by, through, or under them; we utterly dissolve and break off all political connection which may have heretofore subsisted between us and the people or parliament of Great Britain; and finally we do assert and declare these colonies to be free and independent states, and that as free and independent states they shall herafter have [full] power to levy war, conclude peace, contract alliances, establish commerce, and to do all other acts and things which independent states may of right do. And for the support of this declaration we mutually pledge to each other our lives, our fortunes and our sacred honor.

See text prepared by GMW for *From Revolution to Reconstruction* –an HTML project. Last update: 2003-3-6 time: 10:02 © 1994- 2005. All rights reserved. Department of Humanities Computing.

7. See, e.g., 2 Kings 2:11-13 (King James Version, 1611).

8. Ellis Washington, *Uncollected Papers* (2007).

CHAPTER 1

1. Charles Krauthammer, "The Axis of Petulance," Washington Post, March 1, 2002, p. A25.

2. Henry L. Stimson, [Secretary] of War 1911-1913, 1940 -1945, Secretary of State 1929-1933, was very influential. In fact, he recommended the use of the atomic bomb to Truman (as chair of the Interim Committee). Stimson was encouraged by Conant to publish an article in Harper's Magazine explaining the decision to drop the bomb. Stimson and Conant were both concerned that without public support for a willingness to drop the bomb in the future and the decision to drop it on Hiroshima and Nagasaki in the past, the US would lose clout against the Soviets in UN negotiations and in vies for attracting third world nations (this is also a reason nuclear power was encouraged commercially, to increase U.S. international prestige) see. e.g., Henry L. Stimson, *Essay 1*, *at* www.people.virginia. edu/~ejk4e/hius316/answers.htm. Henry Lewis Stimson was born in New York City on 21st September, 1867. After attending Phillips Andover Academy he graduated from Yale University in 1888. He also studied at Harvard Law School before becoming a lawyer. In 1895 Theodore Roosevelt appointed him as a US District Attorney for the Southern District of New York. He also served as Secretary of War under President William Taft (1911-1913). A member of the New York National Guard (1898-1907) Stimson served in the

United States Army in the First World War. Stimson served as a lieutenant colonel in France before being promoted to command the 31st Field Artillery. A member of the Republican Party, Stimson was appointed by Calvin Coolidge as General Governor of the Philippines (1927-1929) and served as Secretary of State under Herbert Hoover (1929-33).

Stimson left public office when the Democratic candidate, Franklin D. Roosevelt, was elected president in 1933.

Stimson wrote extensively about foreign affairs and books published by him include *American Policy in Nicaragua* (1927), *Democracy and Nationalism in Europe* (1934) and *The Far East Crisis* (1936). On the outbreak of war in Europe in 1939, Stimson was an outspoken advocate of support for the Allies against Nazi Germany. In an attempt to gain political unity for his policies Franklin D. Roosevelt appointed Stimson, a prominent member of the Republican Party, as Secretary of War in his Democratic Party administration.

After the United States entered the Second World War in December, 1941, Stimson, who was now seventy years old, energetically organized America's industrial and economic resources in the fight against Japan and Germany. When the Allies gained the upper hand in 1944 Stimson became an opponent of what he believed were needless bombing attacks on Germany. Stimson, who feared the dangers of communism in post-war Europe, argued that it was not in the long-term interests of the United States for the German economy to be completely destroyed. However, he had little impact on the policies of Curtis LeMay, the US Bomber Commander.

Stimson also objected on moral grounds to terror bombing and feared that the creation of firestorms in the cities of Germany and Japan would lead to charges of war crimes. He was particularly concerned about the United States Army Air Force bombing raid on Tokyo on 9th March, 1945, and told Robert Oppenheimer that he was appalled that there was so little protest in the United States about the tactics being used. Stimson also had strong doubts about the use of the atom bombs on Hiroshima and Nagasaki. Stimson, who did not enjoy a good relationship with President Harry S. Truman, retired from office on 21st September 1945. His memoirs, *On Active Service in Peace and War*, was published in 1948. Henry Lewis Stimson died in Washington on 20th October, 1950. See article on Henry Lewis Stimson at: http://www.spartacus.schoolnet.co.uk/SAstimson. htm. *See also* Robert H. Jackson, *Opening Address for the United States, Nuremberg Trials, in* David M. Adams, Philosophical Problems in the Law, 7, 12 (1992) (describing Henry Stimson's views on war).

3. Martin Luther King, Jr., "Letter from the Birmingham jail," cited in David M. Adams, Philosophical Problems in the Law Belmont: Wadsworth Publishing, 1992, 1996). ELLIS WASHINGTON, "What is Plantation Liberalism?": http://worldnetdaily. com/ news/article.asp?ARTICLE_ID=55553

4. Ann Coulter, *Godless: The Church of Liberalism* (New York: Crown Forum, 2006).

5. IBID.

6. Paul Johnson, *A History of the American People* (New York: HarperCollins, 1998), pp. 800-06, for a engagingly prescient section relating the impact of Progressivism on the political landscape during the late nineteenth and early twentieth century American history; Rebecca Brooks Gruver, *An American History* (New York: Alfred A. Knopf, 2d ed. 1976), pp. 992-95. Shortly after the meeting in Potsdam, Sir Winston Churchill was replaced as Prime Minister by Clement Attlee, following the election victory by the British Labour Party in July, 1945. This replacement in leadership at such a crucial time in history was both shocking and ironic. Shocking, because never in the history of British politics had a sitting wartime Prime Minister not been reelected by a large margin. Ironic, because Churchill, arguably the greatest statesman and political leader of his time, brought England from the brink of annihilation during the almost incessant bombings of Hitler's infamous Luftwaffe by his steely demeanor and the sheer moral force of his will.

7. Ann Coulter, "Liberals: Born to Run," *Human Events*, 7/19/06.

8. For Niebuhr quote see citation posted at: http://www.uusc.org/blog/ 2006/ 07/bad- company.html, UUSC Hotwire: A Human Rights Weblog, 7/27/06.

9. Martin Niemoller, *Why the Church is Not Pacifist: Christianity and Power Politics* (1940) at: http://www.billnourse.com/ QUOTES.HTM. I first heard of Pastor Niemoller's words while listening to my favorite radio talk show host, intellectual, and prolific cultural and political commentator, Dr. Michael Savage. (See www.Michaelsavage.com). He quoted Niemoller in the context of that contemporary societies modern-day Hitler and Minister of Propaganda and hatred of the Martin Goebbels (= Mahmoud Ahmadinejad) and his patron country who holds the distinction of being the largest supplier of world-wide terrorism (= Iran).

10. Hal Lindsey, "Armageddon looms large," http://www.worldnetdaily. com/ news/article.asp?ARTICLE ID=50591, July 7, 2006, at p.1-3.

11. Rebecca Brooks Gruver, *An American History, supra* note 6, at 992-95.

12. Johnson, *supra* note 5, at 804-06; Gruver, *supra* note 3, at 992-96. An important agreement that came out of the Potsdam Conference was the creation of a Council of Foreign Ministers to work out the peace treaties for Italy, Austria, Hungary, Rumania, Bulgaria, and Finland. *Id.* Meetings between July and August 1946 produced peace treaties with all these countries except Austria. *Id.* A treaty with Austria was finally worked out in 1955, and only then were Soviet troops removed. *Id.* at 995.

13. After the London Agreement in August 1945, the Allied Powers drafted an agreement called The Prosecution and Punishment of the Major War Criminals of the European Axis. *Id.* In this document they stated that the reasoning and scope behind the creation of a special International Military Tribunal was to try the twenty-four Nazi defendants "whose offenses have no particular geographical location." "Agreement on the Prosecution and Punishment of Major War Criminals of the European Axis," August 8, 1945, 59 Stat. 1544, 3 Bevans 1238 [hereinafter Treaty of London]. The plan followed the Moscow Declaration, October 30, 1943, 9 Dept. of State Bulletin 307, 310-11. The Charter of the Tribunal, detailed in the Treaty of London articles 6(a), 6(b) and 6(c), listed three specific crimes with which the Nazi defendants were to be charged: crimes against peace, war crimes and crimes against humanity. Treaty of London, *supra* art. 6. However, a fourth charge, common plan or conspiracy, was integrated into the language of count one in the indictment and is generally regarded as applying to all three of the previously cited offenses. 1 International Military Tribunal at Nuremberg, Blue Series, at 29, 226 [hereinafter IMT, with volume number preceding and page number(s) following]. Gruver, *supra* note 6, at 994-95.

14. An original primary source for those interested in this topic is, of course, the comprehensive, *Proceedings of the International Military Tribunal.* All of the references to this trial material are from the November 1945-October 1946 proceedings of the International Military Tribunal at Nuremberg, reported in the first twenty-two volumes of Trial of the Major War Criminals Before the International Military Tribunal (Nuremberg, 1947-1949). Additional material, which also supports the position I argue may be found in the October 1946-April 1949 proceedings of the United States Military Tribunal at Nuremberg, reported in the fifteen volumes of "Trials of the War Criminals Before the Nuremberg Military Tribunals," *Control Council Law* No. 10 (Washington, 1949-1953) [hereinafter NMT, with volume number preceding and page number(s) following].

15. *See generally* Townsend Hoopes & Douglas Brinkley, *FDR and the Creation of the UN* (New Haven: Yale Univ. Press, 1997), pp. 184-87 (stating that Truman was a convinced internationalist). *See generally* Richard C. Hottelet, "Ups and Downs in UN History," 5 *WASH. U. J.L. & POL'Y 17* (2001) (discussing Truman's address to the San Francisco conference).

16. David Golove, "From Versailles to San Francisco: The Revolutionary Transformation of the War Powers," 70 *U. COLO. L. REV.* 1491, 1493-96 (1999) (stating that Roosevelt "undertook the monumental task of vindicating Wilson's vision through the creation of a new league"). The League of Nations was the multi-national globalist organization President Woodrow Wilson helped create to bring peace to the world after World War I.

17. Ibid. (discussing Franklin Roosevelt's role in the creation of the United Nations and his desire to build upon the efforts of Woodrow Wilson).

18. *See generally* Townsend Hoopes & Douglas Brinkley, *FDR and the Creation of the UN* (New Haven: Yale Univ. Press, 1997), pp. 184-87 (stating that

Truman was a convinced internationalist). *See generally* Richard C. Hottelet, "Ups and Downs in UN History," 5 *WASH. U. J.L. & POL'Y 17* (2001) (discussing Truman's address to the San Francisco conference).

19. *See* UN Charter arts. 39-51 (providing that the UN will not have a standing army, however forces will be composed of member states if called upon by the Security Council). *See also* Hoopes & Brinkley, *supra* note 6, at 205 (discussing the UN Charter).

20. U. N. Charter art. 42.

21. For Truman's hopeful assessment regarding the necessity of the UN in maintaining world peace, see Hoopes & Brinkley, *supra* note 13, at 185.

22. UN Charter arts. 9 & 23.

23. Id. at arts. 61, 86, 92.

24. *Cf.* Gruver, *supra* note 6, at 992-96.

25. UN Charter art. 97; *See Maurice Bertrand, The United Nations: Past, Present, And Future* 31-36 (Paris: Editions la Dicouerte, 1997) (discussing the various roles of the organs of the UN).

26. The ideas found in this section of the book outlining the history of international war crimes law, was largely relied upon and/or paraphrased from an excellent article by John Fried's article titled, "GI—World War II Commemoration," at http://www.grolier.com/wwii/_warcrimes.html. Fried was an Adjunct Professor of Political Economy at New York University and formerly Special Legal Consultant to the United States War Crimes Tribunals in Nuremberg. His succinct and broad grasp of international law, particularly as it applies to the history of warfare and war crimes rules, traditions, customs and law going back to antiquity is without parallel in my legal research on this subject.

27. Ibid., quoted by John Fried in his article on International law.

28. Kellogg-Briand Pact of August. 27, 1928.

29. Ibid.; Fried, *supra* note 26.

30. Daniel Jonah Goldhagen, *Hitler's Willing Executioners: Ordinary Germans and the Holocaust* (New York: Knopf, 1996), pp. 9-10. Daniel J. Goldhagen is Assistant Professor of Government and Social Studies at Harvard University and an Associate of Harvard's Minda de Gunzburg Center for European Studies. His doctoral dissertation, which is the basis for his book "Hitler's Willing Executioners: Ordinary Germans and the Holocaust," was awarded the American

Political Science Association's 1994 Gabriel A. Almond Award for the best dissertation in the field of comparative politics.

31. Ibid.; Fried, *supra* note 26.

CHAPTER 2

1. In chapter 18 of Machiavelli famous treatise on political statescraft, *The Prince*, 'What Mode Faith Should Be Kept By Princes,' (chapter 18), Machiavelli posses the polarity of combat—*law* and *force*, and in his treatise seems to appreciate the former, but for pragmatic reasons, favor the latter—force. Niccolo Machiavelli, *The Prince* (Penguin Books, New York, 1952), p. 69. Hitler, with his egregiously discriminatory and racist Nuremberg Laws, his singular war against Europe, Russia and the United States, and his apotheosis, the Holocaust, took Machiavelli's political and legal theories to nihilistic levels.

2. Some classics on the subject of legal philosophy and the history of law are the following works: Sir Henry Maine, *Lectures on the Early History of Institutions* chs. 12-13 (4th ed., Gaunt 1998) (London: John Murry Ltd., 1875) (discussing English sovereignty and empire); 2 James Bryce, *Studies in History and Jurisprudence*, ch. 10 (New York: Oxford Press, American Branch, 1901) (explaining the nature of legal and practical sovereignty); H. L. A. Hart, *The Concept of Law*, chs. 2-3 (1961) [hereinafter Hart, Concept of Law] (addressing the variety of laws and commands in society); Roger Fisher, "Bringing Law to Bear on Governments," 74 *Harvard Law Review* 1130, 1130-40 (1961) (suggesting that a realistic approach to international law should understand motivations for domestic governmental compliance). Ronald Dworkin called legal positivism the form of law "accepted in one form or another by most working and academic lawyers who hold views on jurisprudence." Ronald M. Dworkin, "The Model of Rules," 35 U. CHI. L. REV. 14, 17 (1967), *reprinted as* "Is Law a System of Rules?," *in* Essays in Legal Philosophy 25, 28 (Robert S. Summers ed., 1968). *See also* John W. Salmond, *The First Principles of Jurisprudence*, 97-98 (London: Stevens & Haynes 1893) (giving definitions of law by famous scholars). In his writings Salmond protested against "the creed of what is termed the English school of jurisprudence" because it "attempted to deprive the idea of law of that ethical significance which is one of its most essential elements." *Id.* at 9, 10.

3. *See infra* notes 57-65 and accompanying text (discussing articles that get bogged down with such minutiae).

4. *See* Robert H. Jackson, *Opening Address for the United States, Nuremberg Trials, in* David M. Adams, Philosophical Problems in the Law, 14-20 (1992)(stating the basis on which the Tribunal will achieve justice).

5. *Common Law*:

> The system of jurisprudence, which originated in England and was later applied in the United States, which is based on judicial precedent rather than statutory laws . . . the Common law is generally derived from *principles* rather than *rules*; it does not consist of absolute, fixed, and inflexible rules, but rather of broad and comprehensive principles based on justice, reason, and common sense. It is of judicial origin and promulgation. Its principles have been determined by the social needs of the community . . . .

Barron's Law Dictionary 81 (Steven H. Gifis, ed., 2d ed. 1984) (italics mine). *See also Miller v. Monson*, 37 N.W.2d 543, 547 (1949) (defining common law).

6. See Adams, *supra* note 4, at 20. *See generally* Hans Kelsen, *General Theory of Law and State* (Cambridge: Harvard University Press, 1945), pp. 58-61, 143-44 (stating that all laws, not only those granting rights and powers, can be reduced to such "primary norms" whereby sanctions can be imposed).

7. Martin Luther King, Jr.'s, "Letter from Birmingham Jail," at http://almaz.com/nobel/peace/MLK-jail.html. Written on slips of toilet paper and other scap pieces of paper while King and some of his colleagues were unjustly imprisoned for marching in Birmingham, Alabama on April 16, 1963. A little later in this magnificent essay King quotes a famous poet: "As T. S. Eliot who presciently intoned: "The last temptation is the greatest treason: To do the right deed for the wrong reason."

8. ADAMS, *supra* note 4, at 20. A well-known precept of English Common law held that if an official abused the power of his office, he would lose the protection of his office and become liable to the citizen right-holder whose rights would be upheld by the sovereign (the Tribunal, court, etc.). *See, e.g., Johnstone v. Pedlar*, [1921] 2 A.C. 262, 275 (appeal taken from Ir.).

> When a wrong has been done by the King's officer to a British subject, the person wronged has no legal remedy against the Sovereign, for "the King can do no wrong"; but he may sue the King's officer for the tortuous act, and the latter cannot plead the authority of the Sovereign, for from the maxim that the King cannot do wrong it follows, as a necessary consequence, that the King cannot authorize wrong.

Id. at 275 (citations omitted).

9. David Barton, The Myth of Separation: What is the Correct Relationship Between Church and State? A Revealing Look at What the Founders and Early Courts *Really Said*, 196-97 (6th ed. 1992).

10. ADAMS, *supra* note 4, at 20.

11. John Hobbes, *Levianthan: Or the Matter, Form, and Power of a Commonwealth Ecclesiastical and Civil* [1651] (New York: Oxford University Press, 1988). As used by Thomas Hobbes in his treatises *Leviathan* and *De Cive*, natural law is a precept, or general rule, found out by reason, by which a man is forbidden to do that which is destructive of his life, or takes away the means of

preserving the same; and to omit that by which he thinks it may best be preserved. There are nine Laws. The first two are expounded in chapter XIV ("of the first and second natural laws; and of contracts"); the others in chapter XV ("of other laws of nature").

1. His first Law of nature is that every man ought to endeavour peace, as far as he has hope of obtaining it; and when he cannot obtain it, that he may seek and use all helps and advantages of war.

2. The second Law of nature is that a man be willing, when others are so too, as far forth, as for peace, and defence of himself he shall think it necessary, to lay down this right to all things; and be contented with so much liberty against other men, as he would allow other men against himself.

3. The third Law is *that men perform their covenants made*. In this law of nature consisteth the fountain and original of justice... when a covenant is made, then to break it is unjust and the definition of injustice is no other han the not performance of covenant. And whatsoever is not unjust is just.

4. The fourth Law is that a man which receiveth benefit from another of mere grace, endeavour that he which giveth it, have no reasonable cause to repent him of his good will. Breach of this law is called ingratitude.

5. The fifth Law is complaisance: that every man strive to accommodate himself to the rest. The observers of this law may be called sociable; the contrary, stubborn, insociable, forward, intractable.

6. The sixth Law is that upon caution of the future time, a man ought to pardon the offences past of them that repenting, desire it.

7. The seventh Law is that in revenges, men look not at the greatness of the evil past, but the greatness of the good to follow.

8. The eighth Law is that no man by deed, word, countenance, or gesture, declare hatred or contempt of another. The breach of which law is commonly called contumely.

9. The ninth Law is that every man acknowledge another for his equal by nature. The breach of this precept is pride.

12. Adams, *supra* note 4, at 20. *See also* Hagerstrom, *Inquiries into the Nature of Law and Morals* (Olivecrona ed.) (Translated by C. D. BROAD) (Stockholm: Almquist & Wiksell, 1953), p. 217 ("[T]he whole theory of subjective rights of private individuals . . . is incompatible with the imperative theory."). "The description of them [claims to legal protection] as rights is wholly derived from the idea that the law which is concerned with them is a true expression of rights and duties in the sense in which the popular notion of justice understands these terms." *Id.* at 221.

13. According to Hart, "[Hagerstrom] insisted that if laws were merely com-

mands the notion of an individual's right was really inexplicable, for commands are, as he said, something which we either obey or we do not obey; they do not confer rights." H. L. A. Hart, "Positivism and The Separation of Law and Morals," 71 *Harvard Law Review* 593, 605 (1958) [hereinafter Hart, "Positivism and Separation"].

14. George Orwell, *Animal Farm* (New York: Harcourt, Brace & Co., 1946); *1984* (London: Penguin Books, 1949).

Selected Salient Quotes from Orwell's 1984–Book One, Chapter 1

> "The thought police would get him just the same. He had committed—would have committed, even if he had never set pen to paper—the essential crime that contained all others in itself. Thoughtcrime, they called it. Thoughtcrime was not a thing that could be concealed forever. You might dodge successfully for a while, even for years, but sooner or later they were bound to get you."

> "People simply disappeared, always during the night. Your name was removed from the registers, every record of everything you had ever done was wiped out, your one-time existence was denied and then forgotten. You were abolished, annihilated: vaporized was the usual word."

Book One, Chapter 2

> "Nearly all children nowadays were horrible. What was worst of all was that by means of such organizations as the Spies they were systematically turned into ungovernable little savages, and yet this produced in them no tendency whatever to rebel against the discipline of the Party. On the contrary, they adored the Party and everything connected with it... All their ferocity was turned outwards, against the enemies of the State, against foreigners, traitors, saboteurs, thought-criminals. It was almost normal for people over thirty to be frightened of their own children."

> "Thoughtcrime does not entail death: thoughtcrime *is* death."

Book One, Chapter 3

> "If the Party could thrust its hand into the past and say this or that even, *it never happened*—that, surely, was more terrifying than mere torture and death."

Book One, Chapter 5

> "Don't you see that the whole aim of Newspeak is to narrow the range of thought?... Has it ever occurred to your, Winston, that by the year 2050, at the very latest, not a single human being will be alive who could understand such a conversation as we are having now?...The whole climate of thought will be different. In fact, there will *be* no thought, as we understand it now.

Orthodoxy means not thinking—not needing to think. Orthodoxy is unconsciousness." - Syme

Book One, Chapter 6

"Your worst enemy, he reflected, was your nervous system. At any moment the tension inside you was liable to translate itself into some visible symptom."

Book One, Chapter 8

"...to do anything that suggested a taste for solitude, even to go for a walk by yourself, was always slightly dangerous. There was a word for it in Newspeak: *ownlife*..."

Book Two, Chapter 9

"In Oceania at the present day, Science, in the old sense, has almost ceased to exist. In Newspeak there is no word for 'Science.' The empirical method of thought, on which all the scientific achievements of the past were founded, is opposed to the most fundamental principles of Ingsoc."

"The citizen of Oceania is not allowed to know anything of the tenets of the other two philosophies, but he is taught to execrate them as barbarous outrages upon morality and common sense. Actually, the three philosophies are barely distinguishable..."

"Oceania has no capital, and its titular head is a person whose whereabouts nobody knows."

"Sanity is not statistical."

Book Two, Chapter 10

"It was curious to think that the sky was the same for everybody, in Eurasia or Eastasia as well as here. And the people under the sky were also very much the same—everywhere, all over the world, hundreds or thousands of millions of people just like this, people ignorant of one another's existence, held apart by walls of hatred and lies, and yet almost exactly the same—people who had never learned to think but were storing up in their hearts and bellies and muscles the power that would one day overturn the world."

Quotes from George Orwell's *Animal Farm*

(1) Old Major warns, "Your resolution must never falter. No argument must lead you astray. Never listen when they tell you that Man and the animals have a common interest....we must not come to resemble him...No animal must ever live in a house or sleep in a bed, or wear clothes, or drink alcohol, or smoke tobacco, or touch money, or engage in trade."

(2) Orwell narrates, "Nobody stole, nobody grumbled over his rations, the quarreling and biting and jealousy which had been normal features of life in the old days had almost disappeared."

(3) Squealer consoles the animals, saying, "Do not imagine, comrades, that leadership is a pleasure. On the contrary, it is a deep and heavy responsibility. No one believes more firmly than Comrade Napoleon that all animals are equal. He would be only too happy to let you make your decisions for yourselves. But sometimes you might make the wrong decisions, comrades, and then where should we be?" The classic hypocrisy seen here is too hard to miss.

(4) Orwell explains, "Once again the animals were conscious of a vague uneasiness. Never to have any dealings with human beings, never to engage in trade, never to make use of money—had not these been among the earliest resolutions passed at the first triumphant Meeting when Jones was expelled?"

(5) As Napoleon was deceiving the neighboring farmers he was also tricking his own animals. The scapegoat was again Snowball. "Whenever anything went wrong it became usual to attribute it to Snowball." In fact many of the claims begin to sound ridiculous to the objective mind. Of course, Squealer's mission is to keep everything subjective in the minds of the animals.

(6) So Napoleon, with the help of his dogs, slaughters anyone who is said to be disloyal. "...the tale of confessions and executions went on, until there was a pile of corpses lying before Napoleon's feet and the air was heavy with the smell of blood, which had been unknown there since the expulsion of Jones." To top it off, Napoleon outlaws Beasts of England, which had served as one of the only remaining ties between Animal Farm and old Major.

(7) But when Muriel reads the writing on the barn wall to Clover, interestingly, the words are, "No animal shall kill any other animal without cause."

(8) But to justify this little episode, arrangements to amend the rules are made. "No animal shall drink alcohol to excess."

(9) Orwell states, "Somehow it seemed as though the farm had grown richer without making the animals themselves any richer—except, of course, for the pigs and the dogs."

(10) The 7 Commandments are abridged for the last time, simply reading, "All animals are equal but some animals are more equal than others."

15. Oliver Wendell Holmes served as a United States Supreme Court Justice from 1902-1932, and his opinions (particularly his eloquent dissents), have tremendously shaped the thinking of the modern Court; See, e.g., G. Edward White, *The American Judicial Tradition: Profiles of Leading American Judges* 155-60 (New York: Oxford University Press, 1988).

16. Richard A. Posner, "The Problematics of Moral and Legal Theory," 111 *Harvard Law Review* 1637, 1683, n.88 (1998).

17. *See* Oliver Wendell Holmes, "The Path of Law," 10 *Harvard Law Review* 457 (1897) (viewing law through the utilitarian lens of a tool of social control, experience, and raw, statist power of a sovereign over the people).

18. Ellis Washington, "Reply to Judge Richard A. Posner on the Inseparability of Law and Morality," 3 *Rutgers Journal of Law and Religion* (2001-02), 1.

19. See Holmes, *supra* note 17.

20. Remember Holmes's famous admonition in his seminal work, *The Common Law*, "The life of law has not been logic; it has been experience." Oliver Wendell Holmes, *The Common Law* 1 (Cambridge: Cambridge University Press, 1968) (1881). Justice Holmes' use of the word "logic" has been interpreted to mean:

> [t]he formalistic, religion-based logic that reasoned downward syllogistically from assumed truths about the universe; the proposed counter-system was "experience," the changing "felt necessities" that reflected current social values and were altered by time and circumstances. . . This was merely a fatalistic acceptance that law was not so much the embodiment of reason as a manifestation of dominant beliefs at a given time.

21. G. Edward White, The American Judicial Tradition: Profiles of Leading American Judges (New York: Oxford University Press, 1988), 155-60 (According to Holmes, law "was simply an embodiment of the ends and purposes of a society at a given point in its history.")

22. Albert W. Alschuler, *Life Without Values. The Life, Work, and Legacy of Justice Holmes*, (Chicago: University of Chicago Press, 2000), x.

23. Id. Holmes reduced law to its lowest common denominator to mean "beliefs that have triumphed." 2 *The Holmes-Pollock Letters: The Correspondence of Mr. Justice Holmes and Sir Frederick Pollock* 1874-1932 (Mark DeWolfe Howe ed.) Cambridge: Harvard University Press, 1953) vol. 2, p. 36.

24. Holmes further remarked, "[t]ruth [is] the majority vote of that nation that could lick all others." Oliver Wendell Holmes, "Natural Law," 32 *Harvard Law Review* 40, 40 (1918).

25. Holmes also stressed that "when it comes to the development of a *corpus juris* the ultimate question is what do the dominant forces of the community want and do they want it hard enough to disregard whatever inhibitions may stand in the way." Letter from Oliver Wendell Holmes, Jr., to John C. H. Wu (August 26, 1926), *in* Justice Oliver Wendell Holmes: His Book Notices and Uncollected Letters and Papers 187 (Harry C. Shriver ed., 1936). Holmes re-

marked:

> I see no reason for attributing to man a significance different in kind from that which belongs to a baboon or a grain of sand. I believe that our personality is a cosmic ganglion, just as when certain rays meet and cross there is a white light at the meeting point, but the rays go on after the meeting as they did before, so, when certain other streams of energy cross at the meeting point, the cosmic ganglion can frame a syllogism or wag its tail.

Richard Hertz, Chance and Symbol: A Study in Aesthetic and Ethical Consistency 107 (Chicago: University of Chicago Press, 1948). *See* ELLIS WASHINGTON, *The Inseparability of Law and Morality: The Constitution, Natural Law and the Rule of Law* (Maryland: University Press of America, 2002), *supra* note 18, at n. 26 (discussing in detail the legal writings of Justice Holmes). John Gray's famous is/ought analysis of law expressed the ideas that many legal scholars and jurists held at the turn of the twentieth century stating:

> The great gain in its fundamental conceptions which Jurisprudence made during the last century was the recognition of the truth that the Law of a State . . . is not an ideal, but something which actually exists . . . . It is not that which ought to be, but that which is. To fix this definitely in the Jurisprudence of the Common Law, is the feat that Austin accomplished.

John Chipman Gray, *The Nature and Sources of the Law* 94 (photo. reprint 1972) (2d ed. 1921).

26. Ibid., Holmes, *Uncollected Letters and Papers*.

27. *See generally* Hart, "Positivism and Separation," *supra* note 13, at 593-629 (discussing the positive and negative aspects of legal positivism). H. L. A. Hart's classic writing is still superior to all other attempts on this subject. I am exceedingly indebted to Hart's pioneering work in legal philosophy and this article is heavily reliant on his tremendous contributions to the field, particularly his detailed and copious notes, many of which are referenced in this article. Regarding the writings of Jeremy Bentham on positive law and legal positivism, Hart noted that Bentham, as a personal observer of the anarchy of the French Revolution, sought in his theory of law to expound that certain laws were too morally outrageous and evil and that fighting against such laws had to be seriously considered in any legitimate system of laws. *Id.* at 595-600. Critical questions in separating legality from morality include: (1) If the law is not what it ought to be, if it openly combats what Fuller refers to as the principle of utility, ought we (society) obey it?; (2) Ought we to violate it?; (3) Ought we to remain neutral between the law which commands evil and morality which forbids it? *See* Washington, *Separation of Law and Morality*, *supra* note 1, at 1-15 (discussing a natural law analysis of the exclusionary rule).

28. *See* Edward S. Corwin, "*The "Higher Law" Background of American Constitutional Law*," 42 *Harvard Law Review* 149 (1928) (discussing the evolution of the philosophy of law); Arnold Brecht, "The Myth of Is and Ought," 54 *Harvard Law Review* 811 (1941) (contending that the separation of "is" and "ought" is artificial); Hart, "Positivism and Separation," *supra* note 13, at 593-98 (advocating that there is a division of the law as it is from the law as it ought to be). *But see* Lon Fuller, "Positivism and Fidelity to Law: A Reply to Professor Hart," 71 *Harvard Law Review* 630

(1958) [hereinafter Fuller, "Positivism and Fidelity"] (arguing that Hart's position is contradictory); Lon Fuller, *Anatomy of the Law* (New York: Frederick A. Praeger, 1968), p. 175-86.

29. Bentham's first hand eyewitness account of the horrors of the French Revolution's excesses and his adherence to an exclusionary rule which in essence in an admonition to the verity of natural law as a bulwark against law totally unteethered from morals which Bentham saw failed in the French Revolution. *See supra* note 27. For a short and polemical treatment of this subject see Ellis Washington, "Harvard, the Ivy League & the Forgotten Puritans" http://worldnetdaily.com/news/ article.asp? ARTICLE_ID=56450.

30. With the publication of John Austin's *magnum opus*, *The Province of Jurisprudence Determined*, natural law was now systematically compared and contrasted with what he deemed the superior law—positive law, or law that is posited or delegated by human authority to human subjects, as opposed to the former legal philosophy—natural law, which views law as inseparable from God's universal principles of nature. Austin's work is actually a series of six lectures that were first published in 1832. In the *Province of Jurisprudence*, when Austin writes of law, he refers only to positive law. In this work also originates the dual positive law doctrines of the *command doctrine* (law as a command of a sovereign to its subject that the latter must obey at fear of punishment) and *superior orders* (an order from the sovereign or state must be obeyed). One hundred twelve years after Austin's work on positive law was published, defense attorneys for the Nazi defendants in the Nuremberg Trials so effectively utilized Austin's command and superior orders doctrines as to win the freedom for thirty percent of the defendants from the hangman's noose.

31. Hart, *supra* note 13.

32. Ibid.

33. Austin, *supra* note 30.

34. Ibid.

35. Ibid.

36. Franklin Delano Roosevelt was elected President of the United States for four terms (1933-45). He died in office in 1945, several months into his fourth term and shortly before Germany's surrender. He personally appointed ten (9) Supreme Court Justices–1 Chief Justice and 8 Associate Justices. Here they are named followed by the year of appointment to the Court:

Chief Justice,

1. Harlan Stone (1941)

Associate Justices,

2. Hugo Black (1937)
3. Stanley F. Reed (1938)

4. Felix Frankfurter (1939)
5. William O. Douglas (1939)
6. James F. Byrnes (1941)
7. Robert H. Jackson (1941)
8. Wiley B. Rutledge (1943)
9. Harold H. Burton (1945)

Aside from the launching of the New Deal in 1933, the single most familiar New Deal story is that of the contest between the New Deal and the Nine Old Men. According to this story, the stodgy majority of the Supreme Court, held hostage by the doctrine of laissez-faire, repeatedly shot down New Deal legislation until President Roosevelt, goaded beyond endurance and emboldened by his 1936 landslide majority, challenged the Court directly. Roosevelt proposed that because the Justices were elderly and tired and needed help, he would call for legislation permitting him to appoint new Justices to aid the incumbents with their work. His foes called the plan "Court-packing," and a titanic struggle ensued for the soul of the American Constitution. Finally, the Justices carried out an abrupt "switch in time" that took the steam out of the push to pack the Court. The story ends, as do many great American historical dramas, by giving everybody something. Roosevelt lost his plan but gained a more cooperative Court. The Justices saved the institution of the Court, but gave in to Roosevelt and began upholding New Deal measures. And the people got both a more cooperative Court and a renewed appreciation of their beloved Constitution. *See generally* Barry Cushman, "Rethinking the New Deal Court," 80 *Virginia Law Review* 201 (1994) (detailing the popular story of Roosevelt's court-packing controversy); Marian C. McKenna, *Franklin Roosevelt and the Great Constitutional War: The Court-Packing Crisis of 1937* (NEW YORK: Fordham University Press, 2002) (discussing the Court-packing controversy in great detail). McKenna furnishes a fresh look at the controversy, providing evidence that the Court was not influenced by the re-election of Roosevelt in 1937. *Id.* at xxii. Also detailed is the failure of Roosevelt's attempt to alter the makeup of the Court by way of a convincing defeat of his proposed Judicial Reorganization Bill in the Senate. *Id.* Not quite. First, the myth of the unflinching laissez-faire Court is coming under fire. Professor Barry Cushman of St. Louis University Law School is completing a constitutional history of the New Deal; he rejects as overblown the traditional characterization of the Court as unflinchingly "laissez-faire" until the 1937 "switch in time" that defused the Court-packing plan. Second, many of the New Deal measures that the Court struck down deserved to be struck down—they were badly drafted, violating central constitutional principles and the draftsmen knew or should have known what they were doing. Third, the so-called "switch in time" apparently was not a response to the Court-packing controversy; it represented two Justices' sincere belief that the specific law before them (the National Labor Relations Act) was free of constitutional defect and thus different from the laws they previously had struck down. Cushman's analysis of the actual doctrinal history of the Supreme Court is persuasive, but, nonetheless, the "conventional" story of the battle between creative uses of government power and laissez-faire constitutional theory shaped both American constitutional law and the American people's understanding of how that law has developed over time. Since the 1940s the law academy has been virtually taken over by the positive and has utterly decimated the natural law philosophy which original philosophy of law of the Constitution's Framers.

37. Ibid.

38. Ibid.

39. Holmes, *supra* note 24, at 40.

40. See generally my articles published in www.WorldNetDaily.com on FDR and the tragic legacy of liberalism in modern times in Ellis Washington:

- "FDR's Legacy: Tyranny" – http://worldnetdaily.com/news/article.asp?ARTICLE_ID=54589
- "3 Classical Views on Government" – http://worldnetdaily.com/news/article.asp?ARTICLE_ID=54656
- "Neville Chamberlain's Revenge" – http://worldnetdaily.com/news/article.asp?ARTICLE_ID=55074
- "Is Islam compatible with a Republic?" – http://worldnetdaily.com/news/article.asp?ARTICLE_ID=54848
- "10 Commandments of Post-60s' Liberalism" – http://worldnetdaily.com/news/article.asp?ARTICLE_ID=54952
- "Symposium: Should Public Education be Free?" – http://worldnetdaily.com/news/article.asp?ARTICLE_ID=54467

See also article by Freedom Works cited in *Human Events*, July 24, 2006, titled: "Top 10 Corporate Welfare Queens below for just a small synopsis of FDR's leviathan government legacy":

> Monday, July 24, 2006
> *Top 10 Corporate Welfare Queens Ranked by FreedomWorks.*
>
> These organizations grow fat and rich thanks to special treatment from the federal government. They manipulate the political system to get insider deals, government guarantees, fixed prices and other benefits, paid for by taxpayers and consumers.
>
> 10. *United States Postal Service (USPS)*
> The USPS is a monopoly more interested in job protection than efficiency or innovation. Labor costs consume 80 percent of USPS revenue, while UPS and FedEx spend only 56 percent and 42 percent of their revenue on labor, respectively. Reform would allow competition for mailbox and first-class mail service.

9. *Maritime Shippers and Unions*

The Jones Act mandates that all cargo shipped between U.S. ports—including deep-water shipping to Hawaii and Alaska—must be carried on U.S.-built and flagged vessels. That protectionism costs the economy $1.3 billion a year in higher shipping prices, according to a 1999 study by the International Trade Commission. It's time to repeal the Jones Act restrictions.

8. *National Education Association (NEA)*

The ultimate monopoly is America's K-12 government schools, and the NEA is the gatekeeper that opposes almost any reform. Sheltered from competition, public schools continue to decline despite dramatic increases in per-student spending. States should give all students a voucher that allows them to attend the school of their choice.

7. *FreddieMac and FannieMae*
These are quasi-government companies that purchase wholesale mortgages, but unlike most investment banks, they get special government loans and are backed by an implicit federal guarantee. If the real estate market tanks today, taxpayers could be on the hook for billions. It's time for Freddie and Fannie to grow up and cut the cord.

6. *Big Sugar*

Uncle Sam gives sugar special status and protects growers from competition through import quotas and marketing allotments. A handful of industrial growers dominate the industry and receive more than $1 billion a year in subsidies from rigged prices, according to the GAO. Congress should end sugar's sweet deal.

5. *Big Cotton*

U.S. taxpayers and consumers provide billions of dollars to cotton growers through a numbingly complicated array of programs that violate U.S. trade agreements. One company, Allenberg Cotton of Cordova, Tenn., collected more than $186 million from 1995-2004 just in cash payments, according to the Environmental Working Group. Congress should terminate the cotton program.

4. *Asbestos lawyers*

While trial lawyers of all stripes abuse the legal and political system for personal gain, the asbestos litigation attorneys are a special breed. Runaway asbestos lawsuits have already bankrupted more than seventy American manufacturers, destroying 60,000 jobs and costing billions. Yet most of the litigants aren't sick. Congress should pass medical criteria legislation to stop asbestos pillaging.

3. *Amtrak*

Passenger railroads are a failure in America, and the Amtrak monopoly is the reason. Feather-bedding union rules and money-losing routes to nowhere are the hallmarks of this national embarrassment, which burns through more than $1 billion a year from federal taxpayers. Amtrak should be completely privatized and opened to competition.

2. *Corporation for Public Broadcasting (NPR/PBS)*

Big Bird is on welfare, to the tune of about $347 million a year. While taxpayers foot the bills, Sesame Street's owners make millions from licensing toys and videos. With massive budget deficits and plenty of new channels on cable and satellite radio, it's time for Big Bird and his buddies to get off the dole.

1. *Archer Daniels Midland (ADM)*

From ethanol mandates to sugar subsidies, ADM is a case study in corporate welfare. New studies show that it takes more fossil energy to create corn ethanol than the fuel provides, but Congress is doubling the amount we have to buy anyway.

Wednesday, July 19, 2006
Democrats Unhinged: The Real House Democrat Agenda
Courtesy of the House Republican Conference
The legislation included on *Democrats Unhinged: The Real House Democrat Agenda* has been highlighted because of the considerable support these bills have received from senior members of the House Democrat Caucus, including ranking committee members and members of the elected Democrat leadership.

Each bill highlighted on the agenda is sponsored by a current Democrat ranking member on a House committee of jurisdiction. Many are also cosponsored or supported by members of the House Democrat leadership.

Collectively, these bills provide real insight into the agenda these ranking Democrat members are pursuing.

The legislation listed on *Democrats Unhinged: The Real House Democrat Agenda* is distinct because it shows what Democrat ranking members and elected leaders really support: a radical left-wing agenda that contrasts sharply with the vague and fuzzy public relations agendas that have been (and continue to be) rolled out for public consumption by House Democrat leaders.

10. H.R. 63: Democracy Day Act of 2005 (a.k.a. "The Paid Holiday for Government Union Workers on Election Day Act")

Rep. John Conyers (D.-Mich.), ranking member on the Judiciary Committee, wants government workers to get ANOTHER day off work -- courtesy of the taxpayer - on election day while every other American has to take time away from work or their families to vote ... and everyday taxpayers won't get paid by the federal government to participate in our Democracy like their federal union-member counterparts.

Cosponsors include Democrat leadership and ranking Democrats.

9. H.R. 1018: "The Permanent Welfare Housing Act"

Rep. Charles Rangel (D.-N.Y.), ranking member on the Ways and Means Committee, has ignored all of welfare reform's lessons about helping families exit the cycle of poverty. H.R. 1018 rejects the idea of empowering welfare recipients through the incentives of getting back into the workforce or otherwise giving back to their community.

Public Housing Tenants Respect Act of 2005 amends the United States Housing Act of 1937, removing provisions that residents of public housing are required to participate in eight hours per month of either community service or economic self-sufficiency activities in order to retain their public housing.

Cosponsors include ranking Democrats and other senior Democrats.

8. H.R. Investigate Everything In the current Congress, Rep. Henry Waxman (D.-Calif.), ranking members on the Government Reform Committee, has requested multiple investigations and other information (under the "7 member rule"). Waxman has advocated politically-motivated investigations targeting everything from abstinence-oriented education programs to gun ownership rights for individuals, while criticizing past investigations into serious transgressions of justice like the fiasco at Waco and e-mails that were mysteriously absent from Clinton White House servers as "politically motivated."

7. Massive Tax Increase ActRep. David Obey (D.-Wis.), ranking members on the Appropriations Committee, in the 109th Congress has costly amendments to Budget and various Appropriations bills -- meaning new direct spending offset by increases in taxes.

So far this year, Appropriations Committee Democrats have proposed $45.2 billion in new Democrat spending above and beyond the levels included in FY 2007 appropriations bills -- all of which have been rejected by House Republicans.

6. H.R. 2456: "The Decreased Penalties for Crack Cocaine Act"
Rangel wants to reduce the criminal penalties for crack dealers and users.

H.R. 2456 amends the Controlled Substances Act and the Controlled Substances Import and Export Act to eliminate specified mandatory minimum penalties relating to the trafficking in, and possession, importation, or distribution of, crack cocaine.

Cosponsors include Ranking Democrats and other senior Democrats.

1. H.R. 4683: "The Government-Run Health Care Act"
House Democrats want to create a federal health care system without choices that would combine the efficiency of the DMV and the compassion of the IRS -- and tax you through the nose to get it.

Amends the Social Security Act to add a new title XXII (Medicare for All).
According to the Congressional Research Service, H.R. 4683 amends the Internal Revenue Code to impose: 1) on the income of every individual a tax equal to 1.7 percent of wages received; 2) on every employer an excise tax equal to 7 percent of the wages paid to each employee; and 3) on the self-employment income of every individual, a tax equal to the applicable percentage of the self-employment income for such taxable year.
Cosponsors include ranking Democrats and senior Democrats.

4. H.J.Res. 73: "The Cut-and-Run in Iraq Resolution"

Rep. John Murtha (D.-Pa.), ranking member on the Defense Appropriations Subcommittee, believes that "the presence of U.S. troops in Iraq is impeding this progress" and that "an immediate redeployment of our American forces" is appropriate because "it's time for us to get out." (Press conference, November 17, 2005.)

In an interview with CNN, Murtha was discussing his call for troops to be withdrawn from Iraq. When asked for his thoughts on a timetable for such action, he replied: "I think we cannot win this."

Cosponsors include Democrat leadership, ranking Democrats, and other senior Democrats.

3. H.R. 1300: "The Automatic Voting Rights for Felons Act"

Conyers thinks that murderers, rapists and child molesters aren't having their voices heard by Congress.

H.R. 1300 states that the right of an individual who is a citizen of the United States to vote in any election for Federal office shall not be denied or abridged because that individual has been convicted of a criminal offense.

Cosponsors include ranking Democrats and other senior Democrats.

2. H.Res. 636: "The Second Step in Impeaching President Bush Resolution"

Conyers wishes he could aggressively pursue his legislation to censure, and ultimately impeach, President Bush.

H.Res. 636 seeks to censure President Bush for a slew of unsubstantiated allegations.

Cosponsors include ranking Democrats and other senior Democrats.

1. H.Res. 635: "The First Step in Impeaching President Bush Resolution"

Conyers and House Democrats want to set up a select committee with the purpose of investigating grounds for the impeachment of President Bush.

H.Res. 635 establishes a select committee to investigate the Bush Administration and to make recommendations regarding grounds for possible impeachment.

Cosponsors include Democrat leadership, ranking Democrats and other senior Democrats.

41. *Everson v. Board of Education*, 330 U.S. 1, 13 (1947)(enshrined the judge-created doctrine of 'separation of church and state' into constitutional law)

42. Washington, *Inseparability of Law and Morality*, *supra* note 25, at 1-15.

43. Regarding Darwin, conservative writer, Ann Coulter had her usual circumspect ideas and displayed them with devastating wit and logic:

> On Darwinism and Nazism: Hitler's embrace of Darwinism is not a random fact, unrelated to the reason we know his name. It is impossible to understand Hitler's monstrous views apart from his belief in natural selection applied to races. He believed Darwin's theory of natural selection showed that "science" justified the extermination of the Jews.
>
> On Darwinism's appeal to liberals: Liberals subscribe to Darwinism not because it's "science," which they hate, but out of wishful thinking. Darwinism lets them off the hook morally. Do whatever you feel like doing - screw your secretary, kill Grandma, abort your defective child - Darwin says it will benefit humanity! Nothing is ever wrong as long as you follow your instincts. Just do it - and let Mother Earth sort out the winners and losers.

See "*Where Have You Gone Ronald Reagan: Rants and Reactions to the American Left*," at: Whygrr.blogspot.com/2006/06/ann-coulters-godless-quotes.

44. Kellogg-Briand Pact, August 27, 1928, arts. I-II, 46 Stat. 2343, 94 L.N.T.S. 57.

45. *See* Jackson, *supra* note 4, at 12 (discussing the history of the pre and post

World War I treaties). *See also* English barrister, attorney general, Labor member of Parliament, and chief prosecutor for the United Kingdom, Sir Hartley Shawcross' speeches during the Nuremberg Trials, 3 IMT 91-145. Despite Jackson's impressive skills as a prosecutor, Shawcross was in the opinion of most observers the most philosophically educated of the prosecution counsel who deliberated before the International Military Tribunal. *See* Sir Hartley Shawcross, Opening Statement, 3 IMT 91-145; Closing Statement, 19 IMT 433-529. For subsequent impressions of the Nuremberg Trials, *see* Sir Hartley Shawcross, *International Law: A Statement of the British View of Its Role*, 33 A.B.A. J. 31-35 (1947). For impressions of Robert H. Jackson's contributions during the Nuremberg Trials, *see* Robert Jackson, "Mr. Justice Jackson: Four Lectures in his Honor" 87-136 (1969); Washington, *Inseparability of Law and Morality*, (Maryland: University Press of America, 2002), pp. 1-15.

46. Jackson, *supra* note 4, at 13.

47. Ibid.

48. *Id.* at 14. *See generally* The Hague Convention (IV), October 18, 1907, 36 Stat. 2277, T.S. No. 539, 1 Bevans 631. It is evident, at least by 1907 at the ratification of The Hague Convention, that the illegality of aggressive war was one of the "generally accepted rules of international law."

49. Ibid.

50. Hague Convention (IV), art. I, *supra* note 48. Furthermore, The Hague Convention expressly "prohibited resort to certain methods of waging war."

51. Ibid., (neglecting to provide a workable remedy in the event of a violation); *see also* The Judgment at Nuremberg, 6 *F.R.D.* 69, 1947 Extra LEXIS 1, *113-14 (noting that The Hague Convention did not provide a specific remedy for a violation).

52. Ben Barber, *U.S. Wants UN Tribunals Closed*, WASH. TIMES, March 1, 2002, at A1. Mr. Pierre-Richard Prosper, the United States ambassador-at-large for war crime, has stated that the tribunals for Rwanda and the former Yugoslavia, which cost $100 million a year to operate, should prepare to shut down by 2008. *Id.*

> [A]t the International Criminal Tribunal for the Former Yugoslavia, 117 have been indicted, 67 persons have been brought into custody, 26 have been convicted, 5 acquitted, 11 are currently standing trial, and 1 is awaiting the judgment of the court. At the International Criminal Tribunal for Rwanda, 76 have been indicted, 57 have been brought into custody, 8 have been convicted, 1 acquitted and 17 are currently on trial.

52A. Voice of India, "Slobodan Milosevic Dies in Prison Cell", 03/11/2006, yahoo news.

53. Hart, "Positivism and Separation," *supra* note 13, at 599-600; *accord*

Shartle Hershey Amos, *The Science of Law* (5th ed. 1881), p. 4. *See also* William Markby, *Elements of Law* (5th ed. 1896), pp. 4-5 (noting that by establishing a distinction between positive law and morals Austin created the foundation for a science of law). "Positive laws, as Austin has shown, must be legally binding, and yet a law may be unjust . . . . He has admitted that law itself may be immoral, in which case it may be our moral duty to disobey it . . . ."

54. Ibid.

55. Ibid.

56. Paul Johnson, *Modern Times: The World From the Twenties to the Eighties* (New York: Harper Perennial Modern Classics, 1983), p. 422. *See also* 6 F.R.D. 69, 1947 Extra LEXIS 1, *191-246 (declaring only four of the seven Nazi organizations tried to be criminal organizations).

57. Heide B. Mahotra and Stephen Gregory, "Eager for Profits, U.S. Business Forgets History: Lessons from the Holocaust too inconvenient, *The Epoch Times*," May 25, 2006 at: www.theepochtimes.com/news/6-5-25/41922.html.

58. Ibid.

59. Larry Witham, "Christian Coalition Confident of Gains," Wash. Times, September 17, 1998, at A14.

60. Adolph Hitler's Enabling Act of March 24, 1933, effectively overruled the previous German government of the Weimar Republic including the Weimar Constitution. The Act gave Hitler sweeping and absolute powers to change statutory and constitutional law by decree, which thus gave legal validity to his termination of the separation of powers doctrine previously held under the Weimar Republic. Gesetz zur Behebung der not von Volk und Reich [Law for Eliminating the Distress of People and Reich]. 24. March 1933, RGBl. I, 141. Article 1 provides in part: "Apart from the procedure provided in the Reich Constitution, laws of the Reich can also be decreed by the Reich Government"; and Article 2 provides in part, "Laws decreed by the Reich Government may depart from the Reich Constitution as long as they do not have as their object the institutions of the Reich Parliament [Reichstag] and the Reich Council [Reichsrat] as such." *See also* 3 NMT 252-84 (discussing the legality of laws of the Reich government).

61. *See* William L. Shirer, *The Rise and Fall of the Third Reich: A History of Nazi Germany* (New York: Simon & Schuster, 1959, 1960), pp. 211-13, *also see* 304, 306, 309, 332-33, 357-63, 365-68 (discussing the mind set of the German people and their receptiveness to the Nazi government).

62. *Id.* at 32, 34, 41, 57-60, 152-53, 186-87.
63. *Id.* at 659-65.

64. *Id.* at 870.

65. Johann Wolfgang Von Goethe, *Faust* (David Luke, ed. & trans., Oxford World Classic 1998) (1808). *See generally* Johnson, *supra* note 4; Shirer, *Rise and Fall*, *supra* note 61, at 1114 (describing the fall of the Third Reich and Hitler's fall from power).

CHAPTER 3

1. Quoted in, Alan Westin and Barry Mahoney, *The Trial of Martin Luther King* (New York: The Notable Trials Library, 1997), p. 97.

2. *See* James Popple, *The Right to Protection from Retroactive Criminal Law*, 13 CRIM. L. J. 251, 251-62 (1989) (noting that a total of 177 Germans and Austrians were indicted in 13 separate Nuremberg Trials).

3. The Judgment at Nuremberg, 6 F.R.D. 69, 1947 Extra Lexis 1, *432-34. *See also* Popple, *supra* note 2, at 256. Popple states:

> Thirteen separate trials of war criminals were held in Nuremberg between 1945 and 1947. These trials were presided over by judges from all four major victorious Allied Powers: America, Britain, France and the Soviet Union. A total of 177 Germans and Austrians were indicted. All but thirty-five were found guilty: twenty-five were executed, twenty were sentenced to life imprisonment and ninety-seven were sentenced to shorter prison terms.

Id. See also Indictment, 1 International Military Tribunal [IMT] 27-92 (providing information regarding the twenty-four Nazi leaders who were charged on two or more of the four counts which were under the UN Charter and within the jurisdiction of the UN Tribunal).

4. *See, e.g.*, Charles Wyzanski, Jr., "Nuremberg: A Fair Trial?," The Atlantic Monthly, 66-70 (April 1946), *reprinted* In David M. Adams, *Philosophical Problems In The Law (Belmont: Wadsworth Publishing*, 1992), p. 14.

5. Treaty for the Renunciation of War as an Instrument of National Policy, August 27, 1928, 46 Stat. 2343, T.S. No. 796, 94 L.N.T.S. 57 [hereinafter Kellogg-Briand Pact].

6. Robert H. Jackson, *Opening Address for the United States, Nuremberg Trials*, *in* Adams, Philosophical Problems, *supra* note 4, AT 10-11.

7. For an excellent collection of books and articles on the Nuremberg Trials, see *Nuremberg Trials: The Reader's Companion to American History* (Eric Foner and John A. Garraty eds., 1994).

8. Melvin Sickler and Myron Fagan, *Thirst for Justice: A Satanic Plot for a One World Government*, at http://www.prolognet. qc.ca/clyde /illumin. htm (last

visited on October 7, 2003).

9. *Genesis* 11:4 (King James) ("*And they said, Go to, let us build us a city and a tower, whose top may reach unto heaven; and let us make us a name, lest we be scattered abroad upon the face of the whole earth.*"). This rebellion was in direct defiance of God's command, *"And God blessed Noah and his sons, and said unto them, be fruitful, and multiply, and replenish the earth."* *Genesis* 9:1 (King James).

10. The International Court of Justice is the judicial arm of the United Nations and regularly reports to the General Assembly. *See generally* http://www.ICJ-CIJ.org (discussing among other things, the role of the court in the United Nations) (last visited October 19, 2003).

11. The World Bank is the financial arm of the United Nations with profiles that cover the 208 countries (184 World Bank members and twenty-four other economies with populations of more than 30,000) and eighteen country groups reported on in the World Development Indicators book. *See generally* http://www. worldbank.org (providing information on the World Bank) (last visited October 19, 2003).

12. *See* Ellis Washington, "The Nuremberg Trials: The Death of the Rule of Law (In International Law)," 49 *Loyola Law Review* 417-518 (2003). SEE GENERALLY JUDGE ROBERT BORK'S two excellent books on the role of judges and the art of judging in contemporary society and how far the law community and society have descended from the original intent of the Constitution's Framers: Robert Bork, The Tempting of America: The Political Seduction of the Law (New York: Free Press, 1993); Slouching Toward Gomorrah: Modern Liberalism and American Decline (New York: ReaganBooks, 1996).

13. Regarding the foundational position natural law played as the controlling philosophy of American Constitutional law as well as all of its law related institutions from the rulings of local magistrates to the leading opinion handed down by the United States Supreme Court, Professor Burnham wrote: "The scholars have traced the ideas of the [Founding] Fathers back not only to Locke, Montesquieu, but Aristotle and Cicero and Plutarch, Hobbes, Burlamaqui, Milton, Hooker, Bolingbroke, Blackstone, Burke, Shaftesbury and a score of collateral branches."

14. James Burnham, Congress and the American Tradition (Washington, DC: Regnery, 1959), p. 24, "The Fathers were the masters, not the victims, of these inherited ideas, and sometimes it is the rhetoric more than the ideas that is taken over."

15. Rousas Rushdoony noted that John Witherspoon, a Presbyterian minister, was educated at Edinburgh University. Rousas John Rushdoony, *This Independent Republic: Studies in the Nature and Meaning of American History* (Phillipsburg, NJ: Presbyterian & Reformed Publ. Co., 1986), p. 3.

16. David Barton, *The Myth of Separation* (Texas: Wallbuilders Press, 1992), pp. 92-93.

17. David Barton, *Original Intent* (Texas: Wallbuilders Press, 1997), p. 83; *see also* Barton, *The Myth of Separation, supra* note 16, at 92-95, 117-18 (discussing Witherspoon's views on religion and government and their tremendous influence in shaping the ideas of the Constitution's Framers).

18. H. L. A. HART, *Concept of Law* (New York: Oxford University Press, 1960, 1997) p. 601, n.25 (citations omitted) (citing John C. Gray, *The Nature and Sources of the Law*, (1909), p. 94. Hart noted that "Bentham and Austin held the views described in (1), (2), and (3) but not those in (4) and (5). Opinion (4) is often ascribed to analytical jurists, but I know of no 'analyst' who held this view." (*citations omitted*).

19. Ibid. *S*ee also *supra* note 3 (discussing the International Military Tribunal at Nuremberg). *See also* ADAMS, *supra* note 4 (consisting of a collection of writings and commentary on the Nuremberg Trials); Stanley Paulson, *Classical Legal Positivism at Nuremberg, in* ADAMS, *supra* note 4, at 45 (discussing the convential view of the Nuremberg Trials—punishment to Hitler and his Nazis).

20. 17 IMT 458-94. For an interesting and engaging commentary by Jahrreiss reflecting on his Nuremberg Trial experience, see his testimony before the United States Military Tribunal at Nuremberg as an expert defense witness on German constitutional law. 3 IMT 252-84. *See also* 2 Hermann Jahrreiss, *Die Fortentwicklung des Volkerrechts, Jahrbuch fur Internationales und Auslandisches Offentliches Recht* 654-66 (1949), *reprinted in* Hermann Jahrreiss, *Mensch und Staat* 233-53 (Cologne ed., 1957). *See generally* Jean Bodin, Six Books of the Commonwealth 25, 28 (M. J. Tooley trans., Oxford ed. 1955) (1576) (providing a comprehensive starting point for the study of legal history). The previous Western conception of law as subsequent and superior to man was now beginning to be replaced with law as a mere tool or servant of the state. *Id.* However, in Bodin's work, *The Prince*, though freed from the *law of man* and a law unto himself, medieval understandings of the law still constrained him to the *universal natural law* precepts as well as to certain common ecumenical precepts to which all mankind must adhere. Nonetheless, the break with the medieval world of "the Law of Nature and of Nature's God" as Jefferson codified two hundred years later as natural law philosophy in America's Declaration of Independence, was in the sixteenth century already being rent in two like the Temple veil of the Bible when Christ died on the cross. *Matthew* 27:51 (King James). *See generally* The Declaration of Independence (U.S. 1776) (exposing a natural law philosophy).

21. [NO AUTHOR] "States of Terror, Syria Iran and their proxies wage war on israel" *Opinion Journal.com*, 7/14/06, http://www.opinionjournal.com/ editorial/feature.html?ID=110008658.

23. John Austin, *The Province of Jurisprudence Determined*, at 13-14 (photo. Reprint 1970)(2nd ed. 1861). *Id.* To the substantive question of positive law—

who has the right in a society to be sovereign?—James Bryce makes the following comments: "The person or body to whom in the last resort the law attributes this right is the legally supreme power; or Sovereign, in the State."

24. Hermann Jahrreiss, Professor of Law at Cologne and associate defense counsel for defendant Jodl, skillfully and with some success utilized the "act of state" defense and the doctrine of absolute sovereignty. Both legal philosophies came directly out of John Austin's *Providence.* Jahrreiss presented a lengthy apologetic on jurisprudence considerations of the trial. His discourses epitomize the most extensive attempt by defense counsel to specify a philosophical foundation for the defense's case. 17 IMT 458-94. For an interesting and engaging commentary by Jahrreiss reflecting on his Nuremberg Trial experience, see his testimony before the United States Military Tribunal at Nuremberg as an expert defense witness on German constitutional law. 3 IMT 252-84. *See also* 2 Hermann Jahrreiss, Die Fortentwicklung des Volkerrechts, Jahrbuch fur Internationales und Auslandisches Offentliches Recht 654-66 (1949), *reprinted in* Hermann Jahrreiss, Mensch und Staat 233-53 (Cologne ed., 1957); Austin, *supra* note 23 and *supra* note 24.

25. Juscogens.Org.: "A Commentary on the Justice Case" by Doug Linder© 2000 at 222.aldeilis.net/aldeilis/index2.php?option=content &dopdf=1&id=1616– Supplemental.

26. G. M. GILBERT, *NUREMBERG DIARY* (photo. reprint 1995) (Cambridge: DaCapo Press, 1947).

> Ribbentrop was arguing with Hess but getting nowhere, since Hess has no recollection of the world events recounted in the Indictment. Ribbentrop then remarked to me [G.M. Gilbert] "Why all this fuss about breaking treaties? Did you ever read about the history of the British Empire? Why, it's full of broken treaties, oppression of minorities, mass murder, aggressive wars, and everything."

Id. *See generally* Joseph E. Persico, *Nuremberg: Infamy on Trial* (New York: Penguin Books, 1994) (providing a detailed history of the Nuremberg trials); Michael R. Marrus, *The Nuremberg War Crimes Trial 1945-46: A Documentary History* (The Bedford Series in History and Culture (London: Bedford Books, 1997)); Telford Taylor, *The Anatomy of the Nuremberg Trials: A Personal Memoir* (New York: Knopf, 1992).

27. Albert Speer, *Inside the Third Reich, Memoirs* (New York: The Macmillan Co., 1969), pp. 510-11.

28. Gilbert, *supra* note 26, at 185-216. Note in particular the contrast between Speer's limited contrition for his war crimes and Hermann Goering's bravado: a defense which made a virtual mockery of the Court. *Id.*

29. Harold Berman, *The Interaction of Law and Religion* (New York: Abbington Press, 1974), p. 21. Berman is the Robert W. Woodruff Professor of Law at

Emory Law School. This book was the 1983 winner of the American Bar Association Scribes Award and is dedicated to that great legal scholar Rosenstock-Huessey.

30. Sandy Goldsmith & Barbara Kate Repa, "Are You Using Study Aids as a Crutch?" 16 *STUDENT LAWYER*, September 1987, at 32. *See also* Benjamin N. Cardozo, *The Growth of the Law* 49 (New Haven: Yale University Press, 1924) (discussing the secularization of the law).

31. For an example of the perverse, myopic, and craven tone of the defenses of Nazi defendants Hess, Ribbentrop and Keitel, see Gilbert, *supra* note 26, at 217-54.

32. *See* "Agreement on the Prosecution and Punishment of Major War Criminals of the European Axis," August 8, 1945, art. 6 [hereinafter Treaty of London] (establishing the International Military Tribunal at Nuremberg, the first of its kind); Stanley Paulson, "Classical Legal Positivism at Nuremberg" in David M. ADAMS, *Philosophical Problems in the Law* (Belmont: Wadsworth Publishing Co., 1992), p. 45.

33. Treaty of London, *supra* note 32, art. 6. Paulson, *supra* note 32, at 45.

34. Ibid

35. *See, e.g.*, A. L. Goodhart, "The Legality of the Nuremberg Trials," 58 Jurisprudence Review 1, 1-19 (1946) (discussing the legitimacy of the Nuremberg trials); A. L. Goodhart, "Questions and Answers Concerning the Nuremberg Trials," 1 *INT'L L. Q.* 525, 525-31 (1947); Lord Wright, *Natural Law and International Law: Interpretations of Modern Legal Philosophies* (Paul Sayre ed., 1947), pp. 794-807; See book review of same: Herbert D. Laube, "Interpretations of Modern Legal Philosophies. Essays in Honor of Roscoe Pound" *Harvard Law Review*, Vol. 60, No. 6 (July, 1947), pp. 995-998; Lord Wright, "War Crimes Under International Law," 62 L. Q. REV. 40, 40-52 (1946); Quincy Wright, "Legal Positivism and the Nuremberg Judgment," 42 *AM J. INT'L L.* 405, 405-14 (1948) (stating the differences between positive law and natural law and the effects on the legitimacy of the Nuremberg trials). It was generally left to other conservative or conservative-leaning law academics to outline a defense of the legitimacy of the Nuremberg Trials in terms of "Justice and its handmaid, Natural Law," as Wright puts it. The best and most logically and reasoned exposition of the Nuremberg Trials is still the classic work by Hart. *See* H. L. A. Hart, "Positivism and The Separation of Law and Morals," 71 *Harvard Law Review* 615-21 (explaining the difficult legal issue of whether to declare void every law passed during the Nazi regime), 605 (1958) [hereinafter Hart, "Positivism and Separation"]; Lon Fuller, "Positivism and Fidelity to Law: A Reply to Professor Hart," 71 *Harvard Law Review* 648-61 (1958) (discussing his thesis that Nazi law lacked the vital element of all law—fidelity to law, a deficiency

which precluded it from being considered actual law that one was bound to obey).; *See generally* George Leaman, Heidegger im Kontext: Gesamtüberblick zum Ns-Engagement der Universitäts philosophen [*Heidegger in Context: Overview of the Nazi Involvement of University Professors*] 25-27, 109-33 (1993). Posner rightly notes that "[p]rofessors were notable by their absence from the cells of resistance to Hitler that developed during his rule." Richard Posner, "The Problematics of Moral and Legal Theory," 111 *Harvard Law Review* 1637, 1683 n.88 (1998) (citing Alice Gallin, *Midwives to Nazism: University Professors in Weimar Germany 1925-1933*, (Macon: Mercer University Press, 1986), pp. 4-5, 100-05.

36. Gilbert, *supra* note 26, at 36-39 (discussing the Opening Address by Robert Jackson, Chief Prosecutor for the United States at Nuremberg).

37. *See* Treaty of London, *supra* note 32, §§ II art. 8, VI art. 27.

38. *See* Treaty of London, *supra* note 32, §§ II arts. 9 & 10 (granting the tribunal authority to declare a group or organization criminal).

39. *See* Jackson, *supra* note 6, at 7-13. For the full text of Justice Jackson's Opening Address at Nuremberg, see 2 IMT 98-155. President Truman personally asked Justice Jackson to suspend his tenure on the Supreme Court to represent the United States at London and to function as chief prosecutor of the United States and argue before the International Military Tribunal. *See* Report from Robert H. Jackson to the President, 12 Dept. State B. 1071-78 (1945) (providing an overview of the prosecution's arguments). For Jackson's Opening Address and arguments at trial, see Robert H. Jackson, *The Case Against the Nazi War Criminals* (New York: Knopf, 1946); for his closing statement, see 19 IMT 397-432. Jackson later remarked about his experiences at the Nuremberg Trials in Robert H. Jackson, *Nuremberg in Retrospect*, 27 *CAN. B. REV.* 761, 61-81 (1949), *reprinted in* 35 A.B.A. J. 813, 813-16, 881-87 (1949).

CHAPTER 4

1. *See* Sir Hartley Shawcross, Opening Statement, 3 IMT 91-145; Closing Statement, 19 IMT 433-529. For subsequent impressions of the Nuremberg Trials, see Sir Hartley Shawcross, *International Law: A Statement of the British View of Its Role*, 33 A.B.A. J. 31-35 (1947). For impressions of Robert H. Jackson's contributions during the Nuremberg Trials, *see* Robert Jackson, "Mr. Justice Jackson: Four Lectures in his Honor" 87-136 (1969); Robert H. Jackson, *Opening Address for the United States, Nuremberg Trials*, *in* David Adams, *Philosophical Problems in the Law*, Philosophical Problems (Belmont: Wadsworth Publishing, 1992), p. 12 (discussing the history of the pre and post World War I treaties). *See also* English barrister, attorney general, Labor member of Parliament, and chief prosecutor for the United Kingdom, Sir Hartley Shawcross' speeches during the Nuremberg Trials, 3 IMT 91-145. Despite Jackson's impressive skills as a prosecutor, Shawcross was in the opinion of most

observers the most philosophically educated of the prosecution counsel who deliberated before the International Military Tribunal.

2. Charles Wyzanski, Jr., "Nuremberg: A Fair Trial?," The Atlantic Monthly, 66-70 (April 1946), *reprinted in* David ADAMS, *Philosophical Problems in the Law* (Belmont, CA: Wadsworth Publishing Co., 1992).

3. Wyzanski, *supra* note 2, at 69. Wyzanski warned that if the panel succumbed to (justifiable) feelings of outrage, and indulged an urge to punish without granting the defendants a fair trial, it would establish a dangerous precedent for war crimes retribution.

4. *Id.* Seven months later, however, after the trial had run its course, Wyzanski explained that the exemplary manner in which the trial had been conducted dispelled his skepticism about the feasibility of forging an international legal system.

5. Charles E. Wyzanski, Jr., *Nuremberg in Retrospect*, *ATLANTIC MONTHLY*, December 1946, at 56, *available at* http://www.theatlantic. com/unbound/flashbks/nurember/wyprec.htm. He wrote, "[T]he Nuremberg proceedings were a model of forensic fairness .... But the outstanding accomplishment of the trial ... is that it has crystallized the concept that there already is inherent in the international community a machinery both for the expression of international criminal law and for its enforcement.

6. Wyzanski, *supra* note 2, at 56-59.

7. Wyzanski, *supra* note 2, at 15-18.

8. *Id.*

9. *See generally* pamphlet titled, "Are 'Superior Orders' A Legitimate Defense?" *in* "What Should Be Done with the War Criminals?" at Website: AmericanHistoricalAssociation.org. Constructing a Postwar World—The G.I. Roundtable Series in Context. Abstract of Minutes of Executive Committee Meeting, September 2, 1943, National Archives, Washington, D. C.

> Present: Arthur M. Schlesinger, Solon J. Buck and Guy Stanton Ford, members of the Executive Committee; Louis R. Gottschalk, member of the Council; Mortimer Graves of the American Council of Learned Societies as a guest substitute for Waldo G. Leland; also Colonel Francis T. Spaulding, Colonel John D. Kenderdine and Major Donald W. Goodrich of the Education Section, Special Service Division, War Department. www.historians.org/projects/giroundtable/Criminals/Criminals7.htm.

10. See generally, Niccolo Machiavelli, *The Prince* (1513); The Geneva Conventions of 1949 were integrated into out legal system through the Uniform

Code of Military Justice, passed as federal law on 5 May 1950; the Manual for Courts Martial, which implements the UCMJ, came into effect 31 May 1951. The Law of Land Warfare, para. 509, makes explicit that obedience to an unlawful order is no defense against a charge of war crimes. There is a good deal of supporting case law: *Little v. Barreme*, 6 U.S. (2 Cranch) 170 (1804); *Mitchell v. Harmony*, 54 U.S. (13 Howard) 115 (1851); Judgment in the Case of Lieutenants Dithmar and Boldt, 16 Am J. Int'l L. 708 (1921); *U.S. v. Huet-Vaughn*, 43 M.J. 105 (CAAF 1995). Cited in Gary Solis, "Crimes of War," http://www.crimesofwar. org/expert/solis.html.

11. *Regina v. Smith*, 17 S.C. 561 (Cape of Good Hope, 1900); See also *Little v. Barreme*, et al., *supra* note 10. For a comprehensive treatment of the superior orders doctrine in the context of international war crimes trials and as a primary Nazi defence; See DePaul University Professor M. Cherif Bassiouni, *Crimes Against Humanity in International Criminal Law* (New York, Martinus Nijhoff Publishers, 1999, 2nd ed.).

12. *Mitchell v. Harmony*, 54 U.S. (13 Howard) 115 (1851).

13. *U.S. v. John Jones*, 26 F. Cas. 653, 658 C.C.C.D Pa (1813).

14. Ibid.

15. *Regina v. Smith*, 17 S.C. 561 (Cape of Good Hope, 1900).

16. *Llandovery Castle*, 16 AJIL 708 (1922).

17. Ibid.

18. See superior orders doctrine at *supra* note 2, at 15. Wyzanski states:

> The defense of superior orders is, upon the authorities, an open question. Without going into details, it may be said that superior orders have never been recognized as a complete defense by German, Russian, or French law, and that they have not been so recognized by civilian courts in the United States or the British Commonwealth of Nations, but they tend to be taken as a complete excuse by Anglo-American military manuals. In this state of the authorities, if the International Military Tribunal in connection with a charge of a war crime refuses to recognize superior orders as a defense, it will not be making a retroactive determination or applying an *ex post facto* law. It will be merely settling an open question of law as every court frequently does.

19. Ibid.

20. *See generally* FED. R. EVID. (proscribing the requirements and procedure for the admissibility of evidence at trials).

21. *See generally* David Nelken, "Beyond Compare? Critizing 'The American Way of Law,'" 28 *LAW & SOC. INQUIRY* 799 (2003).

22. *See, e.g.*, William B. Ewald, "What's so Special About American Law?," 26 OKLA. CITY U. L. REV. 1083 (2001).

23. *See* Oscar G. Chase, "American 'Exceptionalism' and Comparative Procedure," 50 *AMER. J. COMP. L.* 277, 283-85 (2002) (discussing "adversarial" v. "inquisitional" systems).

24. *See generally* 1-22 IMT (The transcript contains numerous instances where the German council objected to the legal framework of the trial.).

25. *See* Militarstrafgesetzbuch v. 10.10.1940 (RGBl. I S.1347, 1351). Section 47 prohibited the absolute defense to a person who "went beyond the order as given" or intended "that the superior's order referred to an act aimed at civil or military felony or misdemeanor." *Id.* Although defendant Jodl claimed that he did not recall any charges under section 47 "in his 30 years of service."

26. International Military Tribunal at Nuremberg, Blue Series, at 19 IMT 43, section 47 [hereinafter IMT, with volume number preceding and page number(s) following].

27. See [No author cited], *German War Trials: Judgment in the Case of Lieutenants Dithmar and Boldt*, 16 *American Journal Of International Law* 708, 721-22 (1922) (printing a German court decision where a soldier was prevented from raising the defense of "superior orders"). See also Llandovery Castle, 16 *American Journal Of International Law* 708 (1921).

28. Excerpts from Joseph E. Persico, *Roosevelt's Secret War: FDR and World War II Espionage* (New York: Random House, 2001), pp. 201-05. *Ex parte Quirin*, 317 U.S. 1 (1942) is a Supreme Court of the United States case that upheld the jurisdiction of a United States military tribunal over the trial of several Operation Pastorius German saboteurs in the United States. *Quirin* has been cited as a precedent for the execution of any non-legitimate combatant against the United States. It was argued July 29 and July 30, 1942 and decided July, 1942 with an extended opinion filed October 29, 1942.

This decision states:

> "...the law of war draws a distinction between the armed forces and the peaceful populations of belligerent nations and also between those who are lawful and unlawful combatants. Lawful combatants are subject to capture and detention as prisoners of war by opposing military forces. Unlawful combatants are likewise subject to capture and detention, but in addition they are subject to trial and punishment by military tribunals for acts which render their belligerency unlawful. The spy who secretly and without uniform passes the military lines of a belligerent in time of war, seeking to gather military information and communicate it to the enemy, or an enemy combatant who without uniform comes secretly through the lines for the purpose of waging war by destruction of life or property, are familiar examples of belligerents who are generally deemed not to be entitled to the status of prisoners of war, but to be

offenders against the law of war subject to trial and punishment by military tribunals."

29. Wyzanski, *supra* note 2, at 66-70.

30. Ibid.

31. 3 IMT 106. *Accord* 2 IMT 144 (Jackson arguing before the tribunal); Judgment at Nuremberg, 6 *F.R.D.* 69; Judgment, The Hostage Case (*United States v. Wihelm List*) 11 NMT 1239.

32. 19 IMT 464. Furthermore, Shawcross maintained that "the existence of law has never been dependent on the existence of a correlated sanction external to the law itself."

33. Ibid., at 463.

34. U.S. CONST. art. I, § 9. ("No Bill of Attainder or ex post facto Law shall be passed.").

35. Lon Fuller, *The Morality of Law* (London: Edward Arnold, 1964), pp. 41-44, 51-62. *Compare* Lon Fuller, "Positivism and Fidelity to Law: A Reply to Professor Hart," 71 *Harvard Law Review* 630-72 (1958) (discussing his thesis that Nazi law lacked the vital element of all law—fidelity to law, a deficiency which precluded it from being considered actual law that one was bound to obey).

36. John Austin, *The Province of Jurisprudence Determined,* at 13-14 (photo. Reprint 1970) (2nd ed. 1861), p. 84. *Id.* To the substantive question of positive law—who has the right in a society to be sovereign?—James Bryce makes the following comments: "The person or body to whom in the last resort the law attributes this right is the legally supreme power; or Sovereign, in the State." *See also* Jerome Hall, General Principles of Criminal Law (2d ed.)(Indianapolis: The Bobbs-Merrill Co., 1960), ch. 2 (explaining the principles of legality); JOHN RAWLS, *A Theory of Justice* 238 (Cambridge: Harvard University Press, 1971) (providing a general theory of distributive justice and the social contract).

37. Wyzanski, *supra* note 2, at 66-70.

38. Ibid.

39. Ibid., at 17 ("To some the count may appear as nothing more than the ancient rule that the vanquished are at the mercy of the victor."). This motif by Wyzanski, 'victor's justice', is frequently repeated in his critique against the legitimacy of the Nuremberg Trials.

40. *See* Ibid. ("There is no convention or treaty which places obligations explic-

itly upon an individual not to aid in waging an aggressive war.").

> For those who were not chargeable with ordinary crimes but only with political crimes such as planning an aggressive war, would it not have been better to proceed by an executive determination–that is, a proscription directed at certain named individuals? The form of the determination need not have been absolute on its face. It might have been a summary order reciting the offense and allowing the named persons to show cause why they should not be punished, thus giving them a chance to show any mistake of identification or gross mistake of fact.

41. Ibid. at 19.

CHAPTER 5

1. *U.S. v. John Jones*, 26 F. Cas. 653, 658 C.C.C.D Pa (1813).

2. Charles Wyzanski, Jr., "Nuremberg: A Fair Trial?." THE ATLANTIC MONTHLY, 66-70 [14] (April 1946), *reprinted in* David M. ADAMS, *PHILOSOPHICAL PROBLEMS IN THE LAW* (BELMONT: WADSWORTH, 1992) [HEREINAFTER, WYZANSKI, *NUREMBERG*.

3. Robert H. Jackson, *Opening Address for the United States, Nuremberg Trials, in* David M. Adams, Philosophical Problems in the Law, 7-8 (Belmont: Wadsworth, 1992).

4. Wyzanski, *Nuremberg, supra* note 2.

5. *See id.* at 15 (expressing doubt as to whether the defendants could be tried at the tribunal on the charges that encompassed crimes against German citizens on German soil).

6. See "Agreement on the Prosecution and Punishment of Major War Criminals of the European Axis," August 8, 1945, 59 Stat. 1544, 3 Bevans 1238 [hereinafter Treaty of London]. Treaty of London, § II, art. 7. *See also* Hans Kelsen, *Collective and Individual Responsibility in International Law with Particular Regard to the Punishment of War Criminals*, 31 *CAL. L. REV.* 530, 533 (1943) (defining acts of state as "acts performed by individuals in their capacity as organs of the State and therefore acts imputed to the State."). An interesting historical fact is that Kelsen's paper was cited by associate defense counsel Hermann Jahrreiss as substantive authority for the idea that "in questions of breach of the peace, the liability of the individuals to punishment does not exist according to general international law at present valid . . . "

7. Ibid., Kelson at 530.

8. International Military Tribunal at Nuremberg, Blue Series, at 17 IMT 477. [hereinafter IMT, with volume number preceding and page number(s) follow-

ing]. Kelsen seriously disagreed with Jahrreiss' defense. Anticipating the prosecution of Axis war criminals, Kelsen maintained that the characterization of rules, so as to affirm specific criminal liability retroactively, would be supported on a *moral* foundation.

9. Hans Kelsen, *Peace Through Law* (2nd ed.) (Chapel Hill: University of North Carolina, 1944), pp. 87-88.

10. Wyzanski, *supra* note 2, at 16.

11. Ibid.

12. The British Ministry of Defense, Manual of Military Law pt. I, ¶ 23, pt. III, ¶ 627 (12th ed. 1972) [hereinafter Manual of Military Law]; U.S. Dept. of The Army, Field Manual: The Law Of Land Warfare (FM 27-10) ¶ 509(1) (1956) [hereinafter Field Manual].

13. Field Manual, *supra* note 12, at October 1944 ed., para. 347.

14. Para. 345.1 (change of 15 November 1944). Manual of Military Law, *supra*, pt. I, ¶ 23, pt. III, ¶ 627; Field Manual, *supra* ¶ 509(1). These changes are current military practice.

15. Charles Wyzanski, Jr., *Nuremberg: A Fair Trial?*, The *Atlantic Monthly*, 66-70 (April 1946), *reprinted in* David Adams, Philosophical Problems In The Law (Belmont: Wadsworth, 1992) (commenting that Nuremberg was high politics masquerading as law).

16. Wyzanski, *supra* note 2, at 15.

17. Wyzanski, *supra* note 2, at 15.

18. Wyzanski, *supra* note 2, at 15. Wyzanski is morally uncomfortable with his argument from the start, constantly attempting to distance himself from the actions of the Nazis.

19. Ibid.

20. *See* Wyzanski, *supra* note 2, at 14-16. "Thus in Articles 46 and 47 of The Hague Convention of 1907, the United States and many other countries accepted the rules that in an occupied territory of a hostile state 'family honour and rights, the lives of persons, and private property, *as well as religious conviction and practice, must be respected.*'" (*italics mine*)

21. Ibid., at 14.

22. See *1984* (London: Penguin Books, 1949); See generally George Orwell, *Animal Farm* (New York: Harcourt, Brace & Co., 1946).

23. Ellis Washington, "Excluding the Exclusionary Rule: Natural Law vs. Judicial Personal Policy Preferences," Vol. 10, No. 2, *Deakin Law Review* (Australia) 772-94 (September 2005).

24. Declaration of Independence ¶ 1 (U.S. 1776).

> When in the Course of human events, it becomes necessary for one people to dissolve the Political Bands which have connected them with another, and to assume among the Powers of the Earth, the separate and equal Station to which the Laws of Nature and of Nature's God entitle them, a decent Respect to the Opinions of Mankind requires that they should *declare the causes which impel them to the separation* (e.g., for America to free itself from the tyranny of England and King George III).

Id. (emphasis added).

25. G. M. Gilbert, *Nuremberg Diary*, 37-4037-40 (photo. reprint 1995) (Cambridge: DaCapo Press, 1947).

26. Orwell, 1984, *supra* note 22. See also, Ellis Washington, "Why Does the Left So Hate America?", http://worldnetdaily.com/news/ article.asp? ARTICLE_ID=55973, where I do an engaging comparative analysis of Nathaniel Philbrick's book on the Puritans in the modern context of Orwellian thought-crime.

27. *See, e.g.*, Elinor Langer, *A Hundred Little Hitler's: The Death of a Black Man, the Trial of a White Racist, and the Rise of the Neo-Nazi Movement in American* (New York: St. Martin's Press, 2003).

28. *See* William Drozdiak, "Two German Officers Punished for Neo-Nazi's Speech to Military Academy," *Washington Post*, December 9, 1997, at A26 (reporting that two senior officers were reprimanded for allowing a convicted neo-Nazi to address soldiers at an elite military academy).

29. *See* William Drozdiak, "Haider Plays on Fears of Foreigners, Contradictions, Denials Mark Austrian's History," *Washington Post*, February 6, 2000, at A1 (providing a biography of Haider's past and discussing his political views).

30. William Drozdiak, *Haider Baffled by Western Protests: Austrian Far-Right Leader Predicts Acceptance, Reaffirms some Disputed Stands*, *Washington Post*, February 10, 2000, at A17. Haider has made comments that have sparked protests around the world and caused some countries to break diplomatic ties with Austria. *Id.* Among these comments, he has "praise[d] Nazi Germany's orderly employment policies" and he has characterized veterans of the Waffen SS, a branch of the feared Nazi organization, as "decent men of character." *Id.*

31. Wyzanski, *supra* note 2, at 16; *See also* Edward S. Corwin, "*The "Higher Law" Background of American Constitutional Law*," 42 *Harvard Law Review* 149 (1928) (discussing the evolution of the philosophy of law); Arnold Brecht, "The Myth of Is and Ought," 54 *Harvard Law Review* 811 (1941) (contending that the separation of "is" and "ought" is artificial); *See* H. L. A. Hart, "Positivism and The Separation of Law and Morals," 71 *Harvard Law Review* 615-21 (advocating that there is a division of the law as it is from the law as it ought to be), 593-98 (1958) [hereinafter Hart, "Positivism and Separation"]; See also Lon Fuller, "Positivism and Fidelity to Law: A Reply to Professor Hart," 71 *Harvard Law Review* 630 (1958) [hereinafter Fuller, "Positivism and Fidelity"] (arguing that Hart's position is contradictory); Lon Fuller, Anatomy of the Law (New York: Frederick A. Praeger, 1968), p. 175-86.

32. *Ecclesiastes* 1:9 (King James).

33. *Genesis* 1:3 (King James).

34. *Genesis*: 4:8. (King James) "And now art thou cursed from the earth, which hath opened her mouth to receive thy brother's blood from thy hand." *Id.* at 4:11.

35. *See Exodus* 20 (chronicling the giving of the Decalogue by God to Moses).

36. GILBERT, *supra* note 25, at 36-39 (citing chief prosecutor Robert Jackson's opening remarks at the Nuremberg Trials).

37. Ibid.

38. Gilbert, *supra* note 25, at 36-39.

CHAPTER 6

1. Allen M. Dershowitz, *America on Trial: Inside the Legal Battles that Trans*

formed our Nation (New York: Warner Books, 2004) [Hereinafter, Dershowitz, America on Trial].

2. Robert H. Jackson, *Opening Address for the United States, Nuremberg Trials, in* David M. Adams, *Philosophical Problems in the Law* (Belmont: Wadsworth, 1992), pp. 7-8 (stating that the tribunal is justified under current international law).

3. Ibid. (emphasis added).

4. Ibid. at 9 (emphasis added).

5. Ibid. at 8 (emphasis added).

6. Daniel Jonah Goldhagen, *Hitler's Willing Executioners: Ordinary Germans and the Holocaust* (New York: Knopf, 1996), pp. 10-14. Daniel J. Goldhagen is Assistant Professor of Government and Social Studies at Harvard University and an Associate of Harvard's Minda de Gunzburg Center for European Studies. His doctoral dissertation, which is the basis for his book "Hitler's Willing Executioners: Ordinary Germans and the Holocaust," was awarded the American Political Science Association's 1994 Gabriel A. Almond Award for the best dissertation in the field of comparative politics.

7. Paul Johnson, *Modern Times: The World from the Twenties to the Eighties* (New York: Harper Perennial Modern Classics, 1983), p. 422.

8. Jackson, *supra* note 2, at 7.

9. Wyzanski, *supra* note 49, 14-16.

10. This information is taken from Justice Jackson's statements to the Tribunal at the Nuremberg Trials. For access to the transcripts of the Nuremberg Trial, see The Avalon Project at http://www.yale.edu/lawweb/Avalon/imt/imt.htm.

CHAPTER 7

1. Allen M. Dershowitz, *America on Trial: Inside the Legal Battles that Transformed our Nation* 13 (New York: Warner Books, 2004) [Hereinafter, Dershowitz, *America on Trial*].

2. Robert H. Jackson, *Opening Address for the United States, Nuremberg Trials, in* David M. Adams, *Philosophical Problems in the Law* (Belmont, CA: Wadsworth, 1992, 1996), p. 10 (stating that the tribunal is justified under current international law).

3. Judgment at Nuremberg, 6 F.R.D. 69, 1947 Extra LEXIS 1, *111.

4. Jackson, *supra* note 2, at 12.

5. Ibid. at 7.

6. *See, e.g., Lochner v. New York*, 198 U.S. 45 (1905) (the Court struck down laws regulating the maximum number of hours a baker could work per week in New York). Writing for the Court, Justice Peckham held that there were no substantive arguments for precluding the right of freedom of contract by regulating the hours of labor. This opinion was the first example in constitutional law of the jurisprudence called substantive due process. The Lochner opinion is an example of an illegitimate jurisprudence not rooted in the plain text of the constitution but a shameful model of conservative judicial legislation from the bench; however, there appears to be little in this opinion that is unthinking or

mechanical, however political it may be. For a list of other opinions that flowed out of the Lochner precedent. This case was the beginning of the rise of what scholars later called "substantive due process." This type of jurisprudence spawned an entire generation of case law where judges used their own subjective views to reach judicial decisions apart from reliance on an explicit text in the Constitution. At the beginning of this century, it was a conservative Supreme Court that frequently looked askance at any federal or state economic regulation—frequently striking it down, not for constitutional reasons, but for political expediency. Lochner and its progeny became the death knell to the long respected judicial doctrines of Natural law, originalism and *stare decisis*. *See also Muller v. Oregon*, 208 U.S. 412 (1908) (upholding maximum working hours provisions for women); *Bunting v. Oregon*, 208 U.S. 412 (1917) (the Court struck down maximum hours regulations); *Coppage v. Kansas*, 236 U.S. 1 (1915); Adair v. U.S. 208 U.S. 161 (1908) (overruled federal laws against "yellow dog" contracts on interstate railroads); *Adkins v. Children's Hospital*, 261 U.S. 525 (1923) (minimum wages). These constitutionally illegitimate decisions lead to a generation of judicial policy-making in the areas of the right of privacy, sex, abortion, and church/state issues. See also *Griswold v. Connecticut*, 381 U.S. 479 (1965); *Roe v. Wade*, 410 U.S. 113 (1973). My mentor, Justice Clarence Thomas has been the Court's most tireless exponent of originalism.

7. *Lochner*, *supra* note 6.

8. See, Roscoe Pound, Mechanical Jurisprudence, 8 Columbia Law Review 605, 615-16 (1908). *See also* Ellis Washington, *Inseparability Of Law And Morality* (Maryland: University Press of America, 2002), at 445, 455 n.19.

9. Ibid., at 7.

10. *See* "Capitalism and the Holocaust: How the Swiss banks aided the Nazis," *The Int'l Workers Bulletin*, June 16, 1997, at 3, *at* www.wsws.org/public_html/iwb6-16/gold.htm (last visited October 31, 2003).

11. Jackson, *supra* note 2, at 8.

12. Ibid., at 9 (emphasis added).

13. Ibid., at 11 (citation omitted).

14. Ibid. at 10 ("Even the most warlike of peoples have recognized in the name of humanity some limitations on the savagery of warfare. Rules to that end have been embodied in international conventions to which Germany became a party.")

15. Citation omitted.

16. William L. Shirer, *The Rise and Fall of the Third Reich: A History of Nazi Germany* (New York: Simon & Schuster, 1960), pp. 211-13, *also see* 304, 306, 309, 332-33, 357-63, 365-68 (discussing the mind set of the German people and their receptiveness to the Nazi government and the aggressive actions of Germany leading to the start of World War II). See generally Daniel Jonah Goldhagen, *Hitler's Willing Executioners: Ordinary Germans and the Holocaust* (New York: Knopf, 1996). For a good article on appeasement see Tony Blankley, "Appeasement—it won't work this time, either," *Washington Times*, September 6, 2006. Blankley, in his inimitable and historically astute manner stated the following prescient remarks on appeasement:

> The use of the term appeasement to describe a nation's foreign policy first emerged in the 1930s in England to describe the Ramsey McDonald/Stanley Baldwin/Neville Chamberlain British governments' policy of avoiding military conflict with Hitler's Germany by yielding to his territorial demands.
>
> Just so, the British governments of the 1930s thought they were acting both ethically and in the best interest of their people. While there were a few pro-Nazis and anti-Semites in Britain (mostly in the upper classes), Chamberlain and most of his government were neither.
>
> They did think Germany had been unfairly dealt with in the Versailles Treaty after WWI. And they did think it reasonable, natural and more or less inevitable that the 80 million German-speaking people of Europe would be re-united under one nation. Thus they appeased Hitler's demand for the Rhineland, anschluss (union) with Austria and the invasion of the Sudetenland (German-speaking part of Czechoslovakia.
>
> And if that were all Hitler had wanted, Chamberlain would have gone down in history as the 20th century's greatest statesman and peacemaker. (And Winston Churchill would have been remembered — if he was remembered at all by the general public — as an antique, Edwardian warmonger and troublemaker.)
>
> But appeasement — in and of itself — is neither inherently unwise nor immoral. It depends on the facts of each case. While the term had not been used before the 1930s, the policy has been a mainstay of both weak and powerful governments throughout history.
>
> In 1862, during our civil war, in the Trent Affair, after a Union ship violated British maritime rights, the British threatened war if Lincoln didn't capitulate on the matter. His cabinet wanted war, but Lincoln "appeased" the British on the theory of "one war at a time." Bravo Abe the appeaser. . . .
>
> As I wrote in my book last year ("The West's Last Chance"), just as Hitler's Nazis, the radical Islamists are irreconcilable and unlimited in their goals. And, they are expanding their reach into the broad grass roots of Islam throughout the world (including in Europe and the United States).

> A maximum effort to extirpate the malignancy is the only and best defense for our way of life.
>
> I'm not against the appeasers because they are immoral or cowardly. I merely disagree with them because I believe that, like Neville Chamberlain, they underestimate the threat, and are thus dangerously wrong.

17. *See generally* Archer Jones, *The Art of War in the Western World* (1987). See also, G. M. Gilbert, Nuremberg Diary (photo. reprint 1995) (Cambridge: DaCapo Press, 1947).

18. Jackson, *supra* note 2, at 13.

19. Specifically, common law tradition going back to the great international law jurists like Hugo Grotius and Samuel de Pufendorf. On this subject legal commentator and constitutional scholar David Barton wrote:

> Hugo Grotius (1583-1645), a Dutch lawyer, theologian, and statesman, authored *Concerning the Law of War and Peace* (1625)—the first definitive text on international law . . . . Grotius' overall philosophy on law and civil government was clear; he argued that, "What God has shown to be his will that is law."
>
> . . . .
>
> Samuel de Puffendorf (1632-1694), a high political figure and Professor of the Law and Nature at universities both in Sweden and Germany . . . . Puffendorf also believed that civil societies and government could not successfully exist apart from God and His principles.

David Barton, *Original Intent* (Texas: Wallbuilders Press, 1997), p. 223.

20. Kellogg-Briand Pact, August 27, 1928, arts. I-II, 46 Stat. 2343, 94 L.N.T.S. 57.

21. Joshua 6:22.

22. Samuel 15:1-3.

23. Dershowitz, *America on Trial*, *supra* note 1.

24. Ibid.

CHAPTER 8

1. 1 Samuel 15: 32-33.

2. Charles Wyzanski, "Nuremberg: A Fair Trial?" *Atlantic Monthly*," 13, 1946 *reprinted in* David M. Adams, *Philosophical Problems In The Law* (Belmont: Wadsworth, 1992) [HEREINAFTER, WYZANSKI, *NUREMBERG*; Ann Tusa and John Tusa, The Nuremberg Trial (New York: Atheneum, 1986), p. 13.

3. Allen M. Dershowitz, *America on Trial: Inside the Legal Battles that Transformed our Nation* (New York: Warner Books, 2004), p. 291 *quoting* Ann Tusa and John Tusa, *The Nuremberg Trial* (New York: Atheneum, 1986), p. 13.

4. Ibid., at 51.

5. Ibid., at 69.

6. Dershowitz, *America on Trial*, *supra* note 3, at 293-94.

7. Tusa and Tusa, *supra* note 2, at p. 121.

8. Ibid., p. 457.

9. Ibid.

10. Ibid.

11. Ibid.

12. Ibid.

13. Dershowitz, *America on Trial*, *supra* note 3, at 295-96.

14. Ibid., at 296.

15. Ibid.

16. Saddam Hussein played a deceitful shell game with the United States and the UN as they searched the Iraqi desert for over twelve years in a futile effort to destroy his *weapons of mass destruction.* Since 1998, Hussein had refused to allow weapons inspectors back into his country and instead argued, quite persuasively in the eyes of the international community, for the UN to lift sanctions against his country even as evidence mounted from a number of political, military and former scientists who worked on Iraq's weapons programs that Saddam was within a year from having his own nuclear, chemical, and biological weapons of mass destruction.

17. One of legal realism's most illogical and entrenched views held by Holmes, Pound, Posner, Tribe, and other left-leaning jurists is that general ideals do not decide hard cases and that rules (morals) should not (or cannot) control court decisions. Professor Karl Llewellyn, to a degree, breaks ranks with these extreme legal realist positions. However, Llewellyn's rather arrogant and cavalier tone of his reasoning is not much better than his fellow academics. In the first edition of *The Bramble Bush*, Llewellyn assigned himself unreservedly to the ideas that "what these officials do about disputes is, to my mind, the law itself" and "rules . . . are important so far as they help you . . . *predict* what judges will do . . . . That is all their importance, *except as pretty playthings*." Karl N. Lle-

wellyn, The Bramble Bush 3, 5 (New York: Oceana, 1st ed. 1930) (emphasis added). In the second edition he said that these were "unhappy words when not more fully developed, and they are plainly at best a very partial statement of the whole truth . . . . [O]ne office of law is to control officials in some part, and to guide them even . . . where no thoroughgoing control is possible, or is desired . . . . [T]he words fail to take proper account . . . of the office of the institution of law as an instrument of conscious shaping . . . ."

18. Ibid., Llewellyn, *Bramble Bush* , at 3, 5.

19. Ibid., at 9.

20. Ellis Washington, *Inseparability of Law and Morality* (Maryland: University Press of America, 2002), pp. 325-26. *Id.* Philosopher, George Santayana's famous maxim is even more prophetic in light of the naive and failed proclamations of the United Nations and its first experiment with an international world court called the Nuremberg Trials: "If we do not learn from history, we are doomed to repeat it." Not following Santayana's wise counsel has been the idiots' refrain of ignominy throughout world civilization as one nation rises and another nation falls only to be succeeded by yet another "superpower." Each nation oblivious of the circumstances that preceded it, like an idiot savant walking in the middle of traffic, each rise of one nation because of some juxtaposition of either a *separation* or a *perversion* of law and morality, leads inexorably to societal implosion, moral decay, and genocide. America, in many respects I am sad to say, is there.

CHAPTER 9

1. Don Feder, *Will Arafat Triumph from Beyond the Grave,* FrontPageMag.com,

11/15/04.

2. Albert Carr, *Napoleon Speaks* (Viking Press, New York, 1941) p. 327.

3. See generally article on the Korean War on Wikipedeia.com at http://en.wikipedia.org/ wiki/Korean War.

4. See generally article on the Vietnam War on Wikipedeia.com athttp://en.wikipedia.org/ wiki/Vietnam War.

5. This section of the Cambodian war crimes trials was reprinted with permission from IDDS. Copyright (c) 2006 Institute of Defence and Strategic Studies, Nanyang Technological University, Blk S4, Level B4, Nanyang Avenue, Singapore 639798. The material from this section was based on an article by J. Eli Margolis for IDSS (28/07/06), *The worth of Cambodia's war crimes trials.*

6. See article *Cambodia Under Pol Pot (1975-1979)* http://en.wikipedia.org/wiki/Cambodian_genocide.

7. See generally article on the Rwandan Genocide on Wikipedeia.com at http://en.wikipedia.org/wiki/Rwanda.

8. Ibid.

9. Ibid.

10. Wilson, Richard 1964- "Judging History: The Historical Record of the International Criminal Tribunal for the Former Yugoslavia" Human Rights Quarterly - Volume 27, Number 3, August 2005, pp. 908-942 The John Hopkins University Press.

11. See generally article on the Former Yugoslavia on Wikipedeia.com at http://en.wikipedia.org/wiki/Yugoslavia

12. Ibid.

13. Ibid.

14. Ibid.

15. Ibid.

16. Ibid.

17. Allen M. Dershowitz, *America on Trial: Inside the Legal Battles that Transformed our Nation* (New York: Warner Books, 2004).

18. See quote by Saddam Hussein's daughter, Ragdah Hussein, regarding her opinion that the war crimes trials against her father are a "farce." http://en.wikipedia.org/wiki/Trial_of_SaddamHussein].

19. Ibid.

20. Ibid., see article: "Saddam upsets Kuwaiti dogs", Guardian.

21. Ibid. See article: Demonstration, statements support Saddam Hussein, at Arabicnews.com.

22. *See* Hussein article, *supra* note 18.

23. Ibid., at article: "Saddam pleads innocent, trial adjourns"

24. Ibid., John Simpson, "Saddam's Trial is not a farce," BBC, 23 December 2005.

25. All quotes relating to the Padilla case are from the Court of Appeals decision at 2003 U.S. App. Lexis 25616.

26. Dershowitz, *America on Trial*, *supra* note 17, at pp. 560-62.

27. Ibid.

28. Dershowitz, *America on Trial*, *supra* note 17, at p. 561.

29. Linda Greenhouse, *New York Times*, January 10. 2004, p. A11.

30. Dershowitz, *America on Trial*, *supra* note 17, at p. 568, n. 27: On February 20, 2004, the Supreme Court agreed to hear the Padilla case. His release has been stayed pending the Supreme Court decision.

31. *Al Odah v. United States*, 124. S. Ct., p. 534 (2003).

32. *Ex parte Milligan*, 71 U.S. 2, 18 L. Ed., p. 281 (1986).

33. Dershowitz, *America on Trial*, *supra* note 17, at p. 296.

34. *See generally* Hussein article, *supra* note 18.

35. Dershowitz, *America on Trial*, *supra* note 17, at p. 296.

36. Posted on WorldNetDaily.com 6/12/07 by John Burke, http://forums. wnd. com/index. php?fa=PAGE.view&pageId=5&forum Page=17.

Index

**N.B: "n" = endnote number*

A

B

C

D

I

J

K

L

O

P

Q

R

S

T

U

V

W

Y

Author's Biography

Ellis Washington, DePauw University; B.A. 1983, University of Michigan; M.M. 1986, John Marshall Law School; J.D. 1994. Currently he a commentator for the online political journal, WorldNetDaily.com. He was an editor at the University of Michigan Law Review and a law clerk for the Rutherford Institute. He was a member of the Board of Visitors at Ave Maria School of Law and taught business law and contracts at Davenport University and analytical writing at Lansing Community College. He has been invited as a lecturer at various secondary schools, universities, and law schools, specializing in constitutional law, jurisprudence, history of law, legal and political philosophy, international law, critical race theory, and feminist theory. He has published over a dozen law review articles and several books including—*The Devil is in the Details: Essays on Law, Race, Politics and Religion* (1999); *Beyond the Veil: Essays in the Dialectical Style of Socrates* (2000, 2004); *The Inseparability of Law and Morality: The Constitution, Natural Law and the Rule of Law* (2002). His writings appear in the chambers library of all three ideological divisions of the U.S. Supreme Court.

*N.B.: This book is based in part on previously published materials by the author. *See* Ellis Washington, *The Nuremberg Trials: The Death of the Rule of Law* (*In International Law*), 49 *Loyola Law Review* 417-518 (2003); Book Chapter 4: Ellis Washington, "The Nuremberg Trials: Birth of the Death of the Rule of Law" in *The Inseparability of Law and Morality* (Maryland: University Press of America, 2002).

Ellis Washington currently resides in Grosse Pointe, Michigan with his wife, Evelyn and his children, Stone Allen and Eden Alice.